Organized Religion is...

Blind, Leading the Blind

by

Frederick J. Azbell

azbellfj@yahoo.com

authorHOUSE®

AuthorHouse™
1663 Liberty Drive
Bloomington, IN 47403
www.authorhouse.com
Phone: 1-800-839-8640

First published by AuthorHouse 8/11/2010

ISBN: 978-1-4520-5367-7 (sc)
ISBN: 978-1-4520-5368-4 (e)

Library of Congress Control Number: 2010910967

Printed in the United States of America

This book is printed on acid-free paper.

A note from
the pessimistically optimistic realist
with a bent of humanistic pragmatism,
the author, a Deist

This work is a compilation of numerous articles which I have written over a period of the last twelve years or so. Very few have ever been published.

Some detractors may say that many of the articles are out of date. That may be true, but the truths, morals and ethics that I have tried to present never change with the passage of time.

My favorite homophobic, bigoted, and hypocritical *"friend"*, Jerry Falwell, has gone to meet his maker! But what I wrote of him and all his "good Christian right buddies", still apply.

Truth cannot be created, altered, or destroyed by any of man's adopted philosophies. Truth stands alone as fact. Truth is reality as reality is truth.

May the creative force be with you!

Frederick J. Azbell

Gods
and religious faiths
are no more or no less
than what is intended by the will
of the one who creates them.

Frederick J. Azbell

Contents: Beginnings

Part One Contents: Faith   1

Part Two Contents: Reality   27

Part Four Contents: Church and State   127

Faith is believing

what you know

ain't so.

Mark Twain

I Think,

Therefore,

I Do Not Believe.

Frederick J. Azbell

**Reality is all there
ever has been and
all there ever will be.**

**Seeking an
Idealistic State
is an exercise of futility,
a waste of valuable time
and resources of the mind.**

Frederick J. Azbell

Organized Religions

are...

the most regressive
and
destructive forces
that man has ever
created.

Frederick J. Azbell

Contents: Beginnings

A partial list of Deists supplied by Wikipedia, the free encyclopedia:

Ethan Allen
Aristotle
George Berkeley
Cicero
Paul Davies
Albert Einstein
Anthony Flew
Benjamin Franklin
Johann Wolfgang von Goethe
Stephen Hawking
William Hogarth
David Hume (also on list of atheists)
Thomas Jefferson
Immanuel Kant
Gotthold Ephraim Lessing
Abraham Lincoln
John Locke
James Madison
Gouverneur Morris
Thomas Paine
Elihu Palmer
Plato
Alexander Pope
Baruch Spinoza
Lysander Spooner
Alfred Lord Tennyson
Matthew Tindal
John Toland
Constantin Francois de Chasseboeuf, Comte de Volney
Voltaire
George Washington
Keith R. Wright

I dedicate this work to all those, who by using rational logic, place as much faith in their natural selves and Mother Nature as they do their supernatural deities and religious faiths.

Acknowledgements

Special thanks to the misguided and fanatic fundamentalists of the Christian right. This work could not have been written without the reality of their psychopathic tirades of supernatural babel. Great thanks to bigots and hypocrites such as Jerry Falwell, Pat Robertson, Albert Mohler Jr., Bob Jones III, James Dobson, the two burning Bushes, the Pope of Rome, plus all their good buddies who preach doctrines and doctrinaires of intolerance, hatred and utter nonsense. Their satanic and spiritless diatribes leave one such as me, dumfounded!

Additional thanks to the same caliber of hate mongers such as Jesse Helms, Bob Barr, Gary Bauer, Henry Hyde, and his unthinking junta of misguided henchmen.

It would be impossible to express fully my appreciation to that sexual pervert Kenny-boy, blabber-mouth Linda, instigator Luci, and all their fellow conspirators.

My warmest regards, hugs and kisses to all of those unfortunate misfits! To those of you that I may have neglected to mention or thank, please accept my apology. I'll make a special effort to catch you next time!

Introduction

I have for a number of years now, since my retirement from teaching elementary school for thirty-three years, contemplated the possibility of writing a book to express a few of my strongly held beliefs.

Events of the recent past had accelerated that urge. The now defunct **immoral** Moral Majority, the **spiritless** Christian Coalition, the **satanic** Southern Baptist, and the **hypocritical** Church of Christ, plus other bigoted and hypocritical religious groups, keep waving their spiritless and satanic doctrines and doctrinaires in my face while wrapping themselves in Old Glory. I must answer some of their diatribes of sinful lies so that I may rest in peace. Their inhumane rituals have no place in this great nation of ours.

My personal philosophy of life is based upon the fact that I am the pessimistically optimistic realist with a bent of humanistic pragmatism. I choose to think that things shall wok out for the better but I know that if there be the slightest opportunity, some detractor is going to throw a monkey-wrench into the machinery. I am a complete non-believer in organized religious faiths and their gods. I am a Deist. I think that man would not have created his gods and religious faiths if he had had more knowledge and understanding of his universe, Mother Nature and his natural self.

I do not wish to be negative, simply realistic. My head is not floating in the clouds or buried in the sod. My mind is open to any logically developed philosophies. My use of rational logic will not allow me to be convinced or swayed by irrational, supernatural, religious faiths. The bigoted and hypocritical faith presented by Christianity is not my idea of the truth of reality or the reality of truth. Satanic, fundamental faiths such as Christianity, Judaism, and Islam have been the greatest forces fomenting most of the hatred, violence, and wars in this world. Organized religions have proven themselves to be the greatest deterrents to the advancement of humanity among the peoples of this world.

Knowing Verses Understanding

I know that I know
little of all there is to know.

I know that I understand
little of what I know.

Knowing can be acquired through
a closed mind of little seasoning.

Understanding requires an
open mind capable of careful reasoning.

Someday I hope to understand
more of that which I presume to know.

Frederick J. Azbell

Forward

Who came first, man or his gods?
Without man, would there be any gods?

While reading this, I am sure there are those who question my having a belief system! Believe me, I am not faithless. I believe in a creator, but I do not believe in any organized religions of man. I do not believe that the creative power speaks to or listens to man. I have faith in the reality of the Universe with its universal law, and Mother Nature and her laws. I remain in awe of the power displayed by the creative force of the universe in that tremendous Big Bang that happened twelve to fifteen billion years ago. No god that man has discovered or created could equal the power of the creative force that created this universe.

With the use of rational logic, I cannot accept organized religions with their spiritless gods and faiths. Faiths and their gods created by men, such as Moses, are based on philosophical and scientific in consistencies which have little in common with the creation of the universe with its natural laws. Moral and ethical mankind does not necessarily have a religious faith. The most bigoted and hypocritically spiritless men are now the leaders of the satanic Christian right in the United States.

The creative force is responsible for all that exists in the universe through its evolutionary processes. I reject the idea that there must be an intelligent design or designer. The present state of evolution could never have been achieved by any previous planning no matter how great the mind. The creative force is no god that man has created or found. The evolution of the creative force has been happening for these twelve to fifteen billion years. It shall remain so for all eternity, with or without the earth, man, or man's gods.

The Bible, as well as all works of religious faiths, was written by mortal men in efforts to find the meaning of life. Religious man's efforts to deny nature shall never permit him to succeed in his quest of finding or understanding his own evolution. The claims of any faith that its book and faith is the work of a god, is the height of fantasy. Man has created his religious faiths and gods as he wishes. Most of what man has written in his books of religious faiths, have no grounds of fact or truth.

Personally, I care not which religious faith one adopts. I simply detest bigoted Christian fundamentalists with all their false doctrines and doctrinaires which they employ in efforts to control my life and my government. The religion of men, such as Jerry Falwell, Pat Robertson, Bob Jones III, Albert Mohler Jr., James Dobson, George and George W. Bush, the Pope of Rome, and their two billion followers, is immoral and unnatural. These men are worshipping a sinful god and they are practicing a satanic faith.

....

"Doubt everything. Find your own light."

Last words of Gotama Buddha, in Theravada tradition

"Men think epilepsy divine, merely because they do not understand it. But if they called everything divine which they do not understand, why, there would be no end of divine things."

Hippocrates

"God either wants to eliminate bad things and cannot, or can but does not want to, or neither wishes to nor can, or both wants to and can. If he wants to and cannot, he is weak - and this does not apply to god. If he can, but does not want to, then he is spiteful - which is equally foreign to god's nature. If he neither wants to nor can, he is both weak and spiteful and so not a god. If he wants to and can, which is the only thing fitting for a god, where then do bad things come from? Or why does he not eliminate them?"

Epicurus

"Nature free at once and rid of her haughty lords is seen to do all things spontaneously of herself without the meddling of the gods."

Lucretius

"Where there is doubt, there is freedom."

Latin proverb

"Argumentation cannot suffice for the discovery of a new work, since the subtlety of Nature is greater many times than the subtlety of argument."

Francis Bacon

"Men never do evil so completely and cheerfully as when they do it from religious conviction."

Blaise Pascal

....

Religious Bigotry

On the morning of August 10, 2005, I had gotten up and started writing another article, the contents of which had come to me in my waking minutes. The article was nearly completed but I felt that I needed a break. So I turned on the TV to CNN and there was "Dubya" giving one of his glorious insincere speeches, so thinking he would be on all the cable stations, I switched to NBC.

Jane Pauley was interviewing a Dutch couple who had a set of bi-racial twins. One boy favored his father who was black. The other twin favored his mother who was of Dutch ancestry.

Jane and they were discussing problems a bi-racial family encounters.

This got me to thinking of the reality of this situation and I immediately turned off the TV to start this article.

These children had been accepted as friends by their peers. The only problems they appeared to face were the result of bigoted and hypocritical beliefs of the adults with which they came into contact.

This fact only proves once more that what is natural and real is made to be supernatural and unreal by the evil biases and prejudices that we are taught by our friends, teachers and preachers.

The supernatural philosophies of bigots and hypocrites who believe that they are superior to others are the cause of the problems which face these twins.

If this world is to be destroyed by man, it will no doubt be that of one religious fundamental faith fighting another over their superiority concepts.

We see fundamentalist faiths fighting one another in Iraq where the Christian fundamentalists are fighting the likes of Islam.

In Ireland, in recent years, we have had Christian fundamentalists of Protestantism and those of Catholicism fighting each other.

In the Middle East, Jewish fundamentalists are fighting Islamic fundamentalists. In Kashmir, we have Islam fighting Hinduism.

We have supernatural, unenlightened, religious man ready to destroy his natural world in efforts to rid the world of the members of a competing religious faith.

Oh, Really!

I keep hearing various Christian fundamentalists declaring that the United States of America was founded on Judeo-Christian principles and values plus a belief in its god. I'm not too sure what Judeo-Christian principles and values are! I do know that the first settlers to America were religious men who were either fleeing from the English king and his church or the Pope of Rome and the Catholic Church. I do know and understand well that many of the morals and ethics displayed for all to see by the Christian leaders of the various churches here in the United States, such as Falwell, Robertson, Jones, Dobson, and the two burning Bushes, are not humane. I also know that the Crusades, the Inquisitions, and the witch hunts were the uncivilized actions of Christian fundamentalists. The present day exorcisms of the Catholic Church are acts of a satanic faith using the art of sorcery to accomplish its goals.

Although there is an expression of God in a few of our governmental documents, many of the men who were responsible for the founding of this country were Deists, such as Thomas Jefferson who proclaimed that, "Reason and free inquiry are the only effectual agents against error."Another time he declared that, "All persons shall have full and free liberty of religious opinion; nor shall any be compelled to frequent or maintain any religious institution."

Jefferson was adamant in stating that religion and government were to be kept separate. He declared that, "The clergy, by getting themselves established by law and engrafted into the machine of government have been a very formidable engine against the civil and religious rights of man."

James Madison declared that, "The civil government...functions with complete success... by the separation of the church from the state."

George Washington expressed his feelings this way, "Every man conducting himself as a good citizen and being accountable to God alone for his religious opinions, ought to be protected in worshipping the Deity according to the dictates of his own conscience."

John Adams made an even more adamant Deist declaration, "The question before the human race is, whether priests and kings shall rule it by fictitious miracles."

Benjamin Franklin stated, "The way to see by faith is to shut the eye of reason," He firmly believed that, "Original sin was as ridiculous as imputed righteousness."

That very influential Thomas Paine made numerous Deist statements. He declared, "God exists and there it lies. Science is the true theology. God is the power of the first cause, nature is the law, and matter is the subject acted upon. The Deist needs none of those tricks and shows, called miracles to confirm his faith, for what can be a greater miracle than the creation itself and his own existence."

The adamant statements that were made by the founders of the United States make it clear that they had believed in a universal god, since not one of them professed a belief in Christianity nor placed a trust in the words and actions of religious men of any faith.

....

"Those who wish to seek out the cause of miracles, and to understand the things of nature as philosophers, and not to stare at them in astonishment like fools, are soon considered heretical and impious, and proclaimed as such by those whom the mob adores as the interpreters of nature and the gods. For these men know that once ignorance is put aside, that wonderment would be taken away, which is the only means by which their authority is preserved."

Spinoza

"Those who would give up essential liberty to purchase a little temporary safety deserve neither liberty nor safety."

Benjamin Franklin

"Those who invalidate reason ought seriously to consider whether they argue against reason with or without reason; if with reason, then they establish the principles that they are laboring to dethrone: but if they argue without reason (which, in order to be consistent with themselves they must do), they are out of reach of rational conviction, nor do they deserve a rational argument."

Ethan Allen

"It is always better to have no ideas than false ones; to believe nothing, than to believe what is wrong."

Thomas Jefferson

"I would rather be exposed to the inconveniencies attending too much liberty, than those attending too small a degree of it."

Thomas Jefferson

"I almost shudder at the thought of alluding to the most fatal example of the abuses of grief which the history of mankind has preserved – the Cross. Consider what calamities that engine of grief has produced."

John Adams

....

One Christian Idiot

On the 22nd of August of 2005, Pat Robertson, the bigoted hypocritical Christian fundamentalist, called for the assassination of Hugo Chavez, the President of Venezuela.

Tell me that these are not the words of a demented one! One of the so-called leaders of the Christians in the United States! Heaven help us! I wonder what Jesus would say!"

Today is the 24th and Pat says that, "The media has misquoted me and taken my words out of context." There is video footage of him saying that the United States of America should assassinate this man because he is a threat to us.

Stupid hypocritical Pat is the satanic antichrist for sure.

Faith
and
Truth

Are Not

Synonymous Facts.

Frederick J. Azbell

Jerry Falwell had possessed one of the most dangerous minds that the United States ever had to contend with. His bigoted and hypocritical Christian fundamentalist views were a challenge to our democracy. Men with like philosophies remain a threat to the liberty and freedom of this nation. Men who display the same qualities of Christian right idealism are Pat Robertson, Bob Jones III, Albert Mohler Jr., the two burning Bushes and millions of other "good buddies."

It would be my earnest desire to free the United States from the influence of people who promote such undemocratic philosophies.

Part One Contents: **Faith**

Seeking a Faith
Blind Leading the Blind
My God!
Origin of Religious Faiths
Philosophy of Religion
My Belief Verses Their Beliefs
Playing God
Understanding Rational Religious Faith

Seeking a Faith

Why does an otherwise seemingly intelligent person
willingly blind the self as to truth of natural reality
in order to adopt a supernatural god and faith?

I have not found any religious faith that I can agree with. I cannot accept any religion or philosophy of life based on faith alone. I do agree with bits and pieces of various faiths but these still place their trust in a supernatural god. The closest belief system to that of mine seems to be Buddhism which is more realistic toward its approaches to the meaning of life for humane mankind.

....

Buddhism teaches that Reality of Self is unfathomable, inconceivable, immutable, inscrutable, deep, boundless, unmeasurable, markless, signless, undefinable, incomprehensible.

Only Self, Supremely Awake, can know Itself. And the self of a given manifested "Being" that is Fully Awake, that is called **BUDDHA**.

The Ten Fetters that "bind" Beings to perpetuating themselves in artificial, manufactured,
Fictitious realities are:

1. Notions of a permanent individual, personality, soul, or self,

2. Attachments to wrong views, rites, rituals, dogmas, superstitions,

3. Doubt and confusion,

4. Liking, attachment, passions, sense desires, lust, greed,

5. Disliking, aversion, hatred, malice, ill-will, spite,

6. Lust and craving for perpetuating formlessness and hereafters of Immateriality,

7. Lust and craving for perpetuating forms and hereafters of Fine Materiality,

8. Wrong views of Conceit plus pride and arrogance, declaring, "I am the doer,"

9. Excitement for constructions and perpetuating artificial realities, Self-Delusions and Self-Illusions,

10. Addiction to Self-Deception and a complete state of Self-Ignorance, necessary for the Illusion of artificial realities and individuality to seem real, necessary for what it is and the pain and peril associated with these

addictive, ill-conceived, conditioned, fleeting states of fabricated fictitious existence.

"The True State of Permanent Reality" is the goal of Buddhism. Things are created, are inherently subject to decay, and then finally are dissolved again. The way to True Reality, the realization of Perfect Wisdom, Total Supreme Enlightenment, is Buddhahood, Knowing truth. No Blind faith.

What has been **CREATED** is **IMPERMANENT**: Whatever is impermanent is inherently ill. No permanent bliss or happiness is to be found in what is impermanent, only pain and peril.

••

These views of Buddhism more closely follow my personal belief than any other faith that I have studied. I believe all truth lies within me. My greatest challenge in this earthly life is to find, know, and try to understand the truths that dwell within me.

Blind Leading the Blind

Only a sadist would adopt a god that would disfigure or kill him
for no logical reason.

The greatest folly that man has created is blind faith. Most of the organized religions of today are based on the condition that one must blind oneself as to reality in order to accept the faith. One is not to question anything which has been written as the truth by the creators of the faith. The individual is thought to be incapable of comprehending truth! As Benjamin Franklin stated, "The way to see by faith is to shut the eye of reason."

Most religious faiths were created when man was ignorant of nature, the universe, or scientific knowledge of any kind. Faiths developed by ignorant man shall not be able to survive much longer in this vastly improved scientific and technological world. Man is no longer totally ignorant of his universe as was Moses who created his lord god or the creators of Jesus Christ and Christianity.

The creators of most religious faiths did not know or understand truth. Faiths can never be truths since they refuse to accept the reality of natural law. Faiths, such as Christianity, denounce science and refuse to accept it because its members know that truth supplied by scientific knowledge has the ability to destroy their religious truths.

I completely agree with that great statesman and lawyer, Clarence Darrow, who said in his *Why I Am an Agnostic,* "The fear of god is not the beginning of wisdom. The fear of god is the death of wisdom. Skepticism is the beginning of wisdom. The modern world is the child of doubt and inquiry, as the ancient world was the child of fear and faith."

There has never been nor ever shall be any gods controlling the life of man. The creative force does not see, hear, or listen to man. All religious faiths and religious gods have been the creations of the unthinking in desperate attempts to escape reality, find themselves, and then explain their own existence. As Long as man chooses to deny or misunderstand his true nature, he never shall find the answer to any questions about the meaning of life.

Most religious faiths and their gods were created during the time in the development of man when he was aware of few truths of the universe. The truth cannot be found in any supernatural religious faith and god that mortal man has created to meet his personal needs. Truth can only be found in the universe, nature, math, and science. All of man's philosophies that he has devised, including his religious faiths, are the result of creative thought, which by its nature is supernatural. Most men are far too biased and prejudiced to know, let alone understand, truth.

The only truth is in the universe, nature, and realistic man. Truth cannot be created, altered, or destroyed by man, his gods, or religious faiths. The exact or complete knowledge of the creation of everything in the universe, man, the flora and fauna of the earth is likely to remain forever a mystery to man.

The universe was created from that tremendous Big Bang twelve to fifteen billion years ago. Man will forever be trying to determine how all the matter which comprises the universe ever got here. We will probably never know the complete answer to this riddle. However, with modern science we are able to get closer to the beginning of it all. Only the foolishly fundamental religious among us claim to know, or better still, understand this riddle of creation.

Man has been creating his religious gods and faiths since his time on earth evolved. The religious faiths of man are the result of his compulsion to find himself. Man will not accept the fact that he naturally exists. Man considers himself the master and of far too importance in the scheme of things. Although man is an example of the evolutionary processes of Mother Nature, he feels the need for a more fanciful explanation for his existence. Most mystifying explanations of man, such as you find in the Bible, were created when man was totally ignorant of his universe.

The Bible was written at a time in the development of mankind when we knew little of the universe and the world around us. Very little of the earth at this time was known to man. Many men at this time believed our lives were controlled by comets and other heavenly bodies. Some of us still believe these falsehoods of faith. Not too long ago, in San Diego, a goodly number of ignorantly devout fanatics of some obscure faith, killed themselves believing that in doing so they would be joining the tail of a passing comet and ride it to heaven!

Self blinded men make statements of faith and then create theories in efforts to **prove** their beliefs. Christians believe that the Bible is a book of truth when in reality it is a book of philosophical fantasy from the minds of mortal men creating a religious faith for themselves as they would like that faith and its god to be. Moses created his lord god after studying the behavior of his people and then believing he could give them a god to fear.

The Bible was written by mortal men over a period of hundreds of years. It was written exclusively by males since at this time in the development of mankind, the female was denied education. Remember Eve had challenged their god! This is the same philosophy of a number of religions today in the twenty-first century. It was a similar philosophy employed against the black slaves in the United States who were denied access to knowledge in efforts to keep them ignorant in order to subjugate them.

Women, in the time of Moses, were no more than slaves to their husbands. Women were considered as chattel and were bought and paid for by their husbands. Women were considered unclean because of their monthly menses, provided by Mother Nature. Eve had sinned against the lord god of Moses by seeking knowledge! Benjamin Franklin stated, "Original sin was as ridiculous as imputed righteousness."

In the United States at this time, we have the Southern Baptists expressing many of these same beliefs which belittle women in efforts to keep them second class citizens. The female must obey the husband and bow to his every need! Women, in most of the world, have only recently been allowed to compete with men. The only country in the Islamic world that gave women any rights was the secular government of Iraq which we destroyed! The female is not treated as an equal to the male in most of today's world, however, because of the inhumane actions of fundamental religious faiths. The female has since the time of her evolution, been considered inferior to the more **physically** powerful male. The dominance of male over female is a matter of physical strength, not that of brain power or divine inspiration.

The Christian statement of faith is: We believe:

1. The Bible is the only word of God;

2. There is one God, eternally existent in three persons of father, son and holy spirit;

3. The deity of Jesus Christ, his virgin birth, his sinless life, his divine miracles, his vicarious and atoning death, his bodily resurrection, his ascension, his return;

4. Man is sinful by nature and needs regeneration by the holy spirit;

5. Continuing ministry of his holy spirit is necessary for a good life;

6. Resurrection for all;

7. Spiritual unity for believers in Christ;

8. Creation of man by God

My own statement of a rational belief is, I believe:

1. A creative force created the universe and all that exists;

2. Man is the product of evolutionary processes of the creative force of the universe through Mother Nature which is the creative force on earth;

3. The belief in man created faiths and gods only draws man further from the truth;

4. Man needs to place his faith in nature and mankind;

5. Humane mankind is capable of developing its own standards of morals and ethics to guide its life.

I believe that the father of Jesus was the mortal man who had sexual intercourse with his mortal mother. Miracles, resurrection, ascension, and the second coming of a Christ are all the creations of those who created Christ and the Christian faith. Sin is no more natural to man than is goodness. Man needs to become humane and have more faith in his own abilities by using the brains given to him by Mother Nature. There are no such places as Heaven and Hell in my world of reality. Such places exist solely in the minds of the faithful who have succeeded in blinding themselves. The individual man creates his own heaven and hell here on earth with the help of others, of course!

The Ten Commandments which Moses created are basically good being humane. The statements concerning the god that he created are nothing more than disillusionments of a self blinded man. The concepts of good as stated in these commandments are moral and ethical but quite often in disagreement with those expressed throughout the Bible. Man does not need a religious faith to know his words and actions are either good or evil. Man's intelligence and his humaneness should tell him just how moral or ethical he is. Of course, one needs to be honest in his assessments of his or other's words and actions!

The conclusion to the Ten Commandments is, "I am the Lord, I am a jealous God, I plague the children, grandchildren, and great grandchildren of those who hate me with their ancestor's sin. But I make whole those who love me for a thousand generations." All of this rhetoric is, of course, a matter of the biased faith of a revengeful and vindictive god. Mother Nature, on the other hand, is not vindictive, unreasonable, or mean spirited!

To be in constant fear of another man or god, when it is not necessary, is not just. This concept is the creation of an ignorant man. No just creator would make itself to be a constant threat to his creations. No rational person would accept the fact that the god he is to adopt will be vindictive and cruel. The lord god of Moses is not humane. A humane god would not slaughter thousands of innocent men, women, and children simply because they do not believe in him and his faith. Mankind is the creation of Mother Nature through the evolution of the creative force of the universe. The creative force has no knowledge of man or his religious faiths and gods. Man's goodness or evilness comes from his own mind which the creative force of nature gave him. One does not need any Lucifer whispering in his ear to cause him to be evil, just as he does not need any angel telling him to be good. One can be the most religious person alive and still treat his fellow man inhumanely. If one needs proof of this last statement of truth, carefully but honestly study the words and actions of the past Popes of Rome, Pat Robertson, Jerry Falwell, Albert Mohler Jr., Bob Jones I, II, and III, the two burning Bushes, (George and George W.), and a host of other Christian men. But please remember, you must be careful, honest and truthful in your searches for information. If one is honest, he will find that many of these Christian men are or were, bigoted, hypocritical, inhumane, and undemocratic toward their fellow man, especially if that fellow man does not follow the doctrines and doctrinaires of the faith.

I do not follow religious beliefs or organized religions since they are not based on the truth of reality, or the reality of truth. The truth of reality is everything that one sees, hears, touches, tastes, or smells in this world, in other words what one senses. Not the supernatural feelings one gets through some phony sixth sense. The reality of truth is the UNIVERSE, MOTHER NATURE, and all that is NATURAL.

Religions which use fantasy, mysticism, and sorcery in the development of the faith, such as Christianity, Judaism and Islam, are basically dishonest and untruthful. I believe as did Karl Marx, "Religion is the opium of the people." Religious faiths are the creations of desperate men who feel the need for a supernatural god to control their behaviors because they have so little faith in themselves. Praying for guidance to a supernatural god is an exercise in self-deception and self-hypnosis.

There are, and have been forever, countless religious faiths and sects each with a god or gods. How can anyone faith discount all other faiths? The only answer is blind faith. There is not now, ever was, or ever will be any way to prove the existence or worth of any god or religious faith. Blind faith is truthfully blind.

One's religious faith should cause him to become a better, more humane person. One needs to become one with his Universe, Mother Nature, and himself in order to become *spiritual*. If a religious faith is only interested in serving a false god or filling empty heads with its own superiority concepts, doctrines and doctrinaires, that faith is useless and no doubt, dangerous. We are not living in any paradise now, nor shall we be in the future. We are on this earth serving ourselves and mankind. Doctrines and doctrinaires written by biased and prejudiced man who has purposefully blinded himself from the reality of truth and the truth of reality, are dishonest and dangerous.

Fairytales and fantasies written in order to confuse, amaze, or awe the ignorant masses into subjugation, are the work of devils, they are evil. The Bible is the greatest collection of religious fantasy ever bound into one book. Such things as men living to be nearly a thousand years, is utterly ridiculous. The Bible is replete with such fantasy from the minds of unknowing and unenlightened man.

The tall tale of one man and his family gathering a female and a male of each species of animals as told in Genesis, is a tragic comedy! At the time of Noah, very little of the geographical earth was known to man. There are countless numbers of land animals and sea creatures that have been discovered since this time. Christianity believes only in creationism of a god, it does not recognize evolution. Where did all these animals, unknown at the time of Noah, come from? If the Bible is a book of truth, where is the believability?

When the Bible is so full of ridiculous fantasy, fairytales, and sorcery, how does one accept any part of it as truth? I do not possess the necessary faith to believe the Bible or any other text on faith alone.

I am basically a Deist, as was Galileo Galilei who stated, "I do not feel obligated to believe that the same god who has endowed us with sense, reason, and intellect has intended us to forgo their use." I am *the pessimistically, optimistic realist with a bent of humanistic pragmatism.* All truth lies within me. Although I am no better than any other, there has never been or ever shall be anyone to walk the face of this earth better than me. Intelligence, wealth, stations in life, or religious faiths do not make one better than others. The individual alone, through the use of words and actions, determines his worth.

....

"Religion is comparable to a childhood neurosis."

Sigmund Freud 1927

"Men will wrangle for religion; write for it; fight for it; die for it; anything but live it."

Charles Caleb Colton

"I do not believe in the creed professed by the Jewish church, by the Roman church, by the Greek church, by the Protestant church, nor by any church that I know of. My own mind is my church."

Thomas Paine

My God!

Why does man create gods and religious faiths?

Mohandas Gandhi stated, "God is that indefinable something which we all feel but which we do not know.

The greatest argument for the non-existence of a religious god is the continual ungodly and spiritless doctrines and doctrinaires flowing from the mouths of such Christian men as Jerry Falwell, Pat Robertson, Bob Jones III, Albert Mohler Jr., James Dobson, George W. Bush and the Pope of Rome. No just god would permit such inhumane bigots and hypocrites to exist.

The Bible, as well as all books, was written by mortal men. Biased mortal men are not known for creating truthful philosophies of life. Mortal men write what they wish and then declare the writings to be truth.

My truths cannot be determined by others. I am the truth! The truth dwells within me. I know much of the truth, however, what I declare to be truth may be falsehoods of wishful dreaming.

Books of religious faiths have been written by mortal man in desperate searches to find himself and the reason for his existence. Man, however, tends to imitate the writings and philosophies of those who have preceded him. Man, as yet, has not found or recognized the truth of his existence.

Truth cannot be created, altered, or destroyed by men or gods. Truth stands alone, by itself, as fact. Man can give his interpretation of truth but is he being honest? Does he really understand truth? Although any number of men might agree on a truth, are these men being truthful? Do they know as well as understand, truth?

Man' religious truths most often are formed as the result of biases and superstitions held by man. What real truth is there in the truth formed by prejudiced man living in a fantasy world of his own creation?

The mortal men who wrote the Bible were doing so in an effort to develop and support a religious faith. These biased men had varying ideas of truth, however. The truth is, there is little truth in the Bible. However, it is the truth that the faithful can reconcile these differences of opinions on truth because they believe in the sanctity of mortal, religious men.

Many Christian fanatics, such as Falwell, constantly refer to their Bible scriptures as the gospel truth. I guess they believe that being the words of the Bible, makes it truth. Jerry can recite his scriptures word for word, verse by verse, chapter by chapter, and book by book. Jerry has memorized his book well but with little understanding of truth. This bigoted and hypocritical homophobe deliberately discounts the reality that his Bible is a book of faith, thus it is not necessarily a book of truth.

Religious fundamentalists, such as Jerry, believe that the writings of their faith are the only truths. These fanatics are not interested in the truths of others. All the truths of the world, fanatics have determined by and for themselves. What they have determined, however, is merely that they will accept only the truths that they have developed, the truths of others, which conflict with their own, are false!

Because the truths expressed in the Bible are not in conformity with nature and natural law, I choose to believe in a creative force of the universe and its Mother Nature. This force may be a god but I am positive it is not any of the gods that man has found or created to suit his personal needs. For some peace of mind, I need an explanation of me.

But I cannot accept any of the religious gods that man serves. I refuse to believe, as Christians do, that I was created in sin by a god. I do believe, however, that all evil, as well as all good, are the creations of mortal man. The creative force does not know the good or bad creations of man. The creative force creates all life on the earth but does not communicate with any of its creations.

Sin is a matter of personal concept. What is sinful to one may not be so to another. When one sins, it is against his fellow man and nature, not any supernatural god. The societies of humanity judge the behaviors of mankind. The judges of man may or may not be humane, honest or truthful, however.

If one says things or does things which are hurtful to others, then he has sinned. Only he knows the total truth of his words and actions. All truth lies within the one. No one can hold another to his own truths, since truths of the one may not be the truths of the other. When we try to be that which are not, by denying nature and natural law, we sin.

I know when I have sinned against my fellow man. The societies of humanity judge my truthfulness and honesty for me, if need be in a court of law. The sinners of this world are those of us who sin against our fellow man and nature. When one sins, he does know the truth. No creator or god of man judges the words and actions of man. Gods and man are not on the same plane and thus never communicate one with the other. Communications between man and his gods are nothing more than acts of self-delusions on the part of the one receiving the messages.

Societies of man make the laws of the land and judge the behaviors of man. Man has never needed any savior from above to show him the errors of his ways. Man knows the truth. It is his denial of the truth which causes man to sin against his fellow man. All sins are against our fellow man and nature, not any non-existent supernatural god that is out of this world!

When I condemn you for being less than me, I sin. I am making a false assumption that I am right and therefore, you are wrong, such as people like George W. Bush constantly do.

I am assuming that what I have adopted as truth is the one and only. If you have adopted another truth, you are inferior to me! Somehow I have convinced myself that I am superior to you and your truths.

Christians, Falwell, Robertson, Jones, Mohler, and Bush, believe that their god is the one and only. They believe all other gods to be sinful. Fundamental Christian fanatics have created their god and truths to be as they wish.

What is the importance of a god? Mother Nature, which is the creative force on the earth, knows nothing of the gods and faiths of man. It is man who has created his gods and religious faiths as a result of his refusal to accept the reality of nature. Man has forever been a dreamer and somewhat idealistic. Idealism is a negative concept since it is supernatural, not realistic.

We have bigots and hypocrites, Robertson, and Falwell, condemning anyone not following their supernatural views of man. These so-called men of Christianity are able to condemn one to their hell and then in the same breath say, "I love you!" They claim this hypocrisy in the name of their faith and god.

The god of men such as Jerry is a devil in disguise. Bob Jones has the hypocrisy of calling the Pope of Rome, the antichrist. I do not agree with most of what the Pope proclaims, but I cannot condemn him as the antichrist since I do not believe in the religion of Bob Jones. For Bob Jones to claim that the Pope is the antichrist, implies that Jones considers his god and faith to be superior to that of the Pope. One Christian fundamentalist hypocrite trying to outdo another, one pot calling the other, black!

I do not believe in the god of Jones anymore than that of the Pope. I do not believe in any of the man created gods or any of the religious faiths that man has created. I choose to believe that there might have been a humane man, called Jesus, who roamed what is now referred to as the Middle East, doing good deeds. The claims of miracles are the self-delusions of the faithful and have never been proven as natural truth. Miracles are matters of a faith held only by its members,

I do not say that any creator made me in its image. I have no idea as to the image of a god! I have adopted my belief in the creative force and its Mother Nature simply because I desire an explanation of me. The idea of nature being my creator is far more plausible than that of a supernatural god. The creative force nor Mother Nature knows of my personal needs and is no judge of me or any other man.

The communications from any god is the result of self-delusions and hypnotic ideas of the one claiming to receive such messages. We are taught how to self-hypnotize ourselves by our religious faiths. There are several faiths that cause their members to go into complete hypnotic trances.

No god could possibly communicate with man since the two are not on the same plane. Man is natural; gods are the result of states of mind, in other words, supernatural. Man is truth or a natural fact, gods and faiths cannot be proven as to truth as they are supernatural. The gods and religious faiths of man are as he wishes them to be. Man has created his gods and religious faiths to serve his particular, personal needs and wishes.

Origin of Religious Faiths

The refusal of man to follow the laws of Mother Nature
has caused him to create all manner of religious faiths and gods
in his search to pacify his selfish needs and desires.

Organized religious faiths and their corresponding god(s) are the personal creations of spiritless man that had little faith in the abilities given to him by Mother Nature. Religious faiths are created as the result of man trying to deny his true nature, natural law, and the laws of the universe. Man has tried to explain himself in a manner using belief systems that he himself has created. Man will not accept the fact that he is the product of the evolutionary processes of nature. For his own greedy needs, man wants a more glamorous and mystifying reason for his existence. Man feels that he is too important in the scheme of things! The creative force is the creator of the entire universe and all that exists. Mother Nature is that creative force at work on the earth. Man did not begin in any fairytale Garden of Eden a few thousand years ago. The earth is over four and a half billion years of age. It has taken millions of years of evolution to bring the world of flora, fauna, and lastly man to its present state.

The major faiths do not agree with one another on many of the most important points on these developments because their arguments are not based on natural truths. Faiths are the result of creative imaginations of man, not truths or facts. Man creates his faiths according to his assumed needs. The spiritual needs of all men are not the same, thus we have all manner of religious faiths each with its own god(s). Men also view their god(s) in various ways. Many religions deny the reality of other faiths by simply proclaiming that their god(s) and its faith are the one and only one.

I think that Moses created his lord god to be as he wanted after he assumed he knew the needs of his people. Moses had determined that his people were not doing as they should. He therefore created a god for them to fear.

Religious faiths swear to being the word of a god. Most religions will not accept the reality of the gods of numerous faiths. **Blind faith is blind as to truth.**

The reality is, the creators of religious faiths create their gods after they *believe* that they understand the needs of those to be served. There are as many or more gods as there are faiths. In *reality,* no one shall ever know a true god since it does not exist as a factual or truthful reality.

The creative force is not the god of any faith. Gods and faiths exist only in the minds of the faithful who have blinded themselves from the truths of the universe, Mother Nature, the truth of reality, and the reality of truth.

....

"I'm completely in favor of the separation of Church and State. My idea is that these two institutions screw us up enough on their own, so both of them together is certain death."

George Carlin

"Why do you write to me, 'God should punish the English? I have no close connection to either one or the other. I see only deep regret that God punishes so many of His children for their numerous stupidities, for which only He Himself can be held responsible; in my opinion, only His nonexistence could excuse Him' ".

Albert Einstein

"Better to be unborn than untaught, for ignorance is the root of all misfortune."

Aristotle

"If Jesus had been killed twenty years ago, Catholic school children would be wearing little electric chairs around their necks instead of crosses."

Lenny Bruce

"The careful student of history will discover that Christianity has been of very little value in advancing civilization, but has done a great deal toward retarding it."

Matilda Joslyn Gage

"A celibate clergy is an especially good idea, because it tends to suppress any hereditary propensity toward fanaticism."

Carl Sagan

"Trust me, I never told a single soul to vote for Bush."

Jesus

"Fundamentalists of all religions keep announcing to the rest of us that they want to attain more and more earthly power--the Pope wants to re-Christianize Europe; Islamic clerics want to Islamicize Europe; American Evangelical missionaries were busy immediately after the first phase of the Iraq war attempting to convert Muslims, Anglican prelates in Africa think they can get rid of more liberal American Episcopalians. None of these efforts demonstrates the "respect" toward others that all of these religions demand for themselves."

Jane Smiley

Philosophy of Religion

Religious faiths are created by mortal man
in his desperate attempts to escape his natural self.

The goal of any religious faith, worth its salt, should be the betterment in the *humanity* of the faithful. If this is not the case, there is no need of the faith! Preparing oneself for a future pie in the sky home is ridiculous. One should be living a "good" life here on earth and if that future fantastic home does prove to exist, after one dies, then he should be prepared. One cannot claim to be religious simply by the fact that he can recite word for word the doctrines and doctrinaires of propaganda that his books of faith proclaim.

Faiths are not facts or truths no matter how much faith is expressed. No amount of memorization of hypocritical doctrines and doctrinaires can make one religious, or better still, spiritual. Those who may doubt this statement of truth, need to study carefully and honestly, the lives, words, and actions of such men as Falwell, Robertson, Jones, Mohler, the numerous Popes of Rome, and our late Presidents, George and George W. Bush. Study very carefully the Crusades, Inquisitions, witch trials, and present day exorcisms.

No one can honestly say that the men listed above were or are *spiritual*. These men may be Christian, however! They would first need to join the human race and become one with nature in order to become spiritual. Spiritual man is at peace with himself, the universe, and nature. No book of religious faith has the knowledge or ability to raise one to the necessary level of pureness to realize the truth of his existence. The ability to become spiritual comes from within one gained through meditation, not from any religious prayers of biased and prejudiced man

If he claims to be Christian, waving ones false book in my face while speaking evil of me, entitles the waver to a place in his own hell. The creative force of the universe and man has made none of the false claims written in any book of faith. The words written in the Bible, as well as any other religious text, are the words of unenlightened and spiritless man.

If one is truly spiritual, he treats others as well or better than himself. Spiritual man does not condemn others for not believing as he. The welfare of others comes first at all times, not just when it is convenient. A spiritual person does not claim superiority, as do the Christian fundamentalists.

According to the fanatic fundamentalists of the Christian faith, most of us are going to their hell. These spiritless ones believe that they can condemn us to their fantasy world. Those who condemn others are the ones who are the wicked. The heaven and hell of the Christian faith do not exist in the world of reality. The life of heaven or hell one chooses to live is here on earth. The wicked treatment of humanity by members of the Christian faith shall never allow the spiritless faithful to reach any *true* or *just* god or paradise if there should happen to be such a place. No *honest* and *humane* god would allow bigots and hypocrites of Christianity to soil *her* home. (*All animal life on earth comes from the female gender.*)

We are not alone here, however. You and I are in the company of billions of others. Our forefathers had developed laws which protect you from me and me from you. These laws from the societies of humane man need to be obeyed or we must be prepared to pay the judge.

Those who follow my one commandment of life (The Golden Rule) shall live a good and honorable life. Once you have proven your goodness by your spirituality, you shall have surpassed levels that belief in any religious doctrinaires could achieve.

I cannot understand how so many so-called Christian leaders read and preach only superiority concepts which are filled with ideas of non-acceptance of other faiths. It is obvious to anyone using common sense that many religions exist in this world. Not one has ever been proven as fact or truth. How can men who promote superiority concepts of one religion over another justify these doctrinaires? How can they proclaim themselves to be men of a god?

Intelligent and realistic men know that the world of man existed for centuries upon centuries before Christians created their savior, Jesus Christ. Thinking men know that there shall be religious faiths long after the death of Christianity. Man's gods and faiths are not lasting realities since they are not based on nature or the truth of the universe. Christianity has existed for a mere two thousand years. Two thousand years when compared to the age of man is nothing more than a microscopic drop in an immense bucket of time.

De we actually believe we know, let alone understand, the reality of a creator? Judaism and Christianity share the god of Moses. Protestants and Catholics share a Christ but they each have varying philosophies of faith. Which of these faiths is the true one? None of them are based on the truths of the universe; therefore, not one of them can claim legitimacy.

The creative force knows nothing of our created gods and faiths. The creative force of the universe is no god or communicator with man. Religious faiths and their gods are the creations of unknowing and spiritless mortal men who lacked confidence in themselves.

Most of the preaching in our churches is directed at one rather than to one. The continual negative message that man is inherently evil; negates any chance for success of the Christian faith. I do not need any imposter reminding me constantly that I am evil. I know that I am no more evil than I am good. If I am honest with myself, I know when I have done evil and when I have done a good thing. I do not require any Calvinist shouting and deriding me in some senseless attempt to drive out a make-believe devil when I do evil. If I deliberately do evil things it is because that is how I choose to be. I do not need any Lucifer whispering in my ear. The evilness in me comes from my evil thoughts. My thoughts are not the fault of some innocent devil that man created to blame for all his misdeeds.

The principle objective of any religious faith should be the improved humanity of its flock. The members of the faith and church should become more humane. The memorization of propaganda such as doctrines and doctrinaires, the fantasy and make-believe of the faith, is not capable of teaching one to become humane. This fact can be proven by the simple but honest study of the words and actions of known Christians. The manner in which one treats his fellow man is the measurement of his humanity and spirituality.

No man can claim to have a *meaningful* faith if he constantly preaches and practices intolerance and superiority concepts toward other religious faiths. One is not a good religious or holy person when he is preaching false doctrines and doctrinaires which have been proven false by science. No matter what mortal man has written in his books of faith, if the messages are unreal, untruthful, or dishonest, the sources of the messages are spiritless and evil. Faiths can never be proven as truth or fact. Science and mathematics are the only provable truths. Most philosophies of man have never been proven as truths. Thomas Paine stated that, "Science is the true theology." He also proclaimed that, "God exists and there it lies."

Our science texts, which are far more truthful than any book of faith, have to be updated constantly as the knowledge of the universe is revealed to man. Knowledge of the universe is forever advancing. Truths are constantly being revealed. The information in most books of religious faiths was written centuries before man had learned much of what we know to be the truth today. Most religious faiths were written hundreds of years ago and are hundreds of years out of date. Man and his universe do not stand still!

No book of religious faith, written thousands of years ago, should pretend to proclaim what one can do with his body. No god or religious faith owns my body. My body belongs to me. Mother Nature gave me my body. Mother Nature has never communicated with man and said some god owns me. No religion that mortal man has created has the right to deny me what nature has given me.

Man was on this earth thousands upon thousands of years before Christianity was forcefully thrust upon the unsuspecting and ignorant masses by the Catholic Church. As a reality of nature, man was enjoying natural sex these thousands of years before the creation of false gods and religious faiths by mortal man. The gods of Judaism and Christianity are the creations of Moses and the creators of Christ, such as Matthew, Mark, Luke, and John. Mother Nature is not the work of an evil and vindictive god. Natural sex was only declared evil by men who understood very little about truth. Today many of us still follow the words of these stupid, unknowing men.

The Bible attempts to make the creation of man a fanciful fairytale devoid of reality. Mother Nature has not approved of or declared as truth anything about man and his sex life as portrayed in the Bible. Rationally intelligent man could not buy into the fanciful approach to life as presented in the unreal Bible. Truly rational man cannot pretend to believe in the fantasy of any Garden of Eden. Those pretending that the Garden of Eden ever existed are denying the intelligence that mother Nature gave them. Blinding oneself from reality is an example of *Blind, Leading the Blind.*

Christians need to recognize the truth of the vast range of knowledge the universe has presented to man. Science has seen to the fact that we are no longer the stupid and ignorant ones that we were in the days of Moses and Jesus. Most of us are now educated and sensible and humane beings able to make rational choices if we have not allowed our religious faiths to blind us from reality. We no longer require the church to be our protector and make all life decisions for us. Many of us are able to see the hypocrisy in the untruthful doctrines and doctrinaires of the false faiths that unknowing man has produced. Christianity cannot save man any more than it is going to be able to save itself. Two thousand years of Christianity is not a long time when compared to the age of man on earth. Organized religious faiths which refuse to recognize the reality of the universe cannot possibly survive the rapid advancement of scientific truths. The reality of the availability of truthful communications through the use of such systems as the internet will seal the demise of organized religions. It is simply a matter of a few years now.

Albert Einstein said, "Science without religion is lame; religion without science is blind." Since most religions, such as Christianity, still deny science, their blindness will lead them to their own destruction.

The Christian right has no right trying to tell me what I should believe or how I should act. Christianity has never been voted in as the government of the people. According to our Constitution, our governmental bodies are supposed to be free of any particular religious faith.

As George Washington believed, "Every man conducting himself as a good citizen and being accountable to God alone for his religious opinions, ought to be protected in worshipping the Deity according to the dictates of his own conscience." Thomas Jefferson declared, "All persons shall have full and free liberty of religious opinion; nor shall any be compelled to frequent or maintain any religious institutions."

The so-called Christian fundamentalists are totally wrong when they declare that the god mentioned in various governmental documents refers to the Christian god. The god mentioned in these documents refers to the universal god of Jefferson, Madison, and others who were mostly Deists. The god mentioned by these men was nature. Our laws also state that the government shall make no laws establishing a religion. Christianity is not mentioned anywhere in our laws as being the law of the land. Christianity has no authority to direct our lives.

Since I believe Christianity to be a detriment, it has no right to be in my life. I believe the Christian faith to be a regressive and destructive force. The Christian faith is only that which some have chosen to adopt. The Christian faith is not the law of the United States or the universe. Since Christianity is not my faith, Christians need to keep their faith out of my life. The tenets of the Christian faith and its inhumane actions that it has employed are proof of the evilness of Christianity.

No book of faith is capable of teaching one to become spiritual. One can memorize all the words of all religious texts of man and still be spiritless. Spirituality is not part of any organized religious faith. Spirituality comes to one who has become one with himself, the universe, nature and the reality of life. It is impossible to become one with any god since man and gods do not exist on the same plane. Faiths are realities of the mind while man is a reality of nature. Religious faiths of mortal man deny reality and the nature of man, thus are incapable of teaching man the necessary truths he needs in order to reach a state of spirituality.

....

"I like your Christ; I don't like your Christians. Your Christians are so unlike your Christ!"

Mahatmas Gandhi

"It never ceases to amaze me at how many religions depend upon circumcised penises."

Dawn Henderson

"It's interesting to speculate how it developed that in two of the most anti-feminists institutions, the church and the law court, the men are wearing the dresses."

Flo Kennedy

"When one person suffers from a delusion, it is called insanity. When many people suffer from a delusion, it is called religion."

Robert M. Persig

"Pray, v. To Ask the laws of the universe be annulled in behalf of a single petitioner confessedly unworthy."

Ambose Bierce

"When did I realize I was God? Well, I was praying, and I suddenly realized I was talking to myself."

--Anon

"The old lady who said there must be a devil, else how could they make pictures that looked exactly like him, reasoned liked a trained theologian – like a doctor of divinity."

Robert Green Ingersoll

"People want to kill people, and they want biblical permission to do so."

Wilma Ann Bailey

"Theocracy has always been the synonym for a bleak and narrow, if not a fierce and blood-stained tyranny."

William Archer

"We positively affirm: When our leaders speak, the THINKING has been done."
Mormon Teacher's Message for June 1945

"The world holds two classes of men: intelligent men without religion, and religious men without intelligence."

Abu'l-Ala-Al-Maarri

"If you love god, burn a church."

Jello Biafra (ex-Dead Kennedy's singer)

"I should like to see, and this will be the last and most ardent of my desires, I should like to see the last king strangled with the guts of the last priest."

J. Messelier of Paris 1773

"Faith: noun. Belief without evidence in what is told by one who speaks without knowledge, of things without parallel."

Ambose Bierce

"If we are going to teach *creation science* as an alternative to evolution, then we should also teach the stork theory as an alternative to biological reproduction."

Judith Hayes

"About thirty years ago there was much talk that geologists ought to observe and not theorize; and I well remember someone saying that at this rate a man might as well go into a gravel-pit and count the pebbles and describe the colours. How odd it is that anyone should not see that all observation must be for or against some view if it is to be of any service!"

Charles Darwin, 1861

"For my part, I would as soon be descended from that heroic little monkey, who braved his dreaded enemy in order to save the life of his keeper; or from that old baboon, who descending from the mountains, carried away in triumph his young comrade from a crowd of astonished dogs – as from a savage who delights to torture his enemies, offers up bloody sacrifices, practices infanticide without remorse, treats his wives like slaves, knows no decency, and is haunted by the grossest superstitions."

Charles Darwin, 1871

"My only wish is...to transform friends of God into friends of man, believers into thinkers, devotees of prayer into devotees of work, candidates for the hereafter into students of the world, Christians who, by their own profession and admission, are *'half animal, half angel'* into whole *persons.*"

Ludwig Feuerbach

"If God has spoken, why is the universe not convinced?"

Percy Bysshe Shelly

My Belief Verses Their Beliefs

Faith is not a synonym of truth.

My belief system does not instruct me that it is the one and only and that if I do not follow it, I go straight to hell! My belief has but one commandment which just happens to be that of the Golden Rule. The total of my belief system is, **'Do unto others as you would have others do unto you!"** That is it, there ain't no more! Anything more than this statement of truth, is nothing more than great sounding rhetoric and a matter of self-delusion. I need no false god and its religious faith to cloud or distort my *natural reality.*

All the fantasy, sorcery, and mysticism which is the greater part of Christianity, is there to amuse, awe, and confuse the unsuspecting and unthinking faithful. There is nothing mystifying about natural life if one is honest, truthful, and up to facing his true nature. If one accepts the creative force of nature, one cannot be mystified or confused. Nature is the reality of truth. Prejudiced and biased views of life are not the stuff of life but merely the stuff of religious faiths and man's attempts to escape his natural reality. Faiths of mortal man are created in his belief that he needs to **subdue** and **subjugate** himself and his fellow man's behaviors. The books of man which promote feelings of superiority are the works of disillusioned and evil man. Those books which proclaim, "I am the light," shall forever hold man in darkness and ignorance of truth.

Most of man's books about his religious faiths are filled with empty words from the creators of the faith. Since man quite often refuses to accept the reality of truth and the truth of reality, most of his words about his faiths are insincere, untruthful, and unknowing or unenlightened. Man's books of faith are filled to over flowing with prejudiced and biased words of bigoted and hypocritical man who is trying to throw off the shackles of truth. The creative force of the universe has not explained himself to man. The creator does not communicate with man. Man is not the only creations of Mother Nature.

I will not pry into your personal life as long as your philosophy of life does not try to negate my natural rights given to me by Mother Nature. Your life is your own as long as it does not interfere with my life. I do not need anyone telling me how to live. In the United States, too many bigots and hypocrites of the Christian right are trying to subjugate me and control all aspects of my personal life according to the sinful doctrinaires of their faith.

John Adams declared, "The question before the human race is, whether the God of nature shall govern the world by His own laws, or whether priests and kings shall rule it by fictitious miracles."

Spirituality cannot be taught. One might be shown the path to reaching spirituality, but the actual finding comes from within oneself through meditation, not any religious prayers to a god. One must first have a positive attitude toward the universe, especially man, himself and nature. Spirituality comes from the realization of self, as relating to the universe, nature and the universal and natural laws.

As John Adams stated, "When philosophical reason is clear and certain by intuition or necessary induction, no subsequent revelation supported by prophecies or miracles can supersede it."

....

"Life in Lubbock, Texas taught me two things, one is that God loves you and you're going to burn in hell. The other is that sex is the most awful, dirty thing on the face of the earth and you should save it for someone you love."

Butch Hancock

"During almost fifteen centuries has the legal establishments of Christianity been on trial. What have been its fruit? More or less in all places, pride an indolence in the clergy, ignorance and servility in the laity; in both, superstition, bigotry and persecution."

James Madison

"There has never been a good war or a bad peace."

Benjamin Franklin

"The only freedom which deserves the name, is that of pursuing our own good in our own way, so long as we do not attempt to deprive other of theirs, or impede their efforts to obtain it."

John Stuart Mill

"When I do good, I feel good; when I do bad, I feel bad. That's my religion."

Abraham Lincoln

"It is best to read the weather forecast before praying for rain."

Mark Twain

Playing God

The cost of adopting a religious faith is the forfeiture
of one's natural humanity and intelligence.

Christians love to play god. Since their faith teaches them that their Christ is the son of the lord god that Moses created, they assume that the creator of the universe and Christ are one and the same. In addition, Catholics throw in Mary and a holy spirit, even though there is very little spirit in Catholicism. They fail to understand that their god is not a reality of the natural world of man. Gods exist solely in the minds of the faithful. The god of Moses is no father of any mortal man. No man on the earth has ever had a supernatural god as a father. No mortal man has ever procreated with a goddess. No mortal woman has ever procreated with a god. This kind of procreation appears only in Greek mythology and unenlightened religious faiths of man. Man and his gods do not exist on the same plane. Man is natural and tangible. Gods dwell only in the heads of the faithful and are intangible. The father of Jesus, if he ever existed, was the mortal man who had sexual intercourse with his mother. Reality and this fantasy mix only in the heads of the fanatic Christian faithful.

Reverends and priests believe themselves to be sent by a god. They believe themselves to be called by their god. Since their faith denies the reality of Mother Nature and the creative force of the universe, these deceived individuals are merely serving the creators of their faith. Yet, they continually bless others in the name of their false god.

Doctors also love to play god. Whenever a doctor saves one from a certain natural death, he has intervened and assumed the role of a god. Doctors are trying to negate nature anytime they save one from a death that would occur from natural causes. Don't get me wrong, I am not against doctors saving lives, but I believe they are acting the role o f a savior like that present in most religious faiths.

In the United States, we had a doctor who went to prison because he tried to play the role of a god one too many times. Dr. Kovorkian was helping the poor unfortunates to escape their suffering and greet death sooner than Mother Nature had decided. Kovorkian made the sad mistake of getting too bold and the State of Michigan finally was forced by the Christian laws of the state to put the godhead of Kovorkian in prison.

Dr. Kovorkian was giving a much needed and vital service. Some wished to die in dignity and escape their needless suffering. The State of Michigan was not interested in the dignity of dying or the humanity of the doctor's actions because Christian Laws were controlling death in Michigan, as in all fifty states. Christians say that one must suffer for his god and such actions as those of Kovorkian are condemned by our Christian courts.

We have in our government, many legislators who love to play god. Anytime a governmental body passes a law that is placed on the books simply because of Christian values alone, rather than the values of natural humanity, it is playing god. Any law passed in the name of any religious faith is illegal. Unfortunately we have many such illegal and unconstitutional laws on our books. America is not a Christian church state although many of our laws would lead one to think so!

....

"Faith is often the boost of the man who is too lazy to investigate."

F. M. Knowles

"Most people would rather die than think; in fact, they do so."

Bertrand Russell

"I will not attack your doctrines, nor your creeds, if they accord liberty to me. If they hold thought to be dangerous – if they aver that doubt is a crime, then I attack them one and all, because they enslave the minds of man."

Robert Ingersoll

"For ages, a deadly conflict has been waged between a few brave men and women of thought and genius upon the one side, and the great ignorant religious mass on the other. This is the war between Science and Faith. The few have appealed to reason, to honor, to law, to freedom, to fear, to miracle, to slavery, to the unknown, and to misery hereafter. The few have said, 'Think!' The many have said, 'Believe!' "

Robert Ingersoll

"If there be gods we cannot help them, but we can assist our fellow-men. We cannot love the inconceivable, but we can love wife and child and friend."

Robert Ingersoll

"Where knowledge ends, religion begins."

Benjamin Disraeli

"I disapprove of what you say, but I will defend to death your right to say it."
Beatrice Hall, 1907 (many times wrongfully attributed to Voltaire)

Understanding Rational Religious Faith

Knowing is not as profound as **Understanding**

For sometime in the recent past here in Ajijic, Mexico, (near where I reside), we have witnessed a running dispute between those of the Christian faith and the secular humanists, of whether the figure of speech, **rational religious faith** is or is not an **oxymoron.**

Bob Harwood, a writer who spends his winters here, declares in his book, *Seeking Common Ground in a Troubled World,* that the statement is rational. The secular humanists declare that it is not. I, being a Deist, believe that Bob and they are both correct. I shall endeavor to explain to you how this is possible.

In order to understand what this discourse consists of, I went to my dictionary, Chambers 1998 edition.

Chambers describes faith as trust or confidence; belief in the statement of another person; belief in the truth of reveled religion; confidence and trust in god; the living reception of religious belief; that which is believed; any system of religious belief, especially the religion one considers true; fidelity to promises; honesty; word of honor pledged; faithfulness.

Chambers describes religious as concerned with, devoted to or imbued with religion; scrupulous; bound to a monastic life; strict; very exact.

Rational is described as that of reason; endowed with reason; agreeable to reason; sane; intelligent; judicious; commensurable with natural numbers.

I, therefore, conclude that it is rational and reasonable that both those of a religious faith and the secular humanists to be correct in their beliefs.

Nowhere in the descriptions of faith, religious, or rational do we find any of them as being absolute truth.

Religion is a belief system based on faith. Faith is no synonym of truth. Faith does not imply truth, contrary to those who believed as jerry Falwell, Pat Robertson, and George W. Bush.

To adopt the Christian faith, one must adopt its god, doctrines and doctrinaires as Bob Harwood has. Secular humanists do not possess that faith in a god.

To anyone of a religious faith, a **rational** religious faith is reasonable since he believes in his god. To a secular humanist, a religious faith is **irrational** since he does not believe in any god.

Therefore, I conclude that Bob and the secular humanists are both correct in their beliefs. Rational religious faith is correct for Bob and the faithful, incorrect for secular humanists and those of my belief, Deism.

As for me, the creative power that created the universe does not communicate with any of its creations.

···

"The only difference between religion and superstition is the spelling."

--Anon

The only difference between a cult and a religion is the amount of real estate they own."

Frank Zappa

"The Bible and the Church have been the greatest stumbling blocks in the way of woman's emancipation."

Elizabeth Cady Stanton

"The Bible teaches that woman brought sin and death into the world, that she precipitated the fall of the race, that she was arraigned before the judgment seat of Heaven, tried, condemned and sentenced. Marriage for her was to be a condition of bondage, maternity a period of suffering and anguish, and in silence and subjection, she was to play the role of a dependent on man's bounty for all her material wants, and for all the information she might desire...Here is the Bible position of woman briefly summed up."

Elizabeth Cady Stanton

"A scientific truth does not triumph by convincing its opponents and making them see the light, but rather because its opponents eventually die and a new generation grows up that is familiar with it."

Maxwell Planck

"If all people learned to think in the non-Aristotelian manner of quantum mechanics, the world would change so radically that most of what we call "stupidity" and even a great deal of what we consider "insanity" might disappear, and the "intractable" problems of war, poverty and injustice would suddenly seem a great deal closer to solution."

Alfred Korzybski

Part Two Contents: Reality

The Greatest Fault
Show Me
The Soul of Man
Reality and Me
Creation
Christianity, Reality, Truth, Fallacy, Fact, and Theory
Religion Verses Reality
Natural and Supernatural
Nature Verses the Catholic Church
Heaven Verses Reality
The Creative Force Verses the Gods of Man
Nature Verses the Gods of Man
The Reality of Life
Christianity and Violence
The Unreality of Christianity
Prophets and Prophecies from Hell
Bigotry and Hypocrisy
The Christian Right Verses Reality
The Audacity of the Religious Right

**Truth in matters of religion
is simply
the opinion that has survived.**

Oscar Wilde

The Greatest Fault

The greatest fault
   of man is his lack of faith in himself;
   of religious faiths is the fact that they are blind;
   of religious fundamentalists is their feeling of superiority;
   of humanity in general is its lack of honesty and truthfulness;
   of many philosophies of man is their lack of reality;
   of religious belief systems is their belief that the tenets of their faith are the only truths;
   of Christian fundamentalists is their belief that the belief in their faith gives them the right to subjugate me as well as all citizens of the United States.

Frederick J. Azbell

Show Me

Show me
a man
that communicates with a god,
I will show you
a man
living in a world
of his own creation.

Show me
a man
that believes his god
is the one and only,
I will show you
a bigot.

Show me
a man
that believes his adoptive faith
makes him better than others,
I will show you
a hypocrite.

Show me
a religious fundamentalist,
I will show you
one that has blinded himself
as to reality.

Show me
a Christian fundamentalist,
I will show you
one who is trying his best
to make my world
a living hell.

Frederick J. Azbell

The Soul of Man

Notions of a permanent individual personality,
soul, or self are examples of fictitious realities.

No such thing as an individual soul exists in this world. There is only one soul for all of mankind. What we have been taught as the soul, is in reality, nothing more than the temporary self.

The self is what others have assigned to the one. One decides his words and actions. Others interpret these words and actions of the individual temporary self, according to their own biases, then, determine the importance of the individual self.

The temporary individual self exists as long as it is alive. When the self dies, it enters the universal soul of mankind.

"In spite of all the yearnings of men, no one can produce a single fact or reason to support the belief in God and in personal immortality."

Clarence Darrow

"If I had been the Virgin Mary, I would have said, 'No.' "

Margaret Smith

"What was it that Adam ate that he wasn't supposed to eat? It wasn't just an apple. It was the fruit of the Tree of Knowledge of Good and Evil. The subtle message? 'Get smart and I'll fuck you over,' sayeth the Lord. God is the smartest, and he doesn't want any competition. Is this not an absolutely anti-intellectual religion?"

Frank Zappa

"You are never dedicated to do something you have complete confidence in. No one is fanatically shouting that the sun is going to rise tomorrow. They know it's going to rise tomorrow. When people are fanatically dedicated to political or religious faiths or any other kind of dogmas or goals, it's always because these dogmas or goals are in doubt!"

Robert M. Pirsig

"If God has spoken, why is the world not convinced?"

Percy Bysshe Shelley

"A believer is not a thinker and a thinker is not a believer."

Marian Noel Sherman

"The Christian resolution to find the world ugly and bad has made the world ugly and bad."
Friedrich Nietzche

"Has science ever retreated? No! It is Catholicism which has always retreated before her, and will always be forced to retreat."

Emile Zola

"I assert most unhesitatingly, that the religion of the South is a mere covering for the most horrid crimes – a justifier of the most appalling barbarity, a sanctifier of the most hateful frauds, and a dark shelter under which the darkest, foulest, grossest, and most infernal deeds of slaveholders find the strongest protection. Were I to be again reduced to the chains of slavery, next to that enslavement, I should regard being the slave of a religious master the greatest calamity that could befall me...I...hate the corrupt, slaveholding women-whipping, cradle-plundering, partial and hypocritical Christianity of this land."

Frederick Douglass (after his escape)

Reality and Me

All truths are reality but not all of reality is the truth.

I am a realist. I walk the face of this earth. I enjoy self-delusions and dreams, fantasies, and make-believe, but I know and understand the reality of each.

I am the pessimistically optimistic realist with a bent of humanistic pragmatism. I choose to believe that most things shall work-out for the better, but I also understand that if there be the slightest opportunity some detractor is going to throw a monkey- wrench into the machinery!

I would be more closely called a Deist. I am a proud heretic by Christian standards. The Christian faith's Bible is, to me, the greatest collection of the fantasies of sorcery, mysticism, make-believe, and fairytales that have ever been assembled into one book of fiction. The Bible was written by biased, unknowing, spiritless, mortal men. All religious faiths are the creations of frustrated man trying to find the meaning of life while denying the reality of his natural existence. Man has been creating these falsehoods of faith since his time on earth evolved. Not one of these faiths has found the true meaning of life because faiths are not based on natural truths.

The creative force continues its work throughout the universe which, of course, includes our earth. Mother Nature and her natural laws is the creative force of the universe at work on the earth. We are the creatures of nature and its evolution, not any false god that unenlightened, biased, mortal, religious men have created to meet their assumed needs or desires.

As far as I am concerned, one can choose to be whomever he wishes and adopt any faiths one desires, just don't bother me with your false faith and god. Don't display your lack of intelligence by telling me that I am going to your hell for not believing in your voodoo religion. In my world of reality, there is no such place as hell. The creative force is not vindictive. Mother Nature has no religious faith and does not see, hear, or judge man. There is no need for the creative force or Mother Nature to be vindictive, such as the lord god of Moses.

Don't be so ignorant as to suggest that some god that man has created is going to punish me. Don't try to suggest that *this* is better than *that*. Only I can determine those things for myself. Critics try to make asinine assumptions as to what is best. Critics cannot possibly know what is best for others unless they would happen to know others better than they know themselves. What critics consider best for themselves is not necessarily best for others. I consider most critics to be nothing more than frustrated dictators such as the character of man-created gods.

Don't be so ignorant as to suggest that your god has the strength to strike me dead for my heresy! The creative force of the universe, nor Mother Nature, has created any god to judge man. The traits of bigoted and hypocritical man and his vindictive gods are not those traits of the creative force of the universe and nature.

I do not walk the face of this earth with my head floating in the clouds or buried in the sod. I walk with my feet planted firmly on the ground. I cannot live this life preparing for a future home in the sky. That life does not exist anymore than pie in the sky. Mother Nature, nor the creative force, has promised me a next life in any sky. The theory of a next life can never be confirmed or proven. Living a good and humane life on this earth should prepare me for the next life if there happens to be such a thing. For me, the religious faiths of man are nothing more than fantasy. I enjoy fantasy but it will never control my life.

....

"Could you take Pat Robertson too? It's my understanding his greatest wish is to meet you, Lord." (After the death of Jerry Falwell)

Seen on Bartcop.com

"God has spoken to me. I listen to God, and what I've heard is that I'm supposed to devote myself to rebuilding the conservative base of the Republican Party, and I think we shouldn't be underestimated."

Tom Delay, from the New Yorker

"To him it's blindly obvious: the great religions all began at a time when we knew a tiny fraction of what we know about the origins of Earth and human life. It's understandable that early humans would develop stories about gods or God to salve their ignorance. But people today have no such excuse. If they continue to believe in the unbelievable, or they do, they are morons or lunatics or liars."

--The New York Times on Christopher Hitchens

Creation

The creative force of the universe, through Mother Nature,
is the creator of all life on earth.

Everything began approximately twelve to thirteen billion years ago with that tremendous Big Bang. The creative matter of which everything in the universe is composed was born at that instant. The evolution of the universe and our solar system continues to this day and shall never cease.

It has taken these past twelve to thirteen billion years to evolve the universe as it is and over four billion years of evolution of the earth. The universe and all its heavenly bodies got its start with that colossal Big Bang. The evolution of matter here on earth is under the control of nature. Mother Nature is the creative force at work here on earth. The evolution of man on earth did not begin in some fairytale Garden of Eden. The evolution of the earth shall never cease as long as our solar system exists. The universe is forever expanding and evolving as life on earth is forever being created and destroyed.

As any reasonably intelligent person knows, life on earth did not begin as fantasy from the minds of mortal man. Man, along with the flora and fauna of this earth, have taken billions of years of evolution. The time of man on earth is infinitesimal when compared to the billions of years since the creation of our solar system.

Man did not appear on the earth until billions of years of evolution of the universe, our solar system, and the earth. It is unknowing and unenlightened man who has tried unsuccessfully to control, deny, or change this evolution of the creative force and nature.

The creative force of nature with its universal and natural laws is no fantasy from the minds of spiritless, unknowing, mortal man. The fanciful creation of man, flora, and fauna in a Garden of Eden has no reality except as a fairytale of unknowing, unrealistic, and supernatural dreams of man.

Man is not likely to ever know exactly how it all got started. The evolution of the earth has been and forever shall be the charge of Mother Nature and her natural law. The evolution has never ceased for these past four billion years or more. Life on earth is constantly evolving as the universe is constantly expanding and our scientific knowledge is ever increasing.

....

"I think every good Christian ought to kick Jerry Falwell's ass."

Senator Barry Goldwater

"Why should we take advice on sex from the Pope? If he knows anything about it, he shouldn't."

George Bernard Shaw

"A'' religions begin with a revolt against morality, and perish when morality conquers them."

George Bernard Shaw

"No theory is too false, no fable too absurd, no superstition too degrading for acceptance when it has become embedded in common belief. Men will submit themselves to torture and to death, mothers will immolate [burn] their children at the bidding of beliefs they thus accept."

Henry George

"The foundation of morality is to...give up pretending to believe that for which there is no evidence, and repeating unintelligible propositions about things beyond the possibilities of knowledge."

T. H. Huxley

"Freethinkers are those who are willing to use their minds without prejudice and without fearing to understand things that clash with their own customs, privileges, or beliefs. This state of mind is not common, but it is essential for right thinking; where it is absent, discussion is apt to become worse than useless."

Leo Tolstoy

"The most heinous and the most cruel crimes of which history has record have been committed under the cover of religion or equally noble motives."

Mohandas Gandhi

"Religion is a disease. It is born of fear; it compensates through hate in the guise of authority, revelation. Religion, enthroned in a powerful social organization, can become incredibly sadistic. No religion has been more cruel than the Christian."

Dr. George A. Dorsey

"It is not the function of our government to keep the citizen from falling into error; it is the function of our government from falling into error."

Robert H. Jackson, U.S. Supreme Court Justice, 1950

Christianity, Reality, Truth, Fallacy, Fact, and Theory

Man chooses his truths.

Christianity, theory, and fallacy are the creations of man. Truth, fact and reality come from universal and natural law. Although man is unable to create, alter, or destroy the truths of the universe or nature, he is constantly trying to do so.

We have our famous House of Representatives, better known as the House of Special and Individual Interests, supposedly trying to find the answer to all the violence and killings in our schools. This house of fools, however, is pretending to find answers to this terrible sin with the use of little truth, reality, fact, or reason. We have this misguided ship of fools blaming everything and everyone except themselves. They are the government but refuse to admit that they are a big part of the problem. Until our government gets real and starts dealing honestly with itself and us, we must pay the consequences.

The killings in our schools are not caused by the lack of Christ in them. The killings are not caused by guns, Hollywood, the media, the lack of parental control, or the failure of church teachings. The fault lies with the total of the above as well as countless other factors. The fault lies with the sum of all the persons, events, and actions our children have been exposed to in their short lifetimes. The creations of man and living have caused the killings. Of course, the greatest fault goes to the warped minded individuals committing these crimes against humanity. Much of the fault goes to those who have blinded themselves from the truth such as Jerry, Pat, Dubya, and all their good buddies who continually preach intolerance and hatred. Intolerance of others and their beliefs are the major causes which drive these emotionally and mentally ill fanatics to commit these crimes against the societies of mankind.

This *House of Dimwits* is not seriously interested in finding any truths or real answers to this perplexing problem of society when it relies on a bigoted and hypocritical religious faith for help. The members of the House are only interested in laying the blame on someone other than themselves. We all need scapegoats when we do not have the foggiest idea of what to do. We shall never have an answer without truth and honesty. Religious faiths cannot solve a problem which they have a great part in creating. No creator or god of man is capable of resolving this issue. Mother Nature supplied us with brains for thinking through these problems created by man trying to live with man. No amount of blind faith and unrealistic praying is going to solve these sins of the troubled.

Two thousand years of Christianity and a host of other religious faiths have not been capable of erasing violence from our world. Many of our religions, such as Christianity,

Judaism, and Islam, have been the greatest fomenters of the hatred and intolerance which causes this violence.

These religions, which preach superiority concepts, are what the world turns to for the elimination of this blight of violence. This trust is not working out because it is unrealistic and supernatural. The answer to the cause of violence is not to be found in any unrealistic and supernatural god or faith that man has created to meet his selfish needs or wants.

Guns, knives, bombs, clubs and like weapons, do not kill without the hand of man. Man does kill man! Only the self blinded among us blame others for the crimes we are helping to foment. We need truth! The truth, or lack of it, is the product of mankind. We are the sinners. The truth is here. It is man who hides from the truth. We are the ones who cannot raise our children properly because we are relying on the teachings and preachings from our books written by unknowing, untruthful, biased, and prejudiced man. We are trying to live in this naturally real world of man with false concepts of a future *pie in the sky home.* We must get real and stop burying our heads in supernatural doctrines and doctrinaires of our unreal religious faiths.

We have drug addicts raising kids. We have alcoholics raising kids. We have emotionally and mentally unstable nuts raising kids. We have kids raising kids. We have worn-out grandparents raising their kids, kids. We have holier-than-thou Christian bigots and hypocrites raising kids while telling the rest of us how to raise our kids. We have Christian fundamentalists, such as Pat Robertson, Jerry Falwell, and George W. Bush preaching false doctrinaires of faith daily. We need to wake up to the fact that if Christianity was worth its salt, half of the Christian marriages in the United States would not end in divorce.

We must get real and become truthfully one with nature, natural law, humane humanity, and reality if we ever expect to be able to solve this or any other evil acts of mankind. We cannot find the truth of these troubling problems until we get rid of the bigotry, hypocrisy, and false feelings of superiority within ourselves. Our religious faiths are the greatest fomenters of intolerance when they preach their superiority doctrinaires. We must get rid of the terms *heretics* and *infidels* and all other such demeaning and ridiculous name callings.

We must realize that a supernatural god is not capable of dealing with natural man. We cannot promote love and respect as long as we are preaching superiority and placing all our faith in bigoted and hypocritical religious faiths. We need to develop more faith and understanding of ourselves and the societies of mankind, We must realize that through the centuries, with all the religions in the world, man has still not found *truth.*

When Albert Mohler and his Southern Baptist friends declare, "Only those who accept Jesus Christ as their personal savior shall enter Heaven," we must inform them that that is fine and dandy with us as we do not wish to spend eternity with bigots and hypocrites such as they.

Albert is trying to force members of Islam, Judaism, and any who believe in Heaven, to give up their faith and join his. Reverend Mohler and his satanic style religion need to practice less false doctrinaires and join the human race. The members of Judaism were speaking of Heaven thousands of years before the Christians created their Christ, if one believes in the Bible.

How can we ever expect to solve any of our major ills with false concepts of reality? There is no reality at all in such asinine statements as that of rev. Mohler. Mohler appears to be living in a fantasy world of his own creation. No wonder some of us have become so lost!

What we need to do is turn this world over to the children and older women. Art Linkletter declares, "The most honest people in this world are children under seven and women over seventy!" I'm with Art! We desperately need more truth and honesty in this world.

A few years ago, I came across this false prophet from HELL on the TV while awaiting my favorite NBC program, *Meet The Press*. I had some time to kill, so I was flipping through the channels of my Dish Network. There on CBS was this gray-haired gentleman being coached by a blond lady on his right who, herself, must have been in her sixties.

This escapee from the happy farm was putting down another false prophet who had declared that the world would end sometime in July of the year 2000. It was the contention of this gray-haired prophet that this could not possibly be true since Jesus Christ was returning to earth on January 1, 2001!

I now wonder how these two false Christian prophets can explain the fact that the earth and we are still here but Christ is nowhere to be found!

I nearly pissed my pants that day! I was in such convulsions of laughter over the stupidity expressed by these two Christian men. But the troubling and disturbing fact remains that we have millions of ignorant faithful who believe in these fruitcakes. When the sun burns out a few billion years from now, those of us still around can kiss our asses goodbye! Until that time, eons from now, the earth shall be here with or without man and his religious faiths.

....

"The memory of my own suffering has prevented me from ever shadowing one young soul with the superstitions of the Christian religion."

Elizabeth Cady Stanton

"To be patriotic, hate all nations but your own; to be religious, all sects but your own; to be mortal all pretenses but your own."

Lionel Strachey

George Bernard Shaw

"I see little divinity about them or you. You talk to me of Christianity when you are in the act of hanging your enemies. Was there ever such blasphemous nonsense!"

"Custom will reconcile people to any atrocity."

"The fact that a believer is happier than a skeptic is no more to the point than the fact that a drunken man is happier than a sober one. The happiness of credulity is cheap and dangerous quality."

"There are scores of thousands of sects who are ready at a moment's notice to reveal the Will of God on every possible subject."

"No man ever believes that the bible means what it says: He is always convinced that it says what he means."

"Common people do not pray, my lord: they only beg."

"No sooner had Jesus knocked over the dragon of superstition then Paul boldly set it on its legs again in the name of Jesus."

"It is not disbelief that is dangerous to our society; it is belief."

"Beware of the man whose God is in the skies."

"What God hath joined together no mail shall put asunder: God will take care of that."

"All great truths begin as blasphemies."

"Martyrdom is the only way in which a person with no ability can become great."

"There is only one religion, though there are a thousand versions of it."

"We have not lost faith, but we have transformed it from God to the medical profession."

Religion Verses Reality

While religious faiths deal with supernatural idealities,
life is a natural reality.

The greatest difficulty that I have in accepting the Christian faith is the fact that religious leaders and their message are so distantly removed from natural reality. Their bodies are here on earth but their minds are dwelling in a distant unknown world of ideality. They appear unable to rationally synchronize their mortal existence with their dream-like state.

Religious fundamentalists, such as Jerry, Pat, and Dubya believe that having the natural ability to memorize word for word the contents of their Bible makes them religious and better than others. They may be Christian! It is doubtful that they are religious. They are a far-cry from being spiritual. There is no spirituality in the majority of the bigoted and hypocritical doctrinaires they are espousing. Their preachings do not contain qualities which a humane person could accept. It is sad that these prophets from HELL can quote words of which they have no understanding. Their interpretations have no meaning for humane, natural man.

Since most religious faiths were created by unenlightened mortal man thousands of years ago, they are subject to unlimited questions. Man and time have moved well passed the contents of the Bible. In this age of mass communication and enlightened scientific knowledge, it is becoming significantly more difficult for rational and intelligent man to accept these philosophical theories of biased, prejudiced, and unknowing mortal men who wrote this spiritless religious textbook.

All of the religious books which many unthinking persons place all their faith in, have to be judged as any philosophical work, they are subject to flaws. They are subject to the passage of time. They are, for the most part, centuries out of date. Man has moved well passed most of the false doctrinaires and misinformation in any two thousand year old book. The promoters of Christianity are nearly as antiquated as the Bible itself.

In reality, a religious faith should make one a better, humane, human being. Faiths and their gods are created by man in his desperate searches and attempts to find himself, control his and mankind's behaviors. Religious faiths must subjugate mankind in order to control these behaviors. Faiths would be more successful in these attempts to control man if they served mankind rather than some supernatural god.

In most religions, individuals willingly self-hypnotize and deceive themselves into following the tenets of their adopted faith. Those persons better able to accept philosophies based on pure faith alone are those better able at immersing themselves into their religion. Religious fanatics, such as Falwell and friends, have sacrificed their natural will and intelligence in order to accept, without question, the doctrinaires of their adopted faith.

However, intelligence is not the sole determining factor limiting the extent of one's acceptance of and the allegiance to the tenets within a religious faith. An **idiot** can be just as devoted as the most intelligent among us.

Many people believe that if they put in their weekly appearance at church, dressed in their Sunday best, they have demonstrated their devotion to their god and faith. These poor lost ones have never realized the fact that attending a service does not make one holy. These are the same quality of persons who believe that they can say or do as they damn well please, be as inhumane as they choose, as long as they later ask their god to forgive their words and actions.

We have, in this computer age, many places on this earth where people are living as those in Europe did in the Dark Ages. These peoples need the assistance of the compassionate among us, yet we are hampered and prevented in disseminating much vital information by the forces of religious personnel such as the Pope of Rome who declares that these unfortunates first need to adopt his god and be saved.

These false prophets from HELL proclaim that the poor unfortunates will find their salvation in Jesus Christ. How sanctimonious can one become! How Christian of the Pope! This is the same philosophical bull shit propaganda that the white man used when he captured other peoples, enslaved them, and then forced them to accept Christianity.

Whether they be Christian or heathens, these destitute ones need education of life, yet they are being denied birth control and other vital information on contraceptives because these truths conflict with the teachings and doctrinaires of the church. Many Christians teach us that sex is only for procreation. How out of date is this crap! Abortions are sinful! Praying to god will protect us from evils of other men! How far from the truth are such teachings for these people? These preachings of false visions of life are having devastating effects on mankind. Rather than providing the necessary humanitarian and natural truth, the Christians are trying to pretend that sex is evil, especially outside of marriage, not for pleasure, and is only for reproduction. These sinful teachings from their Satan are dishonest, untruthful, and inhumane.

No matter what Christianity claims, nature gave us sex and made it enjoyable to the natural ones among us. In reality, procreation is the furtherest thought in the minds of the majority of us indulging in sex. The sexual urge is a natural one given to us by Mother Nature for our pleasure as well as procreation. Nature does not give gifts and then take them away. Nature made sex a gift of pleasure to man. One's adopted religious faith cannot negate the truths of nature.

These kinds of proclamations and doctrinaires along with mass communication are factors that will be spelling the demise of organized religion. Actively thinking individuals are beginning to admit to these false concepts of unenlightened and spiritless religious men. In this twenty-first century of scientific knowledge and understanding of the universe, organized religions will be relegated to their proper unimportance in the life of man.

Catholics say that women are not fit to be priests because Eve was a woman, disobeyed god, and ate from the tree of knowledge. Eve should not have challenged the lord god of Moses with the truth! They also condemn women for being unclean. The monthly menses of women given to them by Mother Nature, so that they can reproduce, is considered dirty by Judaism and Christianity. Also, since women have been slaves to their men since their evolution, as a result of men's physical dominance, the Christians believe they should remain subservient to their husbands forever.

The unenlightened Christians believe that their disapproval of abortions is going to stop them. No religious faith that man has created can ever be successful in negating natural rights. Mother Nature is in charge of such things.

At the present time there is much confusing talk about stem cell research. Many scientists believe that it has great promise for the prevention and cure of a number of dreaded diseases. Stem cell and fetal research are not going to encourage or discourage most women from aborting or carrying the fetus until birth. A woman's personal situation will determine her choice. That choice is hers and is not that of any religious faith or governmental body. Our government should not be controlled by the philosophy of Christianity or any other religious faith. Mother Nature creates life on this earth.

Religious faiths have not saved man or prevented anything of consequence since they were created by superstitious man. Philosophical self deceptions of the faithful cannot be accepted as interventions of a god. Man's gods are incapable of physical changes in anything. One cannot find the truth of reality, the reality of truth, the truths of nature, nor natural or universal law in the Bible.

....

"I don't know if God exists, but it would be better for His reputation if He didn't."

Joseph Ernest Renard

"Oh Lord, if there is a Lord, save my soul, if I have a soul."

Joseph Ernest Renard

"Skeptical scrutiny is the means, in both science and religion, by which deep thoughts can be winnowed from deep nonsense."

Carl Sagan

"A celibate clergy is an especially good idea because it tends to suppress any hereditary propensity toward fanaticism."

Carl Sagan

"Martyrdom has always been a proof of the intensity, never the correctness, of a belief."

Albert Schweitzer

Natural Verses Supernatural

Man enjoys his fanciful creations

It is amazing that in this world, in this twenty-first century, there are millions of us who do not know, understand nor admit to the differences between what is natural and that which is supernatural.

Roget's Thesaurus describes natural as unaffected, spontaneous, artless, unstudied; unsophisticated, naïve, ingenuous; normal, ordinary, regular, unadorned, unadulterated; inherent, innate, inborn. Roget gives natural the antonyms of affection and deception.

The Chambers Dictionary states that natural is relating to, produced by or according to nature; to the natural world or human nature; not miraculous or supernatural; not the work of humans, not artificial; not interfered with by humans; inborn, innate, inherent; having the feelings that may be expected to come by nature, kindly; normal happening in the usual course; spontaneous; not far-fetched; not acquired; without affectation; not fictitious; physical (esp. as opposed to spiritual or intellectual); lifelike, like nature; based on an innate moral sense, innate reason or instinct rather than revelation...

Chambers describes supernatural as above and beyond nature; not according to the laws of nature; miraculous; magical; spiritual; occult.

From these descriptions of natural and supernatural by recognized authorities of language, I deduce the following:

1. All the heavenly bodies of the universe, the flora and fauna of the earth, including man, are the works of a creative force and are natural truth.

2. All philosophies of man, including religious faiths, are supernatural, not necessarily truth.

3. Things natural cannot be created, altered, or destroyed by the philosophies of man.

4. Things supernatural, being philosophical, are created and controlled by man.

5. Natural things being tangible and supernatural things being intangible are not on the same plane.

6. The communications man has with the supernatural are figments of his creative imagination.

7. The supernatural philosophies of man do not possess the naturalness necessary to create, alter, or destroy the truth of the natural universe.

"You find as you look around the world that every single bit of progress in humane feeling, every improvement in the criminal law, every step toward diminution of war. Every step toward better treatment of the colored races, or every mitigation of slavery, every moral progress that there has been in the world, has been consistently opposed by the organized churches of the world. I say quite deliberately that the Christian religion, as organized in its churches, has been and still is the principal enemy of moral progress in the world."

Bertrand Russell

"The twin doctrines of separation of church and state and liberty of individual conscience are the marrow of our democracy, if not indeed America's most magnificent contribution to the freeing of Western man."

Clinton Rossiter, American historian

"Its first and most immediate purpose rested on the belief that a union of government and religion tends to destroy government and degrade religion."

Justice Black describing the Establishment Clause of the 1st Amendment

"Belief is an obsolete Aristotelian category."

Dr. Jack Sarfatti, physicist

"There is no Energy Shortage. There is no Energy Crisis. There is a *Crisis of Ignorance.*"

R. Buckminister Fuller

"I cannot conceive of a God who rewards and punishes his creatures, or has a will of the type of which we are conscious in ourselves. An individual who should survive his physical death is also beyond my comprehension, nor do I wish it otherwise; such notions are for the fears or absurd egoism of feeble souls."

Albert Einstein

"FAITH, n. Belief without evidence in what is told by one who speaks without knowledge, of things without parallel."

Ambrose Bierce

"The principle of science, the definition, almost, is the following: *The test of all knowledge is experiment,* Experiment is the *sole judge* of scientific "truth."

Richard Feynman

Nature Verses the Catholic Church

The truth of reality, the reality of truth, nor nature,
can be created, altered, or destroyed by any religious faith.

Sex is a gift from Mother Nature through the powers of the creative force of the universe. Nature places us on this earth through the act of natural sex. Nature not only makes sex a means of reproduction, she makes it pleasurable and desirable as a means of releasing us from tensions and stress. Nature makes sure that the natural ones among us have a continual desire for sex. Only the supernatural or unnatural ones have declared this gift of nature to be evil. Mother Nature is the creative force of the universe at work on earth.

After centuries of sexual freedom on the earth, along came these evil and unenlightened Christian men pretending that they knew better than nature! They declared that sex was an evil force and was meant for only reproduction. Sex was not to be pleasurable! If one enjoyed sex, he was a sinner!

These same unenlightened ones declared that masturbation was evil. Semen was only for reproduction! Man was not to throw his seed on the ground! These religious fools declared that Mother Nature did not know what she was doing when she created homosexuals. What nature had created, these spiritless men proclaimed as evil. What gave theses unenlightened ones the right to challenge the natural law of the creative power of the universe? How could unknowing man declare the law of nature as evil? Where did these evil men get their authority?

These unenlightened fools of mankind proceeded to set up this false faith based upon the lord god of Moses and the Christ that their faith had created. These ignorant men created fantasies and fairytales full of mysticism and sorcery. How could men take a world of truth and turn it into some fairytale? How is it that they thought of nature as a *he?* What made them so sure that nature was male? All animal life and vegetation on this earth comes from the female gender. Was this mistake made because at this time in the evolution of mankind, women were no more than slaves to their husbands? Was it because a man purchased his wife and sexual partner from the female's father for a swap of some livestock?

Next these ignorant men proclaimed that women were unfit to serve their god. A woman's monthly menses was considered to be a sign of uncleanliness! Also, according to Moses, the creator of their god, Eve had convinced Adam to eat from the tree of knowledge of bad and good. Women were supposed to remain ignorant as to the reality of the world! Only men and the god that Moses had created were to have any knowledge of the world in which they lived! Since women were to be slaves to their husbands, they did not need knowledge! How is this for rational or sane thinking?

These spiritless ones also declared that natural, mortal man was unfit to serve their god. The servants to their god were to be supernatural men, not contaminated with natural but sinful sex! Sex was deemed dirty, sinful, and human, an act beneath the dignity of those who serve their god!

Then, these spiritless men set up this unrealistic but ritualistic mass which was intended to awe the uneducated hordes into subjugation to the Catholic Church. The Pope of Rome became the supreme commander-in-chief and supposedly took his authority, directions, and power directly from the lord god of Moses and their Jesus Christ which they had created to meet their needs.

Of course, the uneducated masses bought these lines of bullshit since they were ignorant of truth and in need of the protection the church was offering them. After all, the masses in these times, were nothing more than lost sheep. As time passed, however, the flock of ignorant began to find the truth and began to revolt against the dictatorship of the Pope and his church. The Pope was now forced to send out his army of loyalists, led by paid mercenaries, on holy wars or crusades to kill all the heretics who dared challenge his complete authority from god!

Muslims and Christians alike keep their flocks in line by the use of threats and other acts of violence. This means of keeping men subjugated and subservient continues to this day. It's a great tragedy that Christianity needs to sanction violence to keep its congregation in subjugation, thus making itself a Fascist style system of religious faith!

We often pick up our newspapers, magazines, or hear the news on the radio or TV that another priest or priests have been found guilty of molesting their flock of altar boys. We hear of brothers having to leave the seminary for homosexual acts. We hear of priests impregnating nuns. Yet, the Catholic Church still refuses to face the truth of reality of natural sex.

In January of 2002, we had a priest in Boston facing charges of having sexually molested 130 altar boys over a period of 30 years in six different dioceses. The bishops, such as Cardinal Law, were aware of these criminal acts but did nothing but transfer this criminal from one diocese to another in order to hide him from the law. The Catholic Church confessional has become a front for hiding sins against mankind!

Sex is natural! Sex is a gift from Mother Nature. The church cannot pretend to know better than Mother Nature and her natural law. Continual denial of the truth of natural law will eventually cause one to pay for his evilness. When one goes against nature and the natural order of the universe and the world in which he lives, he is going to eventually loose. One can write what he wishes in his books of religious faiths; natural law will have its way in the end. Natural law is the law of Mother Nature and it cannot be altered by the words or actions of mortal man. The creative force of the universe is no god beholding to mankind.

It is rather ironic that in Africa, Asia, and Latin America, man is reproducing himself quicker than resources of mankind can take of these masses, yet the Pope of Rome and other Christian leaders deny them the use of condoms or other means of birth control. I guess poverty and starvation are 'givins' in the church.

Remember, Christianity has gone against the natural order of the universe and nature by creating its own laws. "Man was meant to suffer for his god!" How sick and asinine is this logic? How do Christians claim that an individual's body belongs to their god? No one but one of blind faith could accept this kind of ridiculous logic. Nature does not give gifts and then take them away. The creative force of the universe does not legislate such asinine laws.

Many scientists believe that they are on the verge of discovering the cures for some of our most devastating diseases. Diseases which many Christians claim come from their god as punishment to man.

It is ironic that President Reagan had blocked fetal stem cell research, died of complications associated with Alzheimer's disease, and his wife Nancy, is now pushing for that same stem cell research.

Fetal and stem cell research are not going to encourage or discourage a woman to choose between having a full term baby or aborting it. That woman's personal situation will determine her choice. That choice should be hers and not that of any government or religious faith.

I believe that the only reason the Christian church fights fetal and stem cell research is the fact that it may someday prove the non-existence of their god!

....

"Observation, reason , and experiment make up what we call the scientific method."

Richard Feynman

"People may come along and argue philosophically that they like one better than another; but we have learned from much experience that all philosophical institutions about what nature is, is going to fail."

Richard Feynman

"It does not make any difference how beautiful your guess is. It does not make any difference how smart you are, who made the guess, or what his name is – if it disagrees with experiment, it is wrong. That is all there is to it."

Richard Feynman

"Although it is uncertain, it is necessary to make science useful. Science is only useful if it tells you about some experiment that has not been done; it is good if it tells you what just went on."

Richard Feynman

Heaven Verses Reality

Man makes his own Heaven or Hell here on earth.

I am positive that Jerry Falwell and his good buddies, such as George W. Bush, believe that they are going to the heaven which those of their kind created. If their heaven is populated with bigoted, hypocritical, spiritless men such as them, what kind of a paradise can it be? Is there any sensible one that prays to spend eternity with such fundamental fanatics? These lost ones are creating hell for themselves and others right here on earth.

What could be beautiful about spending eternity with those who detest you for not being as good as they? I would not want to spend eternity with those would stab me in the back!

The reality is that one's heaven or hell is what one is living on earth. Life is what one makes of it, with the help of others of course. If we are living bigoted and hypocritical lives on earth, what makes us believe that things will be any different in a future pie-in-the-sky home?

This is all we have right now. If we expect to be living in any paradise after death, we had better start treating our fellow man with more respect and humanity, rather than false religious concepts. If heaven be the home of the good, many of these holier-than-thou Christian fundamentalists who detest people of other faiths, don't have much time to prepare for their future!

The Creative Force Verses the Gods of Man

Man's religious faiths cannot deny the reality of Mother Nature.

The Christian faith teaches man that its god and Christ are one and the same. This is scientifically impossible. But then again, in the world of religious faiths, nearly anything supernatural is possible. The creative force and its nature do not know of the creations of mortal man. Man creates his gods and religious faiths to serve his personal needs.

Mother Nature, the creator of man and all living things on this earth, has no knowledge of the needs of man. She does not communicate with man or any of her creations. The creative force of the universe creates all things but is a slave to none.

Men of reality have no need for false doctrinaires that cloud or confuse their minds. Realistic and humane man knows that he should treat his fellow man justly, morally, and ethically. These qualities are derived from societies of humane mankind. Humane societies teach us to treat our fellow man in an honest and ethical manner. Learning to treat others as you would have others treat you comes from lessons learned by man living with man, humanely.

Religious faiths are not realistic, honest, or truthful enough to deal properly with the realities of the natural laws of the universe and Mother Nature.

The qualities of goodness are to be found in humane societies of man. Morals and ethics are qualities which one finds in civilized mankind. Qualities of truth and honesty are hard to find in most religious faiths since faiths are not based on the truth of reality or the reality of truth. Man is capable of doing equally well good or evil. Man is not inherently evil as the supernatural Christian faith would have one believe.

Since our religious faiths are created without respect for the nature of man, they are ultimately doomed to failure. The natural laws of the universe and nature controls the life of man. Christianity, as well as all organized religious faiths of unenlightened man, has never reached their idealistic goals since the goals are not in harmony with universal law, Mother Nature, and her natural law.

Nature Verses the Gods of Man

At times, I get to thinking, "This world would
be a much better place without man!"

Followers of religious faiths serve a god(s) because they believe more in the supernatural than they do their natural selves. The faithful believe that there has to be a force greater than themselves that is guiding their every word and action from the heavens above. They feel a need to have this supernatural god to protect them and be their fall-guy. They can feel less egotistical or less culpable whichever way natural things flow forth. Many need the constant feeling of being threatened otherwise they cannot control the wickedness that their faith tells them they possess.

The creative force of the universe through Mother Nature is the creator of all that exists on the earth. The creative force, which created not only the earth but the entire universe, is still creating. Natural law controls all life on earth. Nature is constantly evolving as the universe is constantly expanding. Nature is at work creating new life as the creative force is creating new heavenly bodies.

Mother Nature, through evolutionary processes, has created all life on this planet. The interference to nature by man has caused the confusion and troubles that we are experiencing today.

No religious faith of man shall ever control this earth or its nature. Man and his gods cannot control things natural or universal. Man is merely confused or distracted from the truth by teachings of his religious faiths. The control of this universe and this world of ours is in the power of the creative force of the universe and Mother Nature. The refusal of man to accept his true nature is the root of the problems which mankind faces.

Praying to supernatural gods has never, nor ever shall, change the realities of life on this earth. The changes in the feelings of man after adopting a religious faith, is the result of self-deception. Man is his own worst enemy when he places his trust in unknowing supernatural gods and the faiths he himself creates.

The Reality of Life

On earth, nature is the creator of all living things.

Since his evolution, man has been seeking the meaning of his existence. He has developed and created countless gods and religious faiths. Since the creative force of the universe is no god and has not made itself known to man, we can only make assumptions about who, what, and why of our creation. Man creates his gods. He then develops his faiths as his wishes dictates and declares that the tenets of such faiths are the directives of his god

Christians proclaim that man was made in the image of its god. No one has been able to explain logically the meaning of this proclamation during the two thousand years since the Christians created their Christ and faith. Judaism also makes this same claim and has not explained the meaning in a manner other than statements of faith. Such statements as this, makes no sense to a rational mind. Christians also believe that they own their god and heaven. Could man ever own the creative force of the universe? Could the creative force be a slave to man as the Southern Baptists believe their wives to be?

We shall never be able to find the answers to our perplexing questions of creation and our earthly existence until we are willing to accept the reality of Mother Nature as the creator of all life on earth. We shall never gain the necessary knowledge of life by refusing to accept the natural reality of that life.

We need to transcend the limitations that religious man has created with all his false gods and faiths. The creative force and its Mother Nature is limitless. Nature cannot be contained within the confines of any man-created god or faith. The universe and nature are real and they are not man-made entities, controlled by man, his gods or faiths.

We cannot reach our reality through any gods that we have created to meet our wishes. Reality is not a god and has no religious faith. Reality is the truth of universal law. No number of man-made intermediaries shall teach us to understand the creative force of the universe, nature, and the reality of life.

Christianity and Violence

Christianity foments violence through its intolerance of other faiths,
and its refusal to be rational, logical, natural, ethical and moral.

Violence has always been a part of Judaism and Christianity. The god of Moses slew thousands who opposed his directives. The books of Moses have stories of thousands of men, women and children being slaughtered by the god of Moses at his behest. Moses proudly declares that his god is a god of war. Christianity shares this same god and it slew many non-believers which they referred to as heretics. They also slew many *witches* before they discovered there were no such animals.

The Christian doctrinaires condemn anyone not following the teachings and edicts of the faith. A disbeliever, in the Dark Ages of Christianity, was branded a heretic and an enemy of the faith and therefore subject to any means of torture known to man at this time. Christians adopted the same means of torture that they were subjected to by their first enemies, the Romans.

After the Catholic Church, under the pope of Rome, took forceful control of the uneducated masses, Religious wars became common. The Pope would send out his army of the faithful, led by paid mercenaries, to kill the heretics. Church violence continues to this day, not as overtly since man has become somewhat more civilized throughout the passage of time. Still, a woman who dares believe that her body belongs to her is branded a heretic and can be driven from the church. The satanic ones of the Catholic Church call this ridiculous act excommunication. These stupid ones believe that this act can keep one from his god. The Pope of Rome now needs to civilize his doctrinaires.

Hatred is taught daily in many Christian churches. Violent acts against churches of other faiths, individuals, and our legal abortion clinics are the result of religious bigotry and hypocrisy, hatred and intolerance being preached daily in many spiritless Christian churches.

We have fanatic fundamentalist morons, such as Jerry Falwell, Pat Robertson, and George W. Bush, leading sheep in crusades against gays simply because they declare as truth the false doctrinaires written in their Bible. We had bigots such as Jesse Helms and Bob Barr encouraging the passage of hate producing laws into our government. Most of these laws are causing the stupidly faithful to commit acts of violence against innocent members of other faiths, belief systems, and ways of life.

We shall never be able to cure the evils within ourselves and our fellow man as long as these hate mongers and producers of violence are allowed to go on spewing their doctrinaires of untruths and then wrapping themselves in Old Glory and their sinful Christian faith.

These sinful fundamentalist fanatics are driven by the evil within themselves since they haven't a truthful or honest bone in their bodies. Their daily existence is controlled by their false doctrinaires. They are driven by greed and blind faith which are mandates from Satan. These men are being led by the evil forces of the Christian right. These fundamentalist groups do not wish to face the reality of truth or the truth of reality. The qualities of truth and honesty are foreign to them. They would not recognize a *true* or *just* god if it were to bite them on their unholy asses.

Truth is truth. Truth cannot be created, altered, or destroyed by man or his gods. Truth comes from Mother Nature, universal and natural law. Man's efforts to deny nature and its reality are exercises in futility since truth is not controlled by man, There is little truth in the majority of man's religious faiths or his gods. These faiths were created by mortal, biased and prejudiced man in desperate and foolish attempts to escape his true reality. Man shall never be successful in finding himself as long as he refuses to be truthful, logical, and real. Man has succeeded in writing countless false books of biased fantasy. These fairytale books of faith can never be proven to be anything more than exercises in self deception. Man needs to become real if he expects to be successful in controlling himself.

The creative force of the universe is the creator of everything that exists. The creative force is no figurehead that man has created to suit his personal needs. Religious faiths and gods have little in common with the reality of the creative force, nature, and natural law. Christianity has not been given a mandate from any god. The reality of the creative force has existed billions of years. It shall exist billions of years after the death of man, his creations of gods and faiths, and even the earth.

The creative force is evolving this universe at its own pace. It does not work within the confines of any man-made calendar. The earth is a mere pea in a vast pot of universal soup. The creative force is responsible for everything in the universe; it does not mandate instructions to nor listen to man.

Man is not inherently evil although all evil is the creation of man. No man is created more or less than another. One man's false claims of superiority, such as that of Rev. Mohler that, "Only those who accept Jesus Christ as their personal savior; shall enter Heaven," is an evil of unenlightened Christian man. It is not a spiritual statement. Claims of superiority and acts of violence are the words and actions of evil man under the influence of a satanic god and its faith.

I hope the people of this world eventually eclipse the false faith of Christianity and other religious faiths before these faiths destroy man. Modern communications and science will shortly provide man with correct information that shall not allow us to be held back by dishonest, bigoted, and unenlightened men under the influence of false faiths and their evil gods.

Over half the households in the United States own a computer today. The availability of vast amounts of truthful scientific knowledge is going to revolutionize the United States as well as the entire world. Truthful and honest man is going to see through all the falsehoods and fantasy of religious faiths no matter how many flags and religious books are waved in our faces.

Those books of fantasy, sorcery, and dishonesty are no answer to the truth of reality and the reality of truth. We need honesty and truthfulness, something religious faiths do not contain. Christianity, nor any other religious faith, has corrected the sins of man and they never shall since they are not developed to face reality.

In order to save this world from evil man, we need to burn all untruthful, bigoted and hypocritical books of religious bullshit. We need to turn to the reality of Mother Nature and her natural laws. We need to become more humane in our dealings with our fellow man. We need to accept the truth of the universe which has been given to us by men of science. The biased and prejudiced views of life presented to us by the Bible and other false books of unenlightened man, is not the stuff of life. Man shall never be able to save himself until he becomes one with the reality presented to him by nature and the creative force of the universe.

....

"Sunday School: A prison in which children do penance for the evil conscience of their parents."

Henry Louis Mencken

"Science is of value because it *can* produce *something.*"

Richard Feynman

"It is our responsibility as scientists, knowing the great progress which comes from a satisfactory philosophy of ignorance, the great progress which is the fruit of freedom of thought, to proclaim the value of this freedom; to teach how doubt is not to be feared but welcomed and discussed; and to demand this freedom as our duty to all coming generations."

Richard Feynman

"The human mind treats a new idea the way the body treats a strange protein; it rejects it."

Biologist P. B. Medawar

"There was a time when religion ruled the world. It is known as The Dark Ages."

Ruth Hurmence Green

The Unreality of Christianity

Christianity shall never be successful unless and until it decides
to become one with the universe, Mother Nature, and natural law.

Since the promoters of Christianity refuse to accept the reality of nature, Christianity shall never to able to save humanity. This is a real world in which we live, not some creative dream world of the creators of Christ. Christianity has been in existence for two thousand years but has made little to know improvement in the conduct of man. People such as I, believe that religious faiths have been tremendous obstacles in the path of advancement of mankind. The lack of success of Christianity being able to control the behaviors of mankind is the fact that Christianity refuses to accept the evolution of man and the natural law which controls him. The laws of the universe and Mother Nature govern this earth. No man-created doctrinaires of faith can control the forces of the universe and nature.

That fantastic book, which they call their Bible, has little reality. These fantasies from the minds of unenlightened man that have been promoted all these centuries, as the word of a god, have no legitimacy. This world of ours is no fairytale world of dreamers. This is a real world filled with mortal man and other works of Mother Nature. The law of this world is the law of nature through the creative force of the universe.

Nature is reality. Nature is the creative force of the universe at work on earth. The books of religious faiths written by mortal man are too biased and prejudiced to be accepted as truth. These books are filled to overflowing with fantasy from the minds of men who have blinded themselves from truth. These books are shams, created by unknowing, spiritless men of religious faiths. Religious faiths are created regardless of truth in efforts to subdue and subjugate mankind.

Biased and prejudiced men have been trying to promote their charades and creations of gods and faiths since the time of their own evolution. They shall never succeed in their goal of controlling the behaviors of man since their goals are not based on the reality of truth. Man cannot be controlled by fairytale doctrinaires of faith. Supernatural gods do not have the necessary power to control natural man since the two are on separate planes. Being on separate planes does not allow for communication between man and his gods. The world today is not filled with the ignoramuses as in the days of Moses and Jesus. Heads of educated and enlightened man are no longer floating in the clouds or buried in the sod. The only ones to follow organized religions are the ones who have blinded themselves from the truth of the universe in which they live.

The creative force of the universe is real and alive. It is universal. On earth, Mother Nature and her natural law is the reality of the creative force. Religious faiths and their gods are the creations of unknowing and ignorant man. The link between the faiths of man and the realities of life does not exist.

The primary goal of any religious faith, worth its salt, should be the improvement in the humanity of the faithful. The flock should become more humane and spiritual. If the only goal of a religion is to teach its own doctrines and doctrinaires, that faith is providing a disservice, is useless, and possibly dangerous to the mental health of the faithful.

The nature of the creative force does not know if one adopts any of the faiths of mortal man. Nature is not the fairy god-mother of any faith. One cannot proclaim oneself a truly religious person if he harbors prejudices and feelings of superiority as do the Southern Baptist and many other Christians. Nature does not discriminate. Discrimination is an evil of unenlightened man, foreign to the natural laws of Mother Nature. Man's inhumanity to man does not originate in natural law. Those who are one with nature and natural law are pure and uncontaminated with the evil and unreal philosophies of religious superiority. The bigoted superiority practices of the hypocritical Christian fundamentalists, is the work and actions of their evil faith and satanic god.

The creative force does not judge the words and actions of mortals. The creative force does not play favorites. The sinful idea that Christians are the favored of a creator is the height of fantasy. The levels of good and bad of mankind are judged by mankind itself. What the creative force has created is good. What natural laws of mortal man has tried to negate or change is evil in itself. The unproven religious faiths of man have little to do with the reality of life and natural law.

Christians commit as many sins against their fellow man as do any atheist. Many of the unenlightened Christians commit these sins in the name of their faith. They believe that their faith gives them the right to deny natural rights to whomever they wish because it is written so in the Bible. Most Christians are far too biased and blindly prejudiced to ever be favored by a *true* or *just* god.

No religious faith has the blessings of the creative force of nature. No god has ever been perfect or better than any other. We can strive for perfection but the reality of life does not permit man to create a perfect god. Man is far too prejudiced to ever create or reach perfection.

Not to have faith in natural man and humanity is not to believe in the reality of life. The creative force created everything that exists. Man is real. Only those who do not believe in nature, question the reality of mankind. The gods of man exist solely in the minds of the faithful. Gods are nothing more than the creations of unknowing man in his desperate searches to find himself and control his behaviors. The gods and faiths that mortal man has created only lead him farther from the truth. Man is forever trying to deny the truth of reality and the reality of truth.

We have morons of blinded faith, calling themselves Christians, predicting the end of the world and the return of their Christ. What makes these imbeciles believe that the creative force of the universe is operating within the confines of the Christian calendar?

Would it make sense for the creative force that has been in operation for billions of years to adopt a calendar of a religion of two thousand years? These nincompoops making such predictions should be locked away with others of their intelligence so that they are no further a danger to the sane among us.

Christianity cannot hope to save anyone or anything when it has its head either buried in the sod or floating in the clouds. Trying to live on this real earth while preparing for a pie-in-the-sky future home, is refusing to become part of reality. The creative force of nature is evolving this earth at its own rate. Christianity, nor any other faith of man, shall be able to change the evolution of the universe and earth. The laws of nature are in charge of the evolution of this earth and the lives of man. Interference into the work of nature, by man, only causes confusion.

Christianity is far too negative in its approach to life to be of use to man. Christianity has condemned too many of the creations of nature. The creative force of nature has created everything which exists in our world. Whether man deems the creations of the creative force as good or bad, means nothing to the reality of the universe. The creative force does not create evil. All evil is created by man in his efforts to alter the truth of reality and the reality of truth

Christianity, as well as any religion, can never succeed until it gets real. A belief system cannot create something which does not exist. One may pray until the end of time but never alter the reality that is. One can only change oneself to fit into reality. The creative force does not see nor hear man. The creative force is not here to serve the wishes or answer the prayers of man. Man must serve himself and humanity within the confines of nature and its natural law.

The nature of the creative force has given us the ability to reproduce our kind. It has not, as evil religious man proclaims, condemned we who do not wish to reproduce. Nature has not condemned natural acts of masturbation, gay sex, scientific facts of birth control, nor abortion. These are false doctrinaires written by self-blinded and satanic men trying to deny natural law. These sinful doctrinaires are written in vain attempts to subjugate the ignorant masses. Most of us, however, are no longer lost sheep! Many of us not longer believe that our lives are controlled by comets and other heavenly bodies.

The first Popes of Rome believed that they needed to improve religious faith. They believed that they needed to create a religion that was so highly involved and complicated that the ignorant peons would not be able to question. They created this highly ritualistic mass which awed the masses but which had nothing to do with the reality of their lives. This mass was designed by spiritless men hoping to confuse the uneducated hordes into following the doctrinaires of those in power. The ignorant laity was to accept these man-made falsehoods on faith alone since they did not have the necessary knowledge to question this subjugation of the church. The Pope of Rome was to guide the priests and his flock of lost sheep into a world of fantasy and make-believe.

When the masses began to question his authority, the pope would send out his army of devoted, led by paid mercenaries, to slaughter the heretics. When an individual denounced the authority of the pope, he would be put to death. How Christian can one become?

After years of serving the dictatorial pope and his doctrinaires, educated men began creating other faiths with more tolerance and understanding of human nature and humanity. Luther and Calvin created their faiths. Others began to follow in their footsteps. All of these men were now considered heretics, enemies of the church, and thus they were in constant threats to their lives.

No matter what mortal man has written in his religious books of faith, these are not the words of any god of man. The words written in books by man are simply the words of mortal man trying unsuccessfully to escape his true reality. Biased and prejudiced mortal man is incapable of creating a truthful religious faith. The creative force, billions of years ago, began creating and evolving the universe. Billions of years later the force created our solar system. Christianity has only within the past two thousand years tried to change the works of the creative force and Mother Nature to meet its needs.

The logic of Christianity is greatly flawed. The creative force has written no book of faith. Man with all his human faults wrote the Bible, as he has written all books. The Bible is a prejudiced work created by unenlightened and unknowing men who had *faith* that they knew as well as understood a creator. The Bible is a creation from the vivid imaginations of biased and prejudiced men.

The creative force cannot be contained within the confines of any book of mortal man. One can find the gods of Christianity and Judaism in the Bible but man is not truthful enough or knowing enough to describe the reality of natural law. The universe and Mother Nature are too profound to be explained by desperate man in his need to establish a religious faith in order to control his behaviors.

....

"So long as the universe had a beginning, we could suppose it had a creator. But if the universe is really completely self-contained, having no boundary or edge, it would have neither beginning nor end: it would simply be. What place then, for a creator?"

Stephen W. Hawking

"What I have done is to show that it is possible for the way the universe began to be determined by the laws of science. In that case, it would not be necessary to appeal to God to decide on how the universe began. This doesn't prove that there is no God, only that God is not necessary."

Stephen W. Hawking

"No rational argument will have a rational effect on a man who does not want to adopt a rational attitude."

Karl Popper

The Immorality of Christianity

The false superiority philosophy of Christianity
is an example of the greatest of man's immoralities.

Christians try to deny the natural rights given to man by the creative force of Mother Nature. Nature is the creator of all life on earth. Nature is a reality of truth. Man cannot escape reality by his creation of gods and religious faiths as he wishes them to be.

There are a number of faiths which have heaven as their final resting place, yet the Southern Baptist, led by Albert Mohler Jr. and others, have declared that the members of Judaism and Islam must accept Christ as their personal savior or they will not be able to enter heaven. This fabrication of a falsehood by their ridiculous faith is a directive straight from Satan. It is immoral for Albert and his fellow hypocrites to fabricate doctrinaires of satanic faith and then try to force others to abide by them. The creative force of the universe does not endorse such false propaganda. This hypocrite Mohler needs to alter his sinful and satanic faith. If there should happen to be such a thing as a *just* god, this evil prophet will surely burn in hell.

Judaism and   the Christian faith is immoral for teaching that natural homosexuals are sinful. Nature Mother Nature created all peoples. Where do hypocritical faiths of biased men and their bigoted god get their authority to question or deny the work of nature? Modern science has proven these doctrinaires of unenlightened man to be false. It is the height of immorality to preach as gospel that which has been proven false by science.

For one bigoted faith to place itself above another is immoral. It is sinful and spiritless for anyone to claim religious superiority over another.

It is not only spiritless to preach these doctrinaires of sinful superiority, it is criminal. These teachings of the Pope, Pat Jerry, Dubya and others, are causing the religious lunatics and Christian fundamentalists to bomb churches of other faiths, our legal abortion clinics, and residences of homosexuals. The words and actions of religious bigots encourage attacks upon those who oppose the religious right. All of this violence of the Christian faithful is done in the name of their faith and as they say, the blessing of their god.

Prophets and Prophecies from Hell

Religious prophets do not dwell in the reality of the universe.

In the summer of 1999, in the Holy Lands of Christianity, Judaism, and Islam, there were a number of fanatical Christian groups which caused the mayor of Jerusalem much concern. These Christian fundamental fanatics were threatening to destroy Jewish Temples and Muslim Mosques all in the name of Christianity. These false prophets from hell were proclaiming everything from the coming of Christ to the end of the world with the coming of the new millennium. These Christian idiots believed that the creative force of the universe was keeping time by the Christian calendar!

The creative force of the universe has never operated within the confines of any calendar of man. The creative force was creating and destroying worlds billions of years before it created the earth and its Mother Nature created all life forms on the earth. The Christians created their Christ a mere two thousand years ago. The creative force shall be creating and destroying worlds billions of years after the last Christian has gone to meet his maker.

The earth is not going to be destroyed within the confines of any man-made time table. The earth is going to be here long after Christianity has been forgotten. Life on the earth shall remain as long as the sun is in the sky. Scientists tell us that the sun has several billions of years left. Man may destroy himself before this time, however. The most likely cause of the destruction of the world of man is wars between religious fundamentalists. When the sun burns out a few billion years from now, those unfortunates remaining, can kiss their asses good-bye! Until that sun burns out, most life on earth, with or without man, shall survive.

The second coming of Christ is as likely to happen as you or I returning after we have died. Christ is only an illusion in the minds of the Christian faithful. The creative force of the universe has not created any religious faith or god. The creative force and Mother Nature are not fairy godmothers!

Bigotry and Hypocrisy

If religious faiths were as successful as we are led to believe,
the world would have become a paradise centuries ago.

Why are we so astonished at the violence in our society when many of our religious and governmental leaders and institutions are fomenting the intolerance which leads to this violence? Words and actions of arrogant superiority spoken daily by George W. Bush and his religious right buddies is the cause of much of this violence. The fanatic fundamentalists that listen to this crap believe it to be the gospel. Why are we surprised that the citizenry is constantly so threatening when intolerance is what is being preached to them daily in our churches and governmental agencies?

When our House of Representatives and the Senate is led by bigoted and hypocritical Christian men of faith, the lawless National Rifle Association, and the unethical HMOs and then the Congress refuses to pass legislation to protect us from these predators, why shouldn't we be angry? When Congress refused to seriously study legislation proposed by Clinton simply because the Christian right conservative rednecks could not get rid of that *bastard* in what they considered *their* White House, should we be happy and content? Should we be happy knowing that these *special interest groups* are lining the pockets of our crooked Representatives and Senators in order to receive preferences which are detrimental to the public? Should we be joyous that these Christian hypocrites are passing laws solely in the name of Christianity with no respect for the humane among us?

When Bob Barr and his ilk can plaster offensive, hypocritical, unlawful, Christian propaganda on the walls of our public schools and then declare that this unconstitutional garbage will cure the violence in them, do they expect we thinking public and members of other religious faiths to suffer in silence?

That hypocrite, Barr, financed and paid for by his special interest, the NRA, fought to destroy any and all gun control legislation that was presented to the Congress. He gave us that same line of bullshit the conservatives always give, "Guns don't kill people; people kill people!" Fools, such as Barr, cannot see that the easy accessibility of guns is only one of many factors causing this violence in our society, but it is a major one.

When Bob Jones III, the bigoted Christian president of his own university, can call the Pope of Rome the *antichrist* and many Christian conservatives, such as George W. Bush, beat a path to his university door to receive his money and blessings, what do they believe they are promoting?

When George W. Bush declared that the flying of the Confederate flag over the capitol building in Columbia, South Carolina was a matter of States rights, he was denigrating all of those thousands of Union soldiers who died defeating the Confederacy. George was telling us, "To Hell with the Union soldiers, the African Americans and President Lincoln." Lincoln gave his life for the cause of freedom for all. That rebel battle flag is an affront to all of us who believe in the American way, freedom for all, and are loyal to our federal government.

Jerry Falwell, the hypocrite Christian leader and creator of the now defunct *immoral* Moral Majority, is so bigoted and homophobic that he called a children's TV puppet a homosexual because it is purple, carries a large bag filled with tricks and has and up-side-down triangle on its head. Jerry says that the color purple, the triangle and the *purse* are gay symbols. When we have such lunatics as he leading the Christian faithful, who among us is safe from persecution?

Pat Robertson, the creator of the *spiritless* Christian Coalition, wouldn't recognize a *true* and *honest* god if it were to bite Pat on his unholy ass! Yet, bigoted Pat is one of the Christian leaders in this violent country of ours fomenting us to become more bigoted, hateful, and intolerant of others. His untruth filled messages in the name of Christianity, assures us that Pat does not understand **truth.** Pat has blinded himself from reality and is existing in a world of his own creation.

....

"Christianity – The belief that a cosmic Jewish Zombie who was his own father can make you live forever if you symbolically eat his flesh and telepathically tell him you accept him as your master so he can remove an evil force from your soul that is present in humanity because a rib-woman was convinced by a talking snake to eat from a magical tree...yeah, makes perfect sense."

Anon, found on the web

Henry Louis Mencken

"Not by accident, you may be sure, do the Christian Scriptures make the father of knowledge a serpent – slimy, sneaking and abominable."

"Puritanism:...The haunting fear that someone, somewhere, may be happy."

"There is, in fact, nothing about religious opinions that entitles them to any more respect than other opinions get. On the contrary, they tend to be noticeably silly."

"Sunday: A day given by Americans to wishing that they themselves were dead and in Heaven, and that their neighbors were dead and in Hell."

"I detest converts almost as much as I do missionaries."

"One seldom discovers a true believer that is worth knowing."

"The trouble with Communism is the Communists, just as the trouble with Christianity is the Christians."

"What is the function that a clergyman performs in the world? Answer: he gets his living by assuring idiots that he can save them from an imaginary hell. It's a business almost indistinguishable from that of a seller of snake-oil for rheumatism. "

"God is the immemorial refuge of the incompetent, the helpless, the miserable. They find not only sanctuary in His arms, but also a kind of superiority, soothing to their macerated egos; He will set them above their betters."

"Religion is so absurd that it comes close to imbecility."

"If we assume that man actually does resemble God, then we are forced into the impossible theory that God is a coward, an idiot and a bounder."

"What has 'theology' ever said that is of the smallest use to anybody? When has 'theology' ever said anything that is demonstrably true and is not obvious?...What makes you think that 'theology' is a subject at all?"

Richard Dawkins

"Faith is the great cop-out, the great excuse to evade the need to think and evaluate evidence. Faith is belief in spite of, even perhaps because of, the lack of evidence."

Richard Dawkins

"The universe we observe has precisely the properties we should expect if there is, at bottom, no design, no purpose, no evil and no good, nothing but blind pitiless indifference."

Richard Dawkins

"The observer cannot be left out of the description of the observation."

Dr. John A. Wheeler, physicist

Christ died for our sins. Dare we make his martyrdom meaningless by not committing them?"

Jules Feiffer

"People have murdered each other, in massive wars and guerilla actions, for centuries, and still murder each other in the present, over Ideologies and Religions which. Stated as propositions, appear neither true nor false to modern logicians – meaningless propositions that look meaningful to the linguistically naïve,"

Robert A. Wilson

"And if the Thinker thinks passionately enough, the Prover will prove the thought so conclusively that you will never talk a person out of such a belief, even if it is something as remarkable as the notion that there is a gaseous vertebrate of astronomical heft ("GOD") who will spend all eternity torturing people who do not believe his religion."

Robert A. Wilson

"The Bible tells us to be like God, and then on page after page it describes God as a mass murderer. This may be the single most important key to the political behavior of Western Civilization."

Robert A. Wilson

"There is not the slightest question but that the God of the Old Testament is a jealous, vengeful God, inflicting not only on the sinful "pagans" but even on his Chosen People, fire, lightening, hideous plagues and diseases, brimstone, and other curses."

Steve Allen

The Christian Right Verses Reality

Religious faiths are philosophies of man which have
little truth, factuality or reality, thus have little validity.

There is not much reality in the philosophy of the Christian right. Most of these hypocrites have divorced themselves from this wicked world of man and no longer consider themselves to be on the same plane as the rest of us.

They have divorced themselves from the world of the living by using their holy book of faith. Why do these fundamentalists find only negative thoughts in their books? How can Christians condemn you and me for being human? We are the ones walking the face of the real world while they are the ones who are trying to deny their mortal existence!

The Republican Party of today has sold itself to the fundamentalism of the *spiritless* Christian Coalition, the *immoral* Moral Majority, the *satanic* Southern Baptists, the *hypocritical* Church of Christ and others of their ilk. The Grand Old Party is no longer the honest conservative party of Abe Lincoln. Abe would have told these Christian right devils to go to Hell where they belong. Poor Abe doing flip-flops in his grave!

The Christian right proclaims that it supports less government in our lives, yet it insists that the government pass laws banning abortion, the rights of women to choose what is best for themselves, gay rights, and a host of other rights which their faith has declared evil. They want these laws passed in the name of Christianity. These bigots are trying to take away human rights that man has had long before the Christians created their Christ and faith. These hypocrites of the Christian right are trying to void our natural rights given to us by Mother Nature.

How many of these far right Christian hypocrites exposed themselves during their ill-conceived attempt to overthrow the Clinton administration! It is so sad that Larry Flint stopped his investigations before they were completed. There were many more termites hiding in the framework of our constitution ready to destroy it. These devils are going to continue condemning the rest of us for nearly the same tactics and activities that many of them are engaged in. We need a good and thorough extermination of these termites of the Christian right before they eat up the fabric of our Constitution and destroy our freedoms.

What drives these hypocrites of Christianity? Just what is their end game? Why are they so negative toward the reality of life? Are they trying to save us or simply wanting to subjugate us? I believe it is the latter. I think it is their aim to dominate us. They act as though we are their personal slaves.

These fanatics have no real interest in the salvation of anyone, including themselves. They want the citizens of the United States bowing down to them and doing their evil bidding.

These far right Christian fundamentalists are nothing more than would be Fascist and thus are no better than a Hitler or Mussolini.

The far right Christian quacks, with their religious doctrinaires, will continue their contempt of mankind until they have all been exposed for the hypocrites that they are. I hope America wakes up before it is too late!

Rev. Albert Mohler Jr. of the Southern Baptist, removed himself from this world years ago, yet his senseless and mindless body remains spewing his satanic preachings of untruths of hatred. Mohler denies the existence of Judaism and Islam even though Judaism was a reality thousands of years before the Christians created their Christ.

∙∙

"Nothing is more dangerous than a dogmatic worldview – nothing more constraining, more blinding to innovation, more destructive of openness to novelty."

Stephen Jay Gould

"The most important scientific revolutions all include, as their only common feature, the dethronement of human arrogance from one pedestal after another of previous convictions about our centrality in the cosmos."

Stephen Jay Gould

"Creationist critics often charge that evolution cannot be tested, and therefore cannot be viewed as a properly scientific subject at all. This claim is rhetorical nonsense."

Stephen Jay Gould

"Our creationist detractors charge that evolution is an unproved and unprovable charade – a secular religion masquerading as science. They claim, above all, that evolution generates no predictions, never exposes itself to test, and therefore stands as dogma rather than disprovable science. This claim is nonsense. We make and test risky predictions all the time; our success is not dogma, but a highly probable indication of evolution's basic truth."

Stephen Jay Gould

"No rational order of divine intelligence unites species. The rational ties are genealogical along contingent pathways of history."

Stephen Jay Gould

The Audacity of the Religious Right

Christian fundamentalism is unrelenting!

The Christian religious right followers in the United States have the audacity to believe that their faith is the one and only. They have the audacity to believe that they are the chosen of a god and that their faith controls the gates to heaven. They are demanding that the members of Judaism and Islam become Christian before they can be admitted to their heaven. The Reverend Albert Mohler Jr., President of the Southern Baptist Seminary, states that, "Only those who accept Jesus Christ as their personal savior can enter heaven," even thought the Jews were speaking of heaven thousands of years before the Christians created their Christ and Christianity.

The religious right quite often refers to America's Judeo-Christian tradition. They use this statement to justify their dismissal of other faiths as having any credibility.

It is the truth that the first settlers to the shores of America were basically Christian. They were refugees who had first gone from England to Holland and then to America in an effort to escape the tyranny of the English King and his Church of England. Some were fleeing from the tyranny of the Pope of Rome.

The puritans and Pilgrims, the real settlers of what became the United States, believed the King of England and the Catholic Church were not following the true religion as told in the Bible. The Puritans doubted the truth of Christianity as practiced by the majority of the people following this faith in the 1600's.

The Puritans came out of the Biblical milieu of the Reformation. They had the zeal to reform and to 'purify' the Church of England. They became the leading lights of America, these 'People of the Book.' They practiced a religion more in line with the philosophy of Calvin and Luther.

The religious right is the modern day Puritans. They have set a course of global dominion. They are saying, "Lead, follow, or get out of the way!" The image of the Puritans in their early manifestation is a reflection of much of what we see in the Christian conservative America of today.

The most basic flaw in the belief system of the modern day Puritans, the religious right, is the belief that nothing ever changes. Since the Puritans first came to America, we have become a nation of fifty states. We have immigrants from around the world. These immigrants have made this nation. They have brought us all manner of belief systems and traditions. One religious faith cannot cover the vast number of belief systems practiced in the United States.

There are twenty-two major religions in this world. The Christian faith alone has over

39,000 denominations divided into six ecclesiastical megablocs. There are countless small sects of various religions not listed among the twenty-two major ones.

The estimated population of the world for the year 2008 is 6.684 billion. The estimated number of Christians was 2 billion. Only 15% of the electorate in the United States claim to be associated with the religious right which is a very small number when compared to the population of the world.

No religious faith has ever been voted the one and only in the United States. No religious faith can prove that it is the one and only or the best. The reference to God that appears in several of our governmental documents does not refer to any particular god.

One cannot find the words Christian or Christianity in any document of the United States. However, the Christian right believes that Christianity is the law of the land. The audacity of the Christian right, never ceases.

....

"You don't have to take drugs to hallucinate; improper language can fill your world with phantoms and spooks of many kinds."

Robert A Wilson

"Of course, the United States was not originally intended to be a Christian nation. Jefferson, Washington, Franklin and most of the founding fathers were skeptics or Deists; they especially intended a secular government with an "unbreachable wall" between church and state; they even wrote into the treaty with the Moslem nation of Tripoli a clear statement that, unlike European countries, the "United States is not, in any sense, a Christian nation." (So clearly understood was the principle of separation of church and state in those days that the treaty passed Congress without any debate on that clause, and President John Adams signed it at once, without any fear that it might jeopardize his political future.)"

Robert A Wilson

"Whenever people are certain they understand our peculiar situation here on this planet, it is because they have accepted a religious Faith or a secular Ideology (Ideologies are the modern form of Faiths) and just stopped thinking."

Robert A. Wilson

"One social evil for which the New Testament is clearly in part responsible is anti- Semitism."

Steve Allen

The fact that

a religious faith exists

is no proof

of its truth or

truthfulness.

Frederick J. Azbell

"Don't believe anything.

Regard things on a scale of Probabilities.

The things that seem most absurd, put under 'Low Probability', and the things that seem most plausible, you put under 'High Probability'. Never believe anything. Once you believe anything, you stop thinking about it. The more things you believe; the less mental activity. If you believe something, and have an opinion on every subject, then your brain activity stops entirely; which is clinically considered a sign of death, nowadays in medical practice. So put things on a scale or probability, and never believe or disbelieve anything entirely."

Robert A. Wilson

Part Three Contents: Falsehoods and Truths

Falsehoods and Truths
Religion and Spirituality
Morals and Ethics
Morals, Ethics and Common Sense
Morals and Ethics Verses Truth and Honesty
Truth
Universal Truth
The Reality of Truth
Why Not the Truth?
Truth, Falsehoods, Reality, Ideology, Fact, and Fiction
Faith as Truth
Fact, Fantasy, and Fallacy
Satan: The Devil in Us
Good Verses Evil
Credibility
Compassion
Respect
Insincerity
Futility
Evangelicalism
False Concepts
Fallacies of Christianity
False Books
Judging You, Me, and Them

Falsehoods and Truths

The most important truth in life is the reality
of the natural laws of the universe and nature.

There are millions of us who are planning and living our lives based on falsehoods that have been taught to us and then wondering why our lives are not progressing in a manner for which we have been praying.

We need to realize that the natural law of the universe is no fairy-godmother. When we pray to a false god, we are directing our wishes and needs to a non-existing being. We have been taught to practice self-deception, so why are we surprised that our prayers go unanswered? Prayers are for making right in our head that which has gone wrong in reality. The situation remains, it is only our perspective that has been altered. In other words, we have convinced ourselves to accept on faith that which cannot be accomplished in reality. This is the true reality of religious faiths. Prayers are merely self illusions and the means of self-deception and self-delusions.

Our fates are in our own hands, except for the interference of others. What we do with our lives and the successes or failures we experience depends on our intelligence, talents, and ambitions. The length of our lives and the health that we enjoy depends upon a combination of nature and our personal lifestyle. Thanking an unknowing god for our fortunes and praying for guidance to handle our misfortunes is only a means of deceiving ourselves by taking all responsibility out of our hands. Our successes in life depends mostly upon the brains that Mother Nature gave us and the use we make of that intelligence, plus the good fortunes that come our way. Our fate is the result of natural circumstances, us, and those around us. The more that we are in step with ourselves and reality, the more success we are likely to have.

We practice falsehoods everyday of our lives. Things we cannot explain properly, we devise a theory for. Many of these theories and falsehoods have no logical basis of truth but are promoted as the gospel by religious fanatics.

We cannot live successfully in this world believing in theories and falsehoods of faith. We exist through the grace of Mother Nature and natural law. Nature and the creative force of the universe are constantly at work. Life on the earth is not the paradise that it might be because mankind has chosen to pray to his false gods and refuses to follow the laws of nature and the universe. Man has little respect for the truth of reality and the reality of truth. Man is always creating his own truths.

We choose to believe that our religious faiths and their leaders are promoting truth when, in reality, they are promoting nothing more than religious doctrines and doctrinaires.

Faiths and their gods are not truths or facts of the universe. The adopted faiths of mortal man have little reality. Most truths of our religious faiths have no validity.

Many of us believe that we have chosen the one and only true god, when in reality, there is no such thing. Man-created gods and faiths are fantasies of the mind. The creative force of the universe, nor Mother Nature, has provided man with any deities or religious faiths. Religious faiths and gods are the misguided creations of desperate mortal man.

....

"There are hundreds of millions who believe the Messiah has come. If he did, then it is unfortunately the case that his heroic sacrifice and death have had no effect whatsoever on the very problem his coming might have been expected to address, for history demonstrates, beyond question, that we Christians have been just as dangerous, singly and en masse, as non-Christians."

Steve Allen

"The Bible has been interpreted to justify such evil practices as, for example, slavery, the slaughter of prisoners of war, the sadistic murders of women believed to be witches, capital punishment for hundreds of offenses, polygamy, and cruelty to animals. It has been used to encourage belief in the grossest superstition and to discourage the free teaching of scientific truths. It is therefore not above criticism."

Steve Allen

"Ideas have consequences, and totally erroneous ideas are likely to have destructive consequences."

Steve Allen

"God is by definition the holder of all possible knowledge, it would be impossible for him to have faith in anything. Faith then, is built upon ignorance and hope."

Steve Allen

"No actual tyrant known to history has ever been guilty of one-hundredth of the crimes, massacres, and other atrocities attributed to the Deity in the Bible."

Steve Allen

Religion and Spirituality

Religious faiths have proven to be tremendous obstacles
to the intellectual development and spirituality of mankind.

Thomas Jefferson stated, "The clergy, by getting themselves established by law and ingrafted into the machine of government, have been a very formidable engine against the civil and religious rights of man.

A religious faith is a systematic arrangement of the fantasy of fairytales, make-believe, magic, sorcery, doctrines, doctrinaires, and theories developed by a society of men for the expressed purpose of controlling the thoughts and actions of the faithful. In order to become a member of the faith, one must agree to submit to the subjugation by the faith.

These systems are developed to keep the masses in line since the faithful are thought to have little faith in themselves. Our lives and everyday words and actions are to be in accordance with the dictates written in the books concocted by the creators of the god and faith.

Most religious faiths start out much the same as folklore. Somewhere in the process of creation, men thinking themselves wise, claim a divine connection to a god or gods. If we, the unwashed, do not agree with the theories of the faith, we are deemed enemies, such as Christian heretics or Muslim infidels. In most faiths, one must accept on faith alone what the creators of the religion declare as truth. The use of critical examination would reveal the many flaws in the philosophy of the faith.

As Jefferson stated, "Reason and free inquiry are the only effectual agents against error." How out of date is the philosophy that a faith cannot be questioned! Can't the religious understand why educated and mentally astute men are leaving organized religions because they are not logical? The Catholic Church cannot fill vacancies in its priesthood, yet it still maintains that women are unfit and too impure to serve as priests. Women in the Catholic Church can only serve the church in motherly ways. Mary was the mother of their god but she was a slave to Joseph! This is the third millennium and the Catholic Church is mired in the philosophy of the Dark Ages of Judaism and Christianity! Many of we thinking people are not buying these false doctrinaires any longer. Men who use the intelligence that Mother Nature gave them are rapidly moving passed the spiritless faiths of our fellow Christian brethren.

To deny the existence of something does not make that thing any less so. Praying that something be or not be is an act of futility. We must accept the fact that praying is merely an exercise in self-deception. Prayer changes only that which is in our heads. Prayer cannot alter the reality of truth or the truth of reality; it merely changes our perceptions of them. The faiths of man cannot deny the reality of truth. The truths of nature and the universe cannot be altered by man or his gods. Nature is no slave to man, as is the Christian deity.

Christianity had fought tooth and nail against the early scientific minds such as those of Copernicus and Galileo after they spoke the truth that the sun was the center of the solar system. The Church had already declared that the earth was the center of the universe since that is what is written as gospel in their Bible. The Pope of Rome was compelled to condemn these scientific truths and the men who found them in order to promote his false Christian propaganda. The Church could hardly be expected to declare their book was wrong! The same caliber of thinking comprises most of the *truths* in the Bible. Christians refuse to accept the truth of universal and natural law. The majority of the Christian truths have no validity since the faith does not deal with or recognize reality.

Christianity, since its creation, has tried to keep its flock of sheep ignorant of the truths of natural law. It is written so in Genesis. After Eve coaxed Adam to eat from the tree of knowledge of good and evil, the lord god of Moses drove them from the Garden of Eden. Women were not to be educated in these days. It's such a sad state of affairs that Moses created his lord god to be so afraid of men or women knowing the truth of the world in which they lived!

Religious bigots need to spend less time preaching false doctrinaires of faith and spend more time in learning how to become humane. We of reality are getting extremely tired of being preached at with untruths by bigots and hypocrites of religious faith. Christian leaders need to start preaching the truth of the universe and Mother Nature.

False prophets should stop wasting our time trying to impress us with how much they have memorized from their false books. Religious books of creative but biased and prejudiced minds are crammed full of misinformation and fantasy. Christians need to show the world how reading and following those words of faith have made them more compassionate and humane human beings, not bigots and hypocrites such as Par Robertson, Jerry Falwell, and George W. Bush.

Christians need to become more spiritual. Time and energy spent on memorization of fantasy, false doctrines and doctrinaires would be better spent in learning how to communicate with nature and their fellow man. Their faith should be helping them to face the realities of life and their universe. They cannot escape reality by the use of prayer. Natural law controls the reality of this world and there is no god to hear our prayers. Today we have fundamental religious fanatics all claiming unrealities in the name of Christianity. Jerry and his ilk are preaching hate and bigotry everyday of their existence. Jerry has more than a few marbles missing but is still able to spread his messages of intolerance and hatred. His latest pronouncements about the purple teletubby, proves his fanatic, homophobic, and unrealistic views toward life. How bigoted and irresponsible can one Christian be?

Jokers such as Jerry are the wild cards out here in the darkness of Christianity that we must be on guard against. These spiritless fundamentalists are more of a threat than known hoodlums. The worst dangers facing the world are to be found in the untruthful doctrinaires of all these satanic Christian men.

How do bigots such as Pat and Jerry live with themselves. They certainly have no conscience for selling themselves to Satan! Anyone with a conscience would not declare falsehoods in the name of a religious faith. If there would happen to be such a place as hell, all that I can say is, "Burn, baby, burn! Satan is going to build up his fuel supply when you all arrive!"

I remember that when I was in my twenties, I used to attend mass quite often with Catholic friends of mine. Since I was not attending any church at this time, my friends no doubt thought that they might convert me. At one of these masses, the priest spent considerable time trying to impress his flock of sheep that Catholics were far more devout than Protestants. I had been raised in a United Methodist family. I could hardly wait to exit that evil place and inform my friends that I had attended my last mass. Religious bigots and hypocrites ever where that I go!

How many far right Christian bigots exposed themselves during their ill-fated Impeachment! How many of them showed us their true colors! It did not take a psychologist to detect the hatred and bigotry in the statements, facial, and body language of those so-called House Managers. One could listen to, watch, and sense the arrogance in the haughty behavior and voice of Henry Hyde and his fellow conspirators. These fools were so sure that they had this case all wrapped up. We out here in the boondocks did not know enough to understand the true situation! These bigoted puppets of the Christian right greatly underestimated the savvy and intelligence of we, the peons!

You might preach to us, but you are making a sad mistake when you preach at us with your fabricated doctrinaires of prejudiced faith. We are not as stupid as you may wish! We do not need anyone from the religious right trying to convince us that which is wrong with our government. We know that once we purge the bigots and hypocrites of the Christian right, our government may have a chance to return to normalcy.

"We have seen the enemy and he is us!" Pogo sure had it right. A truly spiritual person would never presume himself superior to another and then make asinine misstatements about another's lifestyle. One does not choose to be straight, bi, or gay. Mother Nature chooses our sexual preferences for us. When we try to be who we are not, we run into problems. To prove this, just look at all those hypocrites who were elected with the guidance of Newt. Many of them have been found guilty of frauds they have been promoting. How irresponsible, unscientific, and hypocritical can one be to pretend that he knows better than Mother Nature. Jerry and his friends need to get a life. Theses satanic Christians are spreading doctrinaires of hatred which causes violence in the name of Christianity.

Many Christians believe that if it is not written in the Bible, it does not exist as truth. How ridiculous is this bigoted nonsense! With logic such as this, one can deny most all knowledge and scientific developments of mankind. Intelligent men no longer believe that comets and other heavenly bodies control the lives of man. Why do so many Christians like to flaunt their ignorance so willingly?

The knowledge of the universe is not written in any book of religious faith. The universe is the work of that creative force billions of years ago. Everything has evolved from that Big Bang. No god of any faith has ever created anything in this universe. Man has created all his gods and faiths to suit his wishes. There is more truth and knowledge in a single scientific book than all the books of faith that man has produced. No religious faith is based on fact or truth of natural law of the universe and thus lacks legitimacy.

Henry Louis Mencken

"The truth is that Christian theology, like other theology, is not only opposed to the scientific spirit; it is also opposed to all other attempts at rational thinking. Not by accident does Genesis 3 make the father of knowledge a serpent – slimy, sneaking and abominable. Since the earliest days the church as a n organization has thrown itself violently against every effort to liberate the body and mind of man. It has been, at all times and everywhere, the habitual and incorrigible defender of bad governments, bad laws, bad social theories, bad institutions. It was, for centuries, an apologist for slavery, as it was the apologist for the divine right of kings."

"The truth is, as everyone knows, that the great artists of the world are never Puritans, and seldom even ordinarily respectable. No virtuous man – that is, virtuous in the Y.M.C.A. sense – has ever painted a picture worth looking at, or written a symphony worth hearing, or a book worth reading, and it is highly improbable that the thing has ever been done by a virtuous woman."

Morals and Ethics

Morals and ethics are concepts of humane mankind.

My dictionary (Chambers) tells me that morals are what is ethical and right. It says that morals and ethics are aside from religion.

Why is it then that Jerry Falwell, plus all his good buddies, constantly talk of morals as though they come from their Bible? Jerry and they are trying to convince us that only that which comes from the Bible is moral or ethical.

No religious text can be accepted as being ethical or moral when it teaches that by believing in the words in such a book, the faithful become superior to others. No religious text can be called ethical or moral when it condemns others for not following its propaganda, doctrines and doctrinaires.

Morals and ethics do not come from any religious textbooks. No religion has an exclusive hold on good. Christianity, such as that practiced by Jerry Falwell, Pat Robertson, Bob Jones, Albert Mohler Jr., the Pope of Rome, George W. Bush, plus nearly two billion others, are the philosophy of false men who have sacrificed their intelligence and self will to a satanic god and its faith.

These devil worshippers are preaching doctrinaires of untruths which were written into their book during the time that heavenly bodies ruled the knowledge of man.

Many of the books written by these unenlightened men of the dark ages of Christianity had statements of misinformation which they used to condemn scientific men such as Copernicus and Galileo. Later these disillusioned and unenlightened men attacked Luther, Calvin, and others for stating the truth about the universe and religion.

Only bigots and hypocrites could call the members of the Christian right moral and ethical. When these satanic men condemn others, they are the ones being unethical and immoral.

Is it moral or ethical for Albert Mohler Jr., the president of the Southern Baptist Seminary, to inform members of Judaism and Islam that they must accept Jesus Christ as their personal savior or he, Mohler, will not allow them to enter Heaven?

Is it moral or ethical for Falwell, Robertson, and their good buddies to deny that the same creator that created them also created homosexuals? Is it moral or ethical that they believe that their Christian faith makes them better than gays?

Is it moral or ethical for Pat Robertson to bilk the unsuspecting anti-abortionist that support him out of millions of dollars for his personal wealth and then invest that money in China, a country where abortions are forced onto women by the government?

Is it moral or ethical for Bob Jones III to call the Pope of Rome the antichrist?

We must remember that morals and ethics are not concepts derived from religious faiths.

Morals and ethics are necessary concepts developed by societies of humane man in efforts to live with his fellow man.

....

"The scientist who yields anything to theology, however slight, is yielding to ignorance and false pretenses, and as certainly as if he granted that a horse-hair put into a bottle of water will turn into a snake."

Henry Louis Mencken

"It's an incredible con job when you think of it, to believe something now in exchange for life after death. Even corporations with all their reward systems don't try to make it posthumous."

Gloria Steinem

"Religion, society and state from none of these do women get their proper honour. It is religion which has created an unparalleled disparity between men and women."

Taslima Nasrin

"Religion is now the first obstacle to women's advancement. Religion pulls human beings backwards, it goes against science and progressiveness. Religion engulfs people with a fear of the supernatural. It bars people from laughing and never allows people to exercise their choice."

Taslima Nasrin

"I don't find any difference between Islam and Islamic fundamentalists. I believe religion is the root, and from the root fundamentalism grows as a poisonous stem. If we remove fundamentalism and keep religion, then one day or another fundamentalism will grow again. I need to say that because some liberals always defend Islam and blame fundamentalists for creating problems. But Islam itself oppresses women. Islam itself doesn't permit democracy and it violates human rights."

Taslima Nasrin

"We are all atheists, some of us just believe in fewer gods than others. When you understand why you dismiss all other possible gods, you will understand why I dismiss yours."

Stephen F. Roberts

Morals, Ethics, and Common Sense

Religious faiths develop many doctrinaires of inhumane morals and ethics.

That great humorist and savvy political analyst, Will Rogers, stated, "There is no argument in the world that carries the hatred that a religious belief does. The more learned a man is the less consideration he has for another man's belief."

I am both amused and amazed at the hypocrisy that we willingly accept as moral or ethical simply because the sources are considered to be virtuous.

George W. Bush has convinced himself and other unthinking conservatives of the Christian right that it is moral and ethical to vanquish our dissenters since we have the physical and technical power to do so. He has unethically changed his reasoning for overpowering Iraq so often that it is difficult for a rational mind to follow his irrationality. Many of us accept any illogical reasoning that he gives us simply because he is the President of the United States and he claims to be a favorite of his god!

Dubya believes, as did Moses, that his god is a god of war. Only a coward would not take advantage of the weak if your god gives you the chance! George W. believes that he has the correct morals and ethics since he is among the chosen of his Christian God. The god of Islam is false!

There are many among us who believe our shit does not stink! Jerry, Pat, and their ilk, blast as evil anyone not following their doctrinaires of bigotry and hypocrisy. However, they always add, "I love you!" We all should know from where that hypocrisy comes.

The Christian right tries to convince us, that a mass of cells in a Petri dish is a human being. If we make use of those cells in the fight against god given diseases, we are murdering babies. This is the kind of hypocrisy of the Pope of Rome and other fanatics of the faith that is preventing the production of much needed drugs to fight some of his god's dreadful diseases.

It is amazing that some of the most tragic wars in the history of mankind have been the result of one religious faith fighting another. Each faith claims that its faith is the one and only. Any logical, truthful and honest person knows that there are many religious faiths each with its god or gods. No one faith can possibly have the sole rights to truth. No religious faith has the blessings of the force of the universe or Mother Nature.

Any faith, worth its salt, would have as its first concern the betterment of humanity. The faith should hope to make its members more humane.

Humane individuals do not condemn others for their varying beliefs. The strong do not vanquish the weak. Morals and ethics are humane concepts developed by civil individuals, civic groups, and responsible governments, not religious faiths. The world is in great need of humane humanity.

Dubya wants a Constitutional ban against gay and lesbian marriages. I, personally, believe that the government should get out of the business of marriage. The government should recognize only civil unions between two individuals be they heterosexual, gay or lesbian. The church should be the institution given the authority to recognize marriages according to its dictates. All civil rights of unions should be based on the civil unions *provided by the government, not the marriages performed by the church.*

No individual, religious organization or governmental agency should have the right to determine with whom someone can have sex as long as the consenting participants are of legal age. If any of the participants in an act of sex is a pedophile taking advantage of a minor, his ass should go to prison, even if he be a priest!

Anyone protecting another, knowing that the one being protected is a pedophile, has no moral authority, he should go to prison, even if he be the Pope of Rome!

···

"The taboos that I have mentioned are extraordinarily harsh and numerous. They stand around nearly every subject that is genuinely important to man: They hedge in free opinion and experimentation on all sides. Consider, for example, the matter of religion. It is debated freely and furiously in almost every country in the world save the United States, but here the critic is silenced. The result is that all religions are equally safeguarded against criticism, and that all of them lose vitality. We protect the status quo, and so make steady war upon revision and improvement."

Henry Louis Mencken

Jerry Falwell

("Mainly for his idiotic homophobic stupidity,
Jerry is my *favorite* Christian hypocrite!")

"If you're not a born-again Christian, you're a failure as a human being."

"I had a student ask me, "Could the savior you believe in save Osama bin Laden? Of course, we know the blood of Jesus Christ can save him, and then he must be executed."

"God continues to lift the curtain and allow the enemies of America to give us probably what we deserve."

"The ACLU's got to take a lot of blame for this."

9/14/2001

"And, I know that I'll hear from them for this. But, throwing God out successfully with the help of the federal court system, throwing God out of the public square, out of the schools. The abortionists have got to bear some burden for this because God will not be mocked. And when we destroy 40 million little innocent babies, we make God mad. I really believe that the pagans, and the abortionists, and the feminists, and the gays and lesbians, who are actively trying to make that an alternative lifestyle, the ACLU, People for the American Way – all of them who have tried to secularize America – I point the finger in their face and say, 'You helped this happen.' "

9/14/2001

"I sincerely believe that the collective efforts of many secularists during the past generation, resulting in the expulsion of God from the schools and from the public square, has left us vulnerable."

9/15/2001

Morals and Ethics Verses Truth and Honesty

Religious faiths have numerous flaws,
the most telling two being the lack of truth and honesty.

There is nothing that would cure quicker our sick Christian family values, morals and ethics than some massive doses of truth and honesty. Many Christians believe that their own codes of truth and honesty, morals and ethics come from their religious faith. This is a sad mistake because Christianity is not based on reality, it therefore contains very little truth and honesty. Without truth and honesty their religion is void of morals and ethics. Christian morals and ethics are based on the supernatural fantasy world of their faith.

Religious faiths are not truths no matter how much faith is expressed. Faiths are the creations of mortal man. Greedy and prejudiced man is known for creating that which benefits himself. Religious man is not known for knowing, let alone understanding, truth. Truth cannot be created, altered, or destroyed by man or his religion. Religious men believe only the truths that they will accept in order to promote their particular faith.

The acceptance of truth and honesty or the denial of the same; comes from men of reality. The nature of reality is truth. Our refusal to accept the truth of natural law has caused man to create all manner of religious faiths. Our faiths are not based on the truth of reality or the reality of truth. The reality of truth is nature and the creative force of the universe.

Man creates his religious faiths to conceal his lack of knowledge of the truth of the universe and world. We do not know or understand truth; therefore we have developed all manner of religious faiths in efforts to explain our existence.

Religious faiths are the creations of self-blinded man serving and unenlightened god. Religious faiths are not developed to serve mankind. The faiths of man are philosophical theories and therefore not necessarily based on known facts or truths. Man has not been honest in his creations of religious faiths, thus man shall never be able to know, let alone understand, himself or his world. The faiths of man need to become more real, truthful, and honest so that their morals and ethics reach a purposeful level of importance.

Truth

What is truth?

Chambers Dictionary defines truth as faithfulness; constancy; accuracy of adjustment, or conformity; a faithful adherence to nature; that which is true or according to facts of the case; the true state of things; the facts; a true statement; an established fact; true belief; known facts, knowledge.

Is it the truth, as Rev. Mohler contends, that only those who accept Jesus Christ as their personal savior shall enter Heaven?

Is it faithfulness to the truth that teaches acceptance of only the faith which one chooses to adopt as his own?

Is it constancy which assures one to believe that he has found the one true god and religious faith?

Is it veracity that tells one that his religious faith is more truthful than that of another?

Are they paying faithful adherence to nature by declaring that sex is only for procreation and that masturbation and homosexuality are evil?

Is it true and according to the facts of the case that Christ shall return?

Is it the true state of things, the facts, that Christ is the son of a god and a mortal woman?

Is it true that there is only one god and that he is the Judeo-Christian one?

Can the Bible, or any religious text, stand an honest test of truthfulness?

Can any adopted religious faith of man pass a test of truthfulness and factuality?

Universal Truth

One's truth is as he perceives it!

Though there may be but one truth, each of us interrupts that truth as we wish. Our past experiences form our biases and prejudices for us.

Christian men, such as Jerry Falwell and Par Robertson, claim that their Bible is the only truth. They have convinced themselves that they know and understand truth.

Truth cannot be created, altered, or destroyed. Truth is independent of the interpretations of man. To suggest that one knows the only truth is to say one knows the universe. To know, let alone understand, the universe; is beyond the present day knowledge of man. To know is not to understand. Understanding what one presumes to know requires a much more profound concept than simply knowing.

Pat and Jerry's book of faith was written by numerous men each believing that he knew and understood the lord god that Moses either found or created. In the second testament, we are lead to believe that Christians knew and understood the reality of their Christ which their faith created.

The truth in the two testaments of the Bible is the truth as the prejudiced and biased writers of these books of faith perceived it. There are as many interpretations of the Bible as there are readers of it. Each man has his own version of truth.

Men of other religious faiths, as those of us without a religious faith, would declare that the Bible is nothing more than a book of fantasy. Non-believers in religious gods, such as Deists, do not believe in any organized religious faiths. For me, the real truth exists in the eleven words of the Golden Rule which are, *Do unto others as you would have others do unto you!* That is the total of truth. Truth is the universal truth of reality of which man and his words and actions are but a microscopic part.

The Deist, Thomas Paine, stated, "The Deist needs none of the tricks and shows called miracles to confirm his faith, for what can be a greater miracle than the creation itself and his own existence."

The earth, which is home to man, is but a microscopic molecule of this great universe, a grain of sand on a vast universal beach. The universe would exist without the miniscule earth. The loss of the earth would be like the passage of a second in the life of a man, of little consequence.

I am quite often amused by men who take themselves so seriously. Some men actually believe that they know, understand, and speak the truth. Some believe that they alone are the important one. Bill O'Reilly, the loud but loose mouthed conservative of Fox News, is constantly saying, "You are entering a no spin zone!" How disingenuous! If one listens carefully to Bill and then honestly interprets his words, one will understand that Bill seldom makes sense and that the total of Bill is a "spin" to promote himself. Little of his philosophy is truth. Men, such as O'Reilly, are not known for speaking the truth. Men with agendas, promote their agendas regardless of truth.

Jerry Falwell speaks of the truth of his Bible and then condemns to Hell anyone not believing as he. The truth is, this world might become a safer and more pleasant place without the truths of Jerry and his ilk.

I am very amused with the many TV shows of the last few years which are called reality. The truth is, that in reality, reality TV is nothing more than a ridiculous depiction of foolish man trying to unsuccessfully escape his reality. Man does not yet understand all that he presumes to know of himself and his naturally real world.

Judaism and Christianity share the lord god of Moses. The Christians later added Christ as their personal savior a few thousand years after Moses had found or created his lord god. Now, however, the Rev. Albert Mohler of the southern Baptist Seminary, informs the members of Judaism and Islam that they must accept Jesus Christ as their personal savior or he will not allow them to enter Heaven! Islam is several hundred years younger than Christianity. But, if we are to believe the Bible, Judaism is several thousand years older than Christianity. The members of Judaism were speaking of going to Heaven thousands of years before the creation of the Christian Christ. Who knows and is speaking the truth?

....

"Could a being create the fifty billion galaxies, each with two hundred billion stars, then rejoice in the smell of burning goat flesh?"

Ron Peterson

"Ideas that cannot be defended by reason and evidence can lead anywhere, and, if there is no warrant for one's belief, there is no telling where it will end."

Paul M. Pfalzner

"There is something feeble and contemptible about a man who cannot face life without the help of comfortable myths."

Bernard Russell

"The old faiths light their candles all about, but burly Truth comes by and puts them out."

Lizette Reese

The Reality of Truth

Universal truths stand alone as **fact.**

A short time ago, I was listening to two Christian fundamentalists, pat Robertson and Jerry Falwell, discuss truth. Of course, the only truth for either of them comes from their individual interpretations of the Bible.

It is astonishing that these two Christian extremists cannot, or refuse to distinguish the difference between ideality, reality, fantasy, or truth.

Ideality can include reality, fantasy, and truth. Reality can include ideality, fantasy, and truth. Fantasy is most often ideality with little reality, seldom truth. Truth is found in reality, occasionally in ideality, seldom in fantasy.

The reality of truth and the truth of reality are not the same. Man is constantly altering his idealities, realities, and fantasies. Persons such as Pat and Jerry are constantly trying to alter truth, not recognizing the fact that truth is independent of thought, not dependent on interpretation.

Truth cannot be created, altered, or destroyed. Truth is a quality of factuality, not a quantity of philosophical thought. Ideality and fantasy are stuff of faiths and dreams. Reality is life as it is. Truth is the veracity of the universe, our solar system, and nature. One man's truth, ideality, or reality can be another's fantasy. Reality has caused man to create all manner of philosophies and religious faiths which he quite often refers to as truth.

Truth is reality, but not all of reality is truth. Man's philosophies, beliefs, faiths, and gods are reality. It is reality also that not all of man's conflicting philosophies, beliefs, faiths, and gods can possibly be truth.

My word for you is, "May the truth of the universe be with you!"

....

"We're fighting against humanism... we're fighting against liberalism...we are fighting against all systems of Satan that are destroying our nation today...our battle is with Satan himself."

Jerry Falwell

"I don't agree with those who think that the conflict is simply between two religions, namely Christianity and Islam...To me, the key conflict is between irrational blind faith and rational, logical minds."

Taslima Nasrin

"We know that the price of seeking to force our beliefs on others is that they might someday force theirs on us."

Mario Cuomo

"A child who is protected from all controversial ideas is as vulnerable as a child who is protected from every germ. The infection, when it comes – and it will come – may overwhelm the system, be it the immune system or the belief system."

Jane Smiley

"Superstitions typically involve seeing order where in fact there is none, and denial amounts to rejecting evidence of regularities, sometimes even ones that are staring us in the face."

Murray Gell- Mann

"The persistence of erroneous beliefs exacerbates the widespread anachronistic failure to recognize the urgent problems that face humanity on this planet."

Murray Gell-Mann

"With or without religion, you would have good people doing good things and evil people doing evil things. But for good people to do evil things, that takes religion."

Steven Weinberg

"The fact is that far more crime and child abuse has been committed by zealots in the name of God, Jesus and Mohammed than has ever been committed in the name of Satan. Many people don't like that statement, but few can argue with it."

Kenneth V. Lanning

"For me, it is far better to grasp the Universe as it really is than to persist in delusion, however satisfying and reassuring."

Carl Sagan

Why Not the Truth?

*If man was truthful, he would feel less need
for the creation of gods and religious faiths.*

Why do we find it necessary to lie about our words and actions? Why can't we tell the truth? What is it that we are trying to conceal, and from whom? Are we actually trying to alter our reality?

Our psychologists and psychiatrists are kept busy by those of us who are trying to escape the realities of life. These doctors of the emotionally disturbed and the mentally impaired are dealing with those of us who are trying desperately to alter our realities since our realities are conflicting with the **truths** that we have been taught. The way of life that we have been taught by society, our adopted faiths and varying philosophies have been revealed to us as being false, we are now desperately confused.

Whether we are lost because of our emotional or mental state, we are now unable to rationalize the conditions of our existence. Our stability has been destabilized since what we have been taught as the truth has not prepared us for the realities of the world in which we now find ourselves. We have been taught to place our faith in false philosophies and doctrinaires of religious faiths and their prophets and now all of these prophets and their prophecies have been proven to be lacking in reality.

The emotional stability of one is not dependent on intelligence. There is little difference between the emotional realities to the brain of a genius or that of an idiot. Our emotional state depends on how well we have been prepared to face our individual realities of life.

Mental illness is beyond our personal control. Unstable mental states are the result of chemical imbalances. The chemical imbalances might possibly be triggered or made worse by the stress associated with learning that one has been fed a continual, philosophical, religious diet of bullshit!

Many of us have been taught to place our lives into the hands of a religious faith and its god. When that faith and its god have failed us, we find that we have not been prepared to face our true reality. No supernatural god is capable of curing the emotionally or mentally unstable person. We may be temporarily comforted by prayer but no supernatural god of mortal man is capable of curing an emotionally or mentally disturbed person that has lost his reality.

The emotionally unstable person must be taught to accept the realities of his life. No amount of praying to a supernatural god is going to alter reality. Truth cannot be created, altered, or destroyed. Praying can only alter our perceptions of reality. Our true reality is not affected by our prayers since the creator of the universe does not hear prayers and is no slave to the wishes of man. Reality therapy and proper medication are the only cures for those of us that have been forced to face the truth of our existence.

. . . .

"If Christian people work together, they can succeed during this decade in winning back control of the institutions that have been taken from them over the past 70 years. Expect confrontations that will be not only unpleasant but at times physically bloody. This decade will not be for the faint of heart, but the resolute. Institutions will be plunged into wrenching change. We will be living through one of the most tumultuous periods of human history. When it is over, I am convinced God's people will emerge victorious."

Pat Robertson Oct-Nov 1992

"Advances in medicine and agriculture have saved more lives than have been lost in all the wars in history."

Carl Sagan

At the extremes it is difficult to distinguish pseudoscience from rigid, doctrinaire religion."

Carl Sagan

"Avoidable human misery is more often caused not so much by stupidity as by ignorance, particularly our own ignorance about ourselves."

Carl Sagan

"Think of how many religions attempt to validate themselves with prophecy. Think of how many people rely on these prophecies, however vague, however unfulfilled, to support or prop up their beliefs. Yet has there ever been a religion with the prophetic accuracy and reliability of science."

Carl Sagan

"Is it fair to be suspicious of an entire profession because of a few bad apples?
There are at least two important differences, it seems to me. First, no one doubts that science actually works, whatever mistaken and fraudulent claim may from time to time be offered. But whether there are *any* "miraculous" cures from faith-healing, beyond the body's own ability to cure itself, is very much at issue. Secondly, the expose' of fraud and error in science is made almost exclusively by science. But the exposure of fraud and error in faith-healing is almost never done by other faith-healers,"

Carl Sagan

Truth, Falsehoods, Reality,
Ideology, Fact, and Fiction

Though there be but one truth,
each man has his own interpretation of that truth.

Jerry Falwell, Pat Robertson, and George W. Bush believe that their book is the truth and the only truth. They have convinced themselves that the universe and all that exists within it was created in six days; man lived to over nine hundred years, and fathered children when he was well over a hundred years of age! This parenting took place thousands of years before the invention of Geritol and Viagra! Their book also declares that adulterers and adulteresses, homosexuals, children who disrespect their parents, those who take the lord god's name in vain, and various others should be stoned to death!

Truth cannot be created, altered, or destroyed. We can, however, create our own falsehoods of faith to alter our reality temporarily. Falsehoods are what man creates in hopes of confusing himself and others in his desperate but ill conceived efforts to avoid facing the truth.

Reality TV is a futile depiction of man trying desperately to alter his reality. Eating grubs, worms, and other such creatures is reserved to but a few uncivilized tribes in this real world of man. Reality TV is stupid men trying desperately to prove how macho they are and women trying to out-macho the men.

Reality is what is! Remember what Clinton said, "That depends on what is, is!" Efforts to change reality usually succeed in deepening our confusion concerning truth.

Ideology is various religious fundamentalists trying to convince each other that only they know truth and that their god and its faith is the one and only. Common sense and rationality should convince us that ideology is no answer to our stupidity. Thousands of years of gods and religious faiths have not shown to have provided us with the necessary wisdom to improve the bigotry and hypocrisy of the common man.

Facts and truths come to us from only two fields of study, science and mathematics. These two fields of science provide us with provable facts and truths. Philosophical studies from the fields of sociology and psychology are based on theories that have to be proven as fact before they can be accepted as truth.

Fiction controls the lives of many people. The world is filled with all manner of fictional ideas that we have created and adopted as truth. Many of us choose what we wish to believe not based on fact or truth, but on unproven ideologies. We have faith that we know what the universe and we are all about.

The world might possibly become a better place when and if we truly understand all that we presume to know.

....

"We at the Christian Coalition are raising an army who cares. We are training people to be effective – to be elected to school boards, to city councils, to state legislature, and to key positions in political parties...By the end of this decade, if we work and give and organize and train. THE CHRISTIAN COALITION WILL BE THE MOST POWERFUL POLITICAL ORGANIZATION IN AMERICA."

Pat Robertson 1980

"If you want to *reason* about faith, and offer a reasoned (and reason-responsive) defense of faith as an extra category of belief worthy of special consideration, I'm eager to play. I certainly grant the existence of the phenomenon of faith; what I want to see is a reasoned ground for taking faith seriously as a *way of getting to the truth,* and not, say, just a way people comfort themselves and each other (a worthy function that I do take seriously). But you must not expect me to go along with your defense of faith as a path to truth if at any point you appeal to the very dispensation you are supposedly trying to justify. Before you appeal to faith when reason has you backed into a corner, think about whether you really want to abandon reason when reason is on your side."

Daniel C. Dennett (Darwin's Dangerous Idea)

"I think that there are no forces on this planet more dangerous to us all than the fanaticism of fundamentalism, of all the species: Protestantism, Catholicism, Judaism, Islam, Hinduism, and Buddhism, as well as countless smaller infections. Is there a conflict between science and religion here? There most certainly is."

Daniel C. Dennett

"There is a significant difference between having no belief in a God and believing there is no God..."

Michael Shermer

"To be a fully functioning moral agent, one cannot passively accept moral principles handed down by fiat. Moral principles require moral reasoning."

Michael Shermer

"Absolute morality leads logically to absolute intolerance."

Michael Shermer

Faith as Truth

Faith and truth are not one and the same.

An artist understands the value of the colors he chooses. He knows and understands the purity, hue, shade, and intensity of each pigment. He knows that black is capable of muddling or darkening the illusion he may wish to convey. He knows that white is capable of lightening a mood and thus make an intended emotional response more pleasant or less morbid.

Black and white, when mixed together in varying amounts, can make countless shades of gray. A wise person, as well as an artist, knows that colors are like the philosophies of man, rarely do either appear as pure. Most philosophical works of man exist as countless shades of gray.

Whenever I hear anyone declare that a given philosophical thought is a matter of pure black or white, I automatically distrust the judgment of that person. Such an individual is not residing in what I consider a world of reality that I am living in. Not all men are known for their honesty and thus they are incapable of truthfully painting life in pure black or white, contrary to those who believe as Bush.

The only truths that man deals with in pure black and white are those in the fields of science and mathematics. The philosophical and sociological fields of study developed by man are the result of man trying to live with his fellow man and thus being philosophical, are never to be a matter of pure black or white. Since the acquired needs of individuals vary greatly, the fields of philosophy are forever muddled in endless shades of gray.

Whenever anyone states that the behavior of another will be such and such, you can be sure that this one understands very little of what he presumes to know about his subject. He is paying little attention to the fact that no two people react in exactly the same manner to a given stimulus. We may say that the average person will typically react to certain stimuli in a given manner, but if we declare that all persons will react exactly alike, we do not understand all that we presume to know of the reality of human behavior.

Truth comes to us in all shades of gray. One man's truth can be another man's fantasy. A humane person is one known for his truthfulness and honesty in dealing with his fellow man. Humane truths are not necessarily those held by men of a religious faith. The truths of men of faith are not based on reality but are the product of philosophical idealities.

President Bush does not live in the reality of gray. Men of faith, such as Dubya, can state, "You are with me or against me!" This statement of faith implies, of course, that Bush believes that he is one hundred per cent correct in his philosophical point of view.

Men of religious faith, such as Jerry Falwell and Pat Robertson, are constantly referring to their Bible as a book of truth. They and their ilk refuse to face the reality that their book was written by mortal men in the process of creating a religious faith. Many men, such as those who wrote the Bible, also believed that heavenly bodies, such as comets, controlled the lives of men.

Religious books of faith were written by mortal men. Mortal men are known for creating belief systems in biased and prejudiced manners to suit their own needs. Religious faiths are mostly created by men of little to no intestinal fortitude or faith in themselves or mankind in general. With so little faith in their own ability, they feel a great need for the intercession of a superhuman god to protect them.

Most books of faith, such as the Bible, were written before man had learned much knowledge or understanding of his universe. Religious men through the centuries have written volumes of information about the possible beginnings of the universe. Men of science have developed theories of the creation of the universe, earth and man. Some religious faiths, such as Christianity, decided years ago to deny scientists and their works knowing that these works could destroy the credibility of their faith. Religious faiths can never provide us with the truths we need since they do not deal with reality.

Religious faiths are philosophies of man developed in desperate attempts to explain his existence, Not all of mankind believe that they have the same needs, thus man has created many different faiths each with its own god(s). Most men feel that they need answers but few men are capable of understanding all they presume to know about the creation of the universe, earth, and man. There is no way to prove any of their faiths and gods. Gods remain a matter of the fantasy of faith.

Many religions will not accept the existence of other faiths and their gods. Most religions teach their faithful that it is the one and only true faith. It should be obvious to all that what we have decided to adopt as truth is not necessarily so. Since we have adopted many gods and religious faiths, we should realize that there is something drastically wrong with the philosophically developed religious belief systems which claim they are the one and only.

If one's religious faith teaches him that he is superior to others because of his faith, that faith is evil. It is unrealistic, and against what we know to be true. One cannot decide that he is right and another wrong simply because an unproven religious belief system teaches him this as fact. Since neither can prove the legitimacy of his religious faith, the one claiming superiority is a bigoted hypocrite, not to be trusted. The world is one of reality rather we like it or not!

It is a known fact that this world has had countless religious faiths and gods since the evolution of man. It is a matter of fact that the belief that a god or religious belief system is the one and only is utterly ridiculous. Faith in a god or religion is not proof of the existence of that god. Supernatural gods are beyond the reality of truth and thus they exist only in the realms of faith and fantasy.

Modern science suggests that this universe has existed for over twelve to thirteen billion years or more. The earth was created over four billion years ago. The Bible would have us believe that the creation of man occurred a few short days after the birth of the universe a few thousand years ago. We know that with modern medicines and scientific research man is living longer as time passes. The Bible has many stories of men living hundreds of years and fathering children after they have reached a hundred years and more. All of this sexual activity took place thousands of years before the invention of Geritol and Viagra!

If we were to be humanitarian here on earth, I'm sure that any compassionate god, worth his salt, were he to exist, would welcome us into his eternal home. If one studies the lives of famous religious men carefully and honestly one finds that many of them, such as numerous Pope of Rome, were not or are not very moral or ethical. There is no way to judge the goodness of a man other than the manner in which he deals with his fellow man. Beasts and man are the only creatures we are required to contend with on earth. From what I understand of Heaven, angels are all that one will need to contend with there since animals on earth are not considered to have souls. So they will not be seen in Heaven. What a pity, as many animals I have known have more respect for humans than does many men, some of whom claim to be Christian!

Angels are the occupants of Heaven and are merely humanitarians who have passed over. A god worth his salt; would recognize the value of black, white, and our multitudinous shades of gray. A *worthwhile* god should be more interested in a man of humanity rather than one that has adopted a fantastic, fundamental, bigoted and hypocritical religious faith.

••

"Men never do evil so completely and cheerfully as when they do it from religious conviction."

Blaise Pascal

"Those who wish to seek out the cause of miracles, and to understand the things of nature as philosophers, and not to stare at them in astonishment like fools, are soo considered heretical and impious, and proclaimed as such by those who the mob adores as the interpreters of nature and the gods. For these men know, that once ignorance is put aside, that wonderment would be taken away, which is the only means by which their authority is preserved."

Spinoza

"I distrust those people who know well what God wants them to do because I notice it always coincides with their own desires."

Susan B. Anthony

Fact, Fantasy, and Fallacy

The greatest threat to our personal freedoms and world security
Is the intolerance of fundamental religious faiths.

Most religious leaders today refuse to distinguish the difference between fact, fantasy, and fallacy since they believe that their interests are being helped by the confusion. It is a sad commentary that most of the writings in our religious texts cannot stand a test of truthfulness or factuality. Religious textbooks are mostly the works of unknowing, unenlightened and poorly educated men who understood very little of or refused to accept reality, science, fact, truth, or the laws of nature and the universe. Most religious texts promote a feeling of life as some would like it to be. These texts have very little in common with reality. Religious faiths teach us to deny reality and live in a make-believe world of fantasy.

The Garden of Eden is awe inspiring for the unthinking, uneducated, or irrational mind. Noah and his ark make a wonderful fairytale for those who prefer to be childlike. Moses and his tablets, the parting of the Red Sea, and like tales must be swallowed along with a few grains of salt from that famous sea.

We gullible ones accept religious fantasies from the minds of creative idealist as fact and then try to convince ourselves and others that we have adopted the one and only god and faith. Theories need to be proven before they can be accepted as fact or truth. For those of us who have self-blinded ourselves or those of little intelligence, education, or reality, it is not too difficult to accept religious fantasies of faith which claim that they are the words of a god.

Men were not very well informed or knowledgeable about the universe and our world two thousand years ago. Few people had any formal education. Not much was known of science or the laws of the universe and nature. Most of the population could be convinced of anything since they knew not fact from fiction. If the pharaoh, king, or religious leader so desired, he could awe the ignorant masses into following false doctrinaires as long as he also promised protection from evil forces real or imagined. This is the manner in which Christianity and other religious systems gained their power over the unsuspecting ones.

As the years passed and the population became more aware of the truth, the teachings of doctrines and doctrinaires of propaganda were questioned. It became more difficult for the Pope of Rome to spread his false teachings. He now was forced to send out his army of the faithful, led by mercenaries, to war against the heretics or non-believers, as Moses had called on his lord god to lead him against the non-believers.

This absolute dictatorship of the Pope continued for hundreds of years until men such as Luther and Calvin came along to challenge his word. All hell broke loose and the Pope was forced to brand these challengers to his absolute power and authority, as heretics. The Pope believed that he had the divine guidance and a right from his lord god to kill whomever would not follow his dictates. In my reality, there are no such places as Heaven or Hell. There is no evil and vindictive god such as that of Moses or the Pope. Mother Nature is the creator on earth and she does not indulge herself in childlike pranks or vindictive acts. The gods, such as the Jewish and Christian ones, are the false visions of unenlightened man. The gods, such as that of the Pope, are inhumane, they are evil. Natural or universal law never forces its will on any of its creatures it has created.

Such men as Jerry Falwell refuse to accept the truths of the laws of nature and science. Jerry tries vainly to refuse science since it proves that his religious faith is false.

The Christian god and faith cannot deny the reality of Mother Nature and her natural law. Jerry, through his false god and faith, is causing moral decay in the United States since he is unwilling to face reality. Refusing to face their reality is the reason Jerry and his good buddies are destroying the morality and ethics of this great nation.

Jesse Helms, the religious right hypocrite that served in the Senate for years, cursed natural homosexuals who are the creations of the same god that made him. When these human beings and citizens ask for the same rights that he enjoys, Jesse declared that they were seeking *special rights*. What kind of lunatic fringe thinking is this! These men passing laws against natural humanity are those whom we need to fear, These Christian fanatics can't distinguish the difference between reality and the fantasies of their religious faith.

The *spiritless* Christian Coalition, the *immoral* Moral Majority, the *satanic* Southern Baptist, and the *hypocritical* Church of Christ believe that the only good people are Christians. Sadly, we have millions of bigots and hypocrites following these devil worshippers. Jerry and Pat spew bigotry and hypocrisy in the name of Christianity and then are praised by the satanic Christian right.

Members of Congress condemned Clinton for his immoral sexual exploits while many of them were involved in similar activities. Henry Hyde remained in his plush office of the people, because he said that his fall from grace was a youthful indiscretion. A short time after he gave this explanation to defend his immorality, we learned that he committed his adultery in his forties! Newt was forced to resign because his wife, who would be suing him for divorce, was about to disclose his fornications with his aide. Livingston had to resign the same post before assuming the office because his sin of omission with a young woman was disclosed by Larry Flint. We have far too many such Christian bigots and hypocrites making laws and passing moral judgments while they are involved in the same activities they are condemning.

America is a beautiful nation. It is full of solid individuals that live lives without condemning others since most of us face our reality and recognize our sins against our fellow man. We also realize that we have bigots and hypocrites of religious faiths condemning us for the same actions that they are involved in. The faithful believe that their **shit** does not stink! If their god does exist, they shall assuredly pay for their sins against their brethren. I hope that they all enjoy Hell!

We need to rid this nation of these hypocrites who try to hide behind Christianity and Old Glory. These bigoted hypocrites are living in a fantasy world of their own creation. These phonies are waving their false Bible in our faces while indulging in the same sinful acts they are accusing the rest of us of committing. These devils are spewing falsehoods, lies, bigotry, and hypocrisy all in the name of Christianity! All that I can say is, "Burn, Baby, Burn!"

· ·

"All through history the ancient gods have found themselves in the trash can of history, eventually discarded. Atheists today are continuing that tradition. We are adding Jehovah, or Yahweh, to the list..."

Dan Barker

"Truth does not have to be accepted on faith. Scientists do not hold hands every Sunday, singing, "Yes, gravity is real! I will have faith! I will be strong! Amen."

Dan Barker

"A" religions are founded on the fear of the many and the cleverness of the few."

Marie Henri Beyle

"God is the only being who does not have to exist in order to reign."

Charles Baudelaire

"The Bible doesn't forbid suicide. It's a Catholic directive, intended to slow down the loss of martyrs,"

Ellen Blackstone

"Anyone who engages in the practice of psychotherapy confronts every day the devastation wrought by the teachings of religion."

Nathaniel Branden, PH.D.

"Appraise the Lord. Tax churches."

Bumper sticker

"Armies of Bible scholars and theologians have for centuries found respected employment devising artful explanations of the Bible often not really meaning what it says."

J. S. Bullion, JR.

"The time has come for honest men to denounce false teachers and attack false gods."

Luther Burbank

"There is no such thing as separation of church and state in the constitution. It is a lie of the Left and we are not going to take it anymore."

Pat Robertson, THE HYPOCRITE

"Vain are the thousand creeds that move men's hearts, unutterably vain, worthless as wither'd weeds."

Emily Bronte

"Truth is the daughter of time, not of authority."

Francis Bacon

"It is proof of a base and low mind for one to wish to think with the masses or majority, merely because the majority is the majority. Truth does not change because it is, or is not, believed by a majority of the people."

Giordano Bruno

"The establishment of religion clause of the First Amendment means at least this: Neither a state nor the Federal Government can set up a church. Neither can pass laws which aid one religion, aid all religions, or prefer one religion over another. Neither can force, not influence a person to go to, or to remain away from church against his will or force him to profess a belief or disbelief in any religion."

Justice Hugo Black

"Everything is more or less organized matter. To think so is against religion, but I think so just the same."

Napoleon Bonaparte

"There is no absolute up or down, as Aristotle taught; no absolute position in space; but the position of a body is relative to that of other bodies. Everywhere there is incessant relative change in position throughout the universe, and the observer is always at the center of things."

Giordano Bruno

"Believe nothing, O monks, merely because you have been told it...or because it is traditional, or because you yourselves have imagined it. Do not believe what your teacher tells you merely out of respect for the teacher. But whatsoever, after due examination and analysis, you find to be conducive to the good, the benefit, the welfare of all beings, - that doctrine believe and cling to, and take it as your guide."

Gautama Buddha

Satan: The Devil in Us

The evilness in the United States population is not the result
of the lack of Christ in our lives, but is the result
of superiority concepts and superstitions within Christianity being preached at us daily.

There are no such animals as Satan, Lucifer, or the Devil! These are the creations of unenlightened mortal man, devised in desperate attempts to explain the evilness within himself. These terms were created by men who understood little about life. Man, at this time, was uneducated as to the true nature of himself. Man refuses to accept the realities of life. Man feels a need to blame something or someone other than himself for his evilness. Much of mankind has, since they evolved, refused to accept themselves as natural creations of Mother Nature.

The creators of most faiths, being dreamers and idealists, developed theories to explain that which they could not comprehend. This is a convenient way of explaining something which is beyond our understanding. We devise stories quite often to hide our shortcomings and mistakes. Try questioning a child as to how your favorite vase got broken! The child suddenly becomes a creative wizard of sorts!

How many criminals has any judge set free because they claimed that Satan or the Devil made them do it? What judge is going to be so foolish as to be swayed by such ridiculous claims? Thank our lucky stars that most of our judges realize that they are to serve society rather than a religious faith and its god.

We can be as evil as we desire. We decide that we are going to do evil as well as good. We do not require any Lucifer whispering in our ear. Like Jerry Falwell, we are the devils, sometimes hiding ourselves in the clothing of sheep. If I decide to injure someone physically or emotionally, I have made that decision by my own free will. My actions and words do not come from any Satan or other scapegoat that my religious faith has taught me. I could, however, be mentally unstable!

Suppose that I rob a store, shoot the clerk, and make off with the cash in the till. When in court, I swear that I saw you commit the crime. When I am finally found guilty, I claim the devil made me do it! What is the poor judge to do? He and all the others in court will no doubt have a good belly laugh and then I will be put away with others of my kind.

Many of these religious fanatics waving their false books in my face are as evil as the worst criminals in our prisons. These false prophets know that they are not being honest and truthful. They know that they are espousing false doctrinaires. They believe, however, that they can hide behind their Christ, Bible, and Old Glory.

I wonder at times if Jerry, Pat, and Dubya are as ignorant as they lead us to believe!

They should realize the stupidity of what they are espousing as truth. They must understand what noted men and women of science have said about sexual choice. Yet they go right on preaching false doctrinaires from their Bible because they believe that the recreation of these words to be truth. Tell me that this dogmatic behavior is not as evil as that of any devil!

Deliberately fabricating untruths and falsehoods to uphold a false concept is being *immoral and unethical .The Christians m*aintaining that they are correct after having been found guilty as hell of lying, are committing a sin of the worst kind. Jerry, Pat and Dubya's Bible and Christ cannot cover their sinful doctrinaires and false propaganda.

The Bible is totally wrong in numerous teachings. The incorrect teachings are too numerous to list. The Bible is hundreds of years out of date. Though much of the text of the Bible may appear on the surface to be moral, it has little to no foundation of truth, fact or reality.

What Christians proclaim of lepers, homosexuals, masturbation, abortions, and sex in general, are complete fabrications and claims made against these actions are a disgrace to Judaism and Christianity. These doctrinaires of faith are pure fantasies created by unenlightened men trying to subjugate themselves and their faithful. Statements such as these spiritless men wrote in their Bible are examples of ignorant man writing his own biases and theories and then claiming these lies to be truth. No *just* god would be so bigoted and inhumane to espouse such falsehoods.

Men wrote this spiritless Bible in the days when they believed that comets and other heavenly bodies controlled the lives of man. The truth of reality and the reality of truth were never considered in any of these fantasies of the mind. Evil men with views toward the subjugation of mankind promoted these fairytales to confuse and awe the ignorant masses. Neither the creators of this fairytale collection of fantasy, or the general public were educated as to the truth of natural law or scientific truths of the universe.

The Bible is void of reality, therefore it shall never succeed in its conquest to dominate and subjugate mankind. It will, however, have a lot of success with those who wish to suppress their intelligence in order to hide their guilt. Make-believe and fantasy can never compete successfully with the truth of natural law. The Bible is a **dead** book. It has no life or future. The Bible deals with the superstitions and make-believe of the ancients. It has nowhere to go. It is two thousand years out of date. The Bible is as flawed as the mortal men who wrote it!

Modern communication with its enlightenments of mankind is going to rapidly awaken the peoples of the world to the hypocrisy of false religious doctrinaires that have been propagated by spiritless men of organized religions. The days of fakery and witchcraft employed by unenlightened men of faith are numbered. Those books which the religious keep waving in our faces will be found to be evil.

Truly knowing persons cannot believe that if they do not accept Christ as their personal savior, they shall be denied entrance to their final resting place. Intelligent persons would not choose to spend eternity with bigots and hypocrites of the Christian faith. Most Jews and nearly all Muslims do not believe in Christ as being anything more than a prophet of the Christians. The Jews had been talking of going to heaven for thousands of years before Rev. Mohler decided that he was the gatekeeper of that mythical location. Heaven is only an illusion in the minds of the faithful of several religions. How could Mohler be so stupid as to believe that he could keep anyone from something that in reality does not exist?

All organized religious faiths are merely philosophies and theories of biased and prejudiced man. There is no way to prove the legitimacy of any god or faith. Religions of biased man are simply falsehoods of faith. Such faiths cannot be considered as truths. The next life theory is just that, a theory. Heaven is a beautiful dream of wishful man. The theory of Jesus being Christ is like all supernatural fairytales. We need to distinguish faith from reality. No religious figure or philosopher has ever been able to show proof of a god although many have tried and there are a few who believe that they have succeeded! Only the very foolish believe that any one has been successful at this goal. It is an impossibility to prove as fact that which by its nature is nothing more than fiction.

If we could truthfully and properly describe nature and natural law, we might possibly become as pure as nature itself. It is for us to live a spiritual rather than religious life, showing the necessary respect for our fellow man in order to find our way in this world of nature and man. No religious faith that man has created can deliver us to any paradise. Nature has not provided man with any final resting place outside of earth. We need to rise above our false faiths and gods that only limit our efforts to live good lives in this world of nature.

There is no true religious faith or god. Theories in the minds of man are not truths until proven to be such. It is asinine to suggest one religion and its god is superior to another. There is no such thing as a single god or a true religion. True religious faiths have never existed. Organized faiths are the creations of mortal man and are not based on the nature of things as they exist. The unwillingness of men of faith to face their reality does not permit them to know truth. Truth cannot be created, altered, or destroyed no matter how much faith is expressed.

....

"As a scientist, I cannot help feeling that all religions are on a tottering foundation...I am an infidel today. I do not believe what has been served for me to believe. I am a doubter, a questioner, a skeptic. When it can be proved to me that there is immortality, that there is resurrection beyond the gates of death, then I will believe. Until then, no."

Luther Burbank

Good Verses Evil

Man is no more evil than he is good.

One of the greatest faults of man is his lack of faith in himself and his fellow man. Man is not inherently good or evil. Good and evil are relative terms describing the qualities that man learns from his society. The qualities of good and evil are concepts adopted by man. The manner in which one deals with his fellow man determines his goodness or evilness. Goodness does not come from a god anymore than evilness comes from a devil.

Somehow Christians and members of Judaism have declared that man is inherently evil because according to Moses Eve convinced Adam to eat from the tree of knowledge of good and evil. Having knowledge of life somehow was an insult to the lord god of Moses! It makes no sense to a rational mind; that knowledge of life could be a sin, but that is what members of Judaism and Christianity believe. In my world of reality and nature, there never was an Adam and Eve, Moses, or Garden of Eden.

We curse our government when it tempts people and then entraps them only for succumbing to these evil schemes and temptations. Why should a *just* god need to stoop to such vile tactics?

There is no reason for a *benevolent* god to create evil. There is no logical reason to make a supernatural devil the scapegoat for the evil thoughts and actions of natural man. Mother Nature created man, gave him brains, thus man is capable of creating his own good and evil.

It is the nature of man which allows him to be both good and evil. Man has never needed a god or devil to guide him in being an angel or a devil. Man decides his behaviors by himself with the brains nature gave him.

No religious faith has been able, nor ever shall be able, to save mankind from anything. Mankind is in no need of being saved. Man is real and natural. Some of us just happen to be more truthful, honest, and humane than others. It is supernatural gods and their organized religions that are out of step with reality. Mankind is living in this natural world of nature, while his gods are living in a superficial world of ideality.

It is impossible to deal with natural man by imposing supernatural standards of behavior. In order to deal successfully with man, one must become real and follow natural law. The Christian faith is far too concerned with preparing for a future pie-in-the-sky home!

Christianity has its supernatural head in the clouds while trying to deal with the natural realities of life on the earth. The mankind which religious faiths claim to be saving has been condemned by their gods and faiths. The false premise of evil man will not allow Christianity to deal honestly with mankind.

Any psychologist or psychiatrist, worth his salt, will tell one that it is impossible to help anyone by preaching to them that they are evil. There needs to be a twinkling of hope in order for the confused mind to strive for improvement. Many of our parents, using their religious faith, have preached to their children that they are evil. We cannot expect to raise emotionally healthy children by constantly reminding them of their evilness. Our religious faiths are the root of these false preachings which are having devastating effects on our children and thus our country.

· ·

"Immorality: A toy which people cry for. And on their knees apply for. Dispute, contend, and lie for. And if allowed would be right proud Eternally to die for."

Ambrose Bierce

"Impiety: Your irreverence toward my deity."

Ambrose Bierce

"Infidel: In New York, one who does not believe in the Christian religion; in Constantinople, one who does."

Ambrose Bierce

"Lord, I do not believe; help thou my unbelief."

Samuel Butler, English author

"To put one's trust in God is only a way of saying that one will chance it."

Samuel Butler

"What, me worry about the historical Jesus? The gospel writers made up their story; the church fathers invented the virgin birth on the winter solstice; the pope thought up the immaculate conception; so I can imagine ant damn thing I please about Jesus, or the Spook, or about the big guy himself."

Theologian Franz Bibfeldt

"When you repeat the same thing over and over, Sunday after Sunday, that makes people believe it whether it is true or not. It also makes writing theology easy."

Franz Bibfeldt

Good, Just, and Evil

There is no black or white in the philosophies of man
since the world of philosophical thought
is a reality of countless shades of gray.

We have a lot of violence in our societies. Many of us seem to have our own theories as to how all this violence has come to be and how it can be corrected. Nobody, however, has come up with a winning solution. We shall never solve this problem by trying to blame any particular person or thing. The solution is going to require honest, truthful, serious, and rational thought and action. The first and most important requirement is honesty. The high-sounding pronouncements and doctrinaires coming from the misguided Christian right with its false family values, is not going to solve anything. So far their philosophy has only succeeded in making things worse. We need to get real! We are living in a real world of nature not some fanciful idea of a remote or supernatural dream world.

Christians proclaim that we need to put Christ back into the public schools. The false and misguided pronouncements from their make-believe faith, is one of the main factors causing this violence. Any reference to a Christian deity has no place in our public schools. Our students are not totally Christian. If Christians can't find enough time to pray in their churches and homes to satisfy their needs, some drastic revisions are needed in their religion. Christianity should not be in our public schools anymore than Judaism, Islam, or any other faith. Christianity is no answer to any problems of violence since many of its leaders are fomenting the bigotry and hypocrisy which causes this violence. The superiority philosophy of Christianity is the leading cause of this violence in our society and the world community. Christianity has proven itself to be ineffective in its teachings over these past two thousand years. The Christian faith shall never be able to alter anything in this real world of man until it is willing to become real itself. When Christians become humane and face their true reality, they may start gaining some progress in the improvement of mankind.

Religion and spirituality should go hand in hand. I know, as well as you, this is not the case with most members of religious faiths. Jerry and his ilk may claim to be Christian but they sure as hell are not spiritual and it is rather doubtful that they are religious. We need to get rid of all these false prophets from hell and become one with nature and reality. We must teach our children to stretch passed the teachings in our false religious faiths.

The answer to violence is not to be found in any book of bigoted religious faith such as that used by the Christian right. Their faith is far too negative to be of any help. The answer to solving the scourge of violence is to be found in us. We are the truth. When we cannot communicate properly with our fellow man, including our offspring, we definitely have a break-down in our society! Quite often I have heard, "I am the light!" yet we are still in the dark, searching for answers in all the wrong places.

Why are we still searching in these false religious faiths of spiritless mortal man? We have not found the truth in our fanatical and senseless searches. Religiously biased and prejudiced men do not write the truth since they are not honest and truthful enough. Meaningful and helpful texts need to present unbiased assessments. One sided views developed in an effort to promote a religious faith are not the reality of truth or the reality of life.

The truth is within us. We are the ones that decide if we want to do good or evil. We are the ones who decide to follow blindly what other deceitful men have written in their books of faith. If we keep waving our various false books of faith in each other's face, we are going nowhere in short order. If the Southern Baptist believe that they own Heaven, we need to tell them that that is fine with us as we will create a new home since we do not wish to spend eternity with bigots and hypocrites such as they. Sharing a home with them would be like spending eternity in Hell!

If I condemn John for being black, John condemns Jack for being homosexual, Jack condemns Joan for being Catholic, and Joan condemns Mary for being a Jew, where is all this condemning leading us? Do any of these condemnations make sense to you? If they do, you are the one that needs to change your satanic beliefs.

The devil; is waving his false religious books at us. These books which are written to save us are being used to tear us apart. These false books are setting me against you and you against your neighbors. I hate you and you hate me! We both hate all those with different faiths than ours. We hate the blacks, Asians, members of Islam or Judaism. We even hate those who do not look like us or act as we do. Hate, hate, hate, and then find someone or something else to hate.

Condemn, condemn, condemn, and then find something else to condemn! Where did all this hatred and condemnation come from and where is it leading us?

Is the Christian religion teaching us to be intolerant? Intolerance is the leading factor in causing violence in our world.

Why do we listen to evil prophets such as Pat Robertson, Jerry Falwell, George W. Bush, the Pope of Rome and others bigots? What do these satanic men do for this world except to cause rancor and unrest? Poor Abe Lincoln twisting and turning over and over in his grave because members of his conservative party have sold themselves to the bigoted, hypocritical, lunatic fringe of the Christian right! Abe was a known Deist such as Jefferson, Adams, Madison, Franklin, and others. These men believed in a god but did not put their faith in any organized religion. In fact, they were very skeptical of Christianity. Jefferson even wrote his own version of the Bible as he was at odds with most of it.

The Republican Party with its fundamental friends of the Christian right are trying to destroy the government of the United States that Abe gave his life to save. They are tearing the United States into bits and pieces of bitterly contested ideologies all in the name of Christianity. They want to make The United States solely a Christian country. Please come back Abe! We need you desperately! We have gone bonkers and are preparing for a holy war. We need an honest realist to save us from these false prophets from Hell who are trying to subjugate the citizens of the United States and make us as unrealistic, bigoted and hypocritical as they.

"I give my money to the church organs in the hope the organ music distract the congregation's attention from the rest of the service."

Andrew Carnegie

"To be an atheist requires strength of mind and goodness of heart found in not one of a thousand."

Samuel Taylor Coleridge

"What's the deal with this Christ fellow? It's not a sacrifice if you get to take it back three days later."

Stephen Carville

"Have you ever wondered why God waited thousands of years, from Adam to Jesus, to tell the world he had a son? He, who begins by loving Christianity more than truth, will proceed by loving his sect or church better than Christianity, and end in loving himself better than all."

Samuel Taylor Coleridge

"Nature ordains that a man should wish the good of every man, whoever he may be, for this very reason, that he is a man."

Cicero

"They came with a Bible and their religion – stole our land, crushed our spirit...and now tell us we should be thankful to the 'Lord" for being saved."

Chief Pontiac

"You say there is but one way to worship the Great Spirit. If there is but one religion, why do you white people differ so much about it?"

Chief Red Jacket

"The trouble with born-again Christians is that they are an even bigger pain the second time around."

Herb Caen

Credibility

The faithfully blind are indeed, blind!

Credibility: the quality of deserving belief or confidence! Where is all the credibility? Where has it gone? Maybe the question is, did we ever have credibility?

Take a look at this Congress which took control with the guidance and leadership of that great hypocrite, Newt! This group of misfits was going to do a much needed House cleaning. With Newt guiding them, they got sidetracked along the road to the Capitol, sold themselves to the *lawless* National Rifle Association, the *hypocritical* Christian right, and the *crooked* Health Management Organizations, thus losing all of their credibility before they were even sworn in! They have proven themselves to be nothing more than hypocritical obstructionists, such as their counterparts in the Senate, Jesse Helms and his good buddies.

This misguided kindergarten class spent their time in the House trying to oust the legally elected President of the United States. It mattered not that Clinton had been elected twice by the voters of this great nation. This House of Numbskulls had been given a mandate from Hell by the Christian right to get rid of that *son-of-a-bitch* in *their*

White House at any cost! The *spiritless* Christian right, the *immoral* Moral Majority, the *satanic* Southern Baptist, and the *hypocritical* Church of Christ, plus others of their ilk, were financed by bigoted and hypocritical religious individuals to get rid of that *bastard,* Bill.

America had never known such prosperity as we enjoyed under the leadership of Clinton. These spiritless Christian right hypocrites decided that Clinton had broken too many of their religious tenets no matter how unrealistic these tenets may be!

They put this misguided sex deviate, Kenneth Starr, to the task of finding any and all misdeeds that Billy had committed. This sexual pervert of the Christian right proceeded to spend millions of our tax dollars on his wild goose chases, tied up the federal government for months, then could find nothing that could be judged illegal.

But then, Billy, this brilliant man, had not been too careful in hiding his blow-jobs! The bimbo that had been servicing him there in the Oval Office of the White House, told all to loose lips Linda. Clinton had handed over his penis on a silver platter to the devil! Clinton had let his cock become his downfall! Satan now had his sinner by the balls, so to speak! Satan was going to have his day! Kenny-boy was going to rid the nation of this bastard!

However, something happened on the way to the execution. America finally awoke and said, "Wait a minute there, Kenny-boy, sex is a normal thing! The President, unlike you and your hypocrites, the Christian right, has done nothing to harm America. Lying about how much or how little sex one is getting is a common practice. Quite a few of us lie about our sex lives in the hope that we will confuse our detractors. Just ask all of those good buddies such as Hyde, Livingston, Gingrich, Swaggert, and other members of the Christian right. The President may have tarnished his own reputation but he has not tried to destroy the government as you have!"

We had become the laughing stock of the world, not because of Billy but rather the words and actions of this extremely zealous group of Christian right bigots and hypocrites in their fanatic and desperate attempt to steal the country and subjugate us all with their religious hypocrisy.

Later, we had this same band of renegades refusing to consider legislation that Clinton was proposing. These obstructionists, controlled by the Christian right, the NRA, and the HMO industry, would not allow the passing of any legislation which would benefit the public because these special interest groups would lose support from their cronies.

Where is the credibility? We vote these servants into office and they immediately inform us that they are going to turn this country over to the special interest groups that are lining their pockets! Our Representatives and Senators are going to do as they damn well please since they know on which side their bread is buttered! They are saying, "Oh by the way, "We'll be looking for your money and votes next time! Thanks a million for your support!"

Jesse Helms, the bigoted one that he is, sat in one of our plush Senate offices making asinine and false statements which had been proven incorrect by many experts in the philosophical fields of sociology and psychology. He got away with these ridiculous tirades of lies simply because he had the seniority to do so by intimidating others in the Senate. This lowest form of mankind spread rumors and doctrinaires of lies in the name of the Christian right. He would then receive the highest praise and blessings of the spiritless religious organizations such as the hypocritical Christian Coalition and the immoral Moral Majority.

We must learn to pay attention to these sly foxes wearing the clothing of sheep who deliberately lie and make false statements of fact and quote passages from their satanic books which defend these inhumane untruths. Those of us who have become wise to these underhanded tactics are able to throw this vomit back into their faces.

We need credibility. In order to achieve the truth, honesty, and the American way, we first need to rid ourselves of these immoral, bigoted, and hypocritical devils from the Christian right. America can never attain its proper place in history as long as it is controlled by the evil force of the Christian right devils.

Compassion

The ridiculous and futile drive to create endless religious faiths and their gods
appears to have removed most truthfulness, honesty, and love from our world.

Whatever happened to compassion? Where has it gone? Our misinformed Christian right President Bush talks constantly about compassion but then in the same breath he condemns others for the moral decay in America which he and his kind are promoting. I cannot seem to find any compassion or understanding in the majority of his doctrinaires or policies which he espouses as the result of his adopted religious faith. Could the moral decay in America be coming from him and his Christian right good buddies?

Compassion, to me, implies that one has feelings for his fellow man. The Christian right philosophy that Bush espouses is only for the members of his faith, not the population in general. Is this what he means by compassionate conservatism?

Where is love in his book? Of course, his good buddy, Jerry, is constantly telling others that he loves them, while condemning them to his hell. Is this love and compassion Christian style? Maybe Bush has learned compassion from his hypocrite friends such as Jerry! Please quote chapter and verse where the Christian right talks about love, compassion, and the acceptance of their fellow man for whom he is.

Fairytales cannot be proven to be anything more than fantasies from the minds of man. Our religious books of faith should teach us more than fantasies and fairytales. Christians have been trying for two thousand years to subjugate man with their books of fantasy but haven't succeeded yet, since their fairytales are void of reality. Natural, mortal man cannot be controlled by supernatural gods and religious faiths.

Many of us rely on these supernatural creations of man to direct our lives. Most of these false doctrinaires written into our books of faith have not one iota of truth. Most are the pipedreams of man lost in the wonderment of nature and its natural law.

Most of these false doctrinaires have been created in an effort to confuse and awe unthinking man into submission and subjugation. There is no factual basis for any of these fantasies of the mind.

When are we going to wake up to reality? When are we going to say, "Enough is enough!" When are we going to make an effort to transcend these dreams of unenlightened, spiritless men of faith and find the truth? The creative force nor Mother Nature has blessed or condoned any of these false gods and faiths.

The creative force will be here long after the religious faiths of man have been thrown on the trash heap of passing philosophical events. The universe will survive with or without the earth, man, or man's religious faiths and gods.

We need to extricate ourselves from the prisons of religious faiths. There is only one creative force of the universe. Nothing has been created by any god that man has found or created. If we stay with the unproven doctrinaires of our false faiths, we are dooming ourselves to useless rituals and nothing more. We are practicing self-deception learned through our spiritless fundamental faiths. If we are trying to find our salvation, we must become one with the laws of the universe and Mother Nature. We need to burn all these false books and eliminate our false philosophies of life. Man did not receive his beginnings from any of the supernatural gods that he has created to fulfill his perceived needs.

....

"Christianity finds it hard to win new converts without reducing them emotionally to such wretchedness of self-deprecation that they surrender the last remnants of reason and human worth..."

Eli Chesen

"Worship God. It's easier than thinking."

Chapman Cohen

"Gods are fragile things; they may be killed by a whiff of science or a dose of common sense."

Chapman Cohen

"Agnostic: One who does not pretend to know what many ignorant men are sure of."

Clarence Darrow

"Just think of the tragedy of teaching children not to doubt!"

Clarence Darrow

"I do not consider it an insult, but rather a compliment to be called an agnostic. I do not pretend to know where many ignorant men are sure – that is all Agnosticism means."

Clarence Darrow

"Reality is that which, when you stop believing in it, doesn't go away."

Philip K. Dick

"Mankind shall not be free until the last king is strangled in the entrails of the last priest."

Diderot

Respect

Dysfunctional individuals
such as Jerry Falwell, Pat Robertson, and George W. Bush
are example of men that have never developed
a meaningful respect for humanity.

Respect, to treat with consideration, refrain from violating, to feel or show esteem, deference, or honor to...

This world of mankind is in great need of a sense of respect. Many of our organizations which are trusted to be models of respect, such as the Christian faith, are the fomenters of intolerance and hatred which causes disrespect. Respect for mankind is not part of most religious faiths. Christians, like most members of religious faiths, reserve their respect only for those with the same believe system.

Violence in our schools is the result of the intolerance and hatred which our children are being taught daily by this Christian society of ours. Jerry declares that a homosexual can be cured simply by finding the Christ of Jerry and accept him as a personal savior. Homosexuals are in no need of being saved. Mother Nature made homosexuals just as she made Jerry. The homosexual is in no more need of being saved than is Jerry.

Jerry is a hypocrite of the highest order that believes his faith makes him better than others. Jerry's sidekick, Rev. Mohler of the southern Baptist Seminary, declares that only those who accept Jesus Christ as their personal savior can enter heaven. Bob Barr believes that the plastering of illegal propaganda, such as the Ten Commandments of Moses, on the walls of our public schools will prevent violence in them. Christian fundamentalists, such as Bob Barr, cannot see that this bigotry is the leading factor causing this violence.

 How can we ever hope to rid violence from our lives when our religious and governmental leaders are fomenting it with their bigoted faiths and untruths. Children are not as stupid as some of us may wish them to be. Most of the youth of today are able to see through all this bullshit that the Christian fanatics are trying to pass off as the gospel truth. These false prophets from hell are making our children angry with their preachings of false doctrinaires of untruthful propaganda.

If one has respect only for those who believe as he, how can he teach his children the proper amount of respect that they need? Christians are trying to force feed our children the pap of hatred and disrespect and then wonder what has gone wrong with their society!

Christians are teaching their children disrespect for anyone of a different point of view or faith. When a number of our most influential Christian faithful in this nation are preaching superiority and untruths, and our children know these doctrinaires to be false, how can we hope to teach them to be respectful? Violence is the result of a lack of respect. If we respect the views of others and others respect our views, we are not likely to attack one another.

If we try to teach our children concepts which they know are not true, we are displaying no respect for their intelligence. If we try to force theory for fact, we are demonstrating to those children how false we actually are. When we try to declare scriptures from the Bible to be facts or truths, we are doing a great disservice to our youth who know that the Bible is a book of faith. Faiths cannot be accepted as facts or truths. If our religious faiths were truths, we would state so. Christianity is known as a faith, not a truth. Only the self-blinded, who do not question, can make statements of faith which are nothing more than unproven truths.

Children know when they are being lied to. My thirty-three years of teaching elementary school prove to me that this is fact. When we declare as fact, that which is faith, we are teaching our children to be untruthful. We are demonstrating no respect for their intelligence and their reasoning ability. Youths in our middle and high schools have learned much of life from living it. They know that there are people of various races, creeds, colors, belief systems, religious faiths, and sexual orientation. If our children have not been taught to hate, they will accept any and all people with equality. If bigots and hypocrites, such as jerry Falwell, Pat Robertson, and George W. Bush have taught them intolerance and hatred, they will hate all equally.

Could we ethically or morally believe in the Christian faith of Rev. Mohler? If we were to follow the teachings of Mohler, all that we are going to learn is bigotry and hypocrisy, hatred and intolerance practiced by the Southern Baptist. What should really matter is that we are good and moral persons who treat our fellow man with respect. We need to show humanity toward all of mankind. If we are good persons, we are not going to condemn others. The religion of another person has no effect on me unless that person is trying to use his religion to control my life.

What kind of religious teaching is it when Bob Jones declares the Pope of Rome to be the antichrist? This Christian hypocrite of the highest order, Jones, is a good example of a pot calling the kettle black! The most important question is, what is he teaching his university students and students everywhere?

Respect means that we accept other for who they are. We do not need everyone believing as we. We only need for others to respect us as we are. If you respect me and I respect you, we are not likely to attack one another. We do not need to **change** each other.

Insincerity

In order to adopt a fundamental religious faith,
one must first remove truth and sensibility from his life.

How can the population of the world take seriously these fundamental faiths such as Christianity?

When the Christian right makes outlandishly false and satanic misstatements of truth, why do we listen to them? Why are these devil worshippers so dishonest, insincere, and inhumane?

Some time ago I heard a doctrinaire so far off the nuthouse wall, that it was hard for me to believe that Rev. Mohler would flaunt his stupidity and hypocrisy so willingly! Mohler declared before his god and the world, "Only those who accept Jesus Christ as their personal savior shall enter Heaven!" Does this idiot with his brains up his ass, realize the ridiculous rhetoric he is espousing?

Here is this moron trying to say that he is replacing Saint Peter as the gatekeeper to the heaven of Judaism, Islam and Christianity! The members of Judaism were speaking of heaven thousands of years before Christian hypocrites such as he created their Christ!

Unfortunates such as he, Pat, Jerry, Bob, and Albert have sold themselves to the Satan their faith created. They have actually convinced themselves that the untruths and lies they find in their Bible are in reality, truth. This is the third millennium and the Christian right hypocrites are living in the Dark Ages of Christianity.

The Christian right is constantly speaking of their morals. Let's get truthful for a minute. Which of the men or philosophies mentioned below are more sincere, insincere, moral, immoral, ethical, or unethical?

1. A man who lies about his extra marital sexual exploits, such as Clinton, or one such as Hyde who conveniently neglects to admit to his sins;

2. The Rev. Mohler who declares that he holds the key to heaven, or one who does not claim to be Christian but lives an Honorable, respectable, and humanitarian life;

3. A person faithful to his fellow man and country or one who is constantly wrapping himself in his religious faith and Old Glory in order to hide his sins?

Jerry Falwell claims that a gay or lesbian that asks for the same rights and privileges that he is receiving is asking for *special rights*. Tom and Dick, Mary and Jane, are not entitled to the same rights as Jack and Jill! How is that for humane, logical, rational reasoning? Of course, these are statements and rationalities from an inhumane, spiritless Christian, not words from a logical mind! There is little humanity or rationality in the majority of Jerry's wild rantings and ravings. Jerry's teachings are satanic doctrinaires from Hell. Christianity is no longer able to control the thoughts and actions of fanatic members such as Jerry and his good buddies. The supposedly *enlightened* ones of Christianity are now the preachers of hate, bigotry and hypocrisy.

Ponder these questions for a few seconds and then answer them honestly for yourself. Which is more moral or ethical?

1. Any rabbi you can name or Rev. Mohler,

2. Barney Frank or Jerry Falwell,

3. Clinton or Hyde,

4. Judaism or Christianity,

5. Islam or Christianity,

6. Adolph Hitler or Jesse Helms,

7. David Duke or Bob Barr?

....

"As nightfall does not come all at once, neither does oppression. In both instances, there is a twilight. And it is in such twilight that we all must be aware of change in the air – however slight – lest we become unwitting victims of the darkness."

Supreme Court Justice William O. Douglas

Eskimo: "If I did not know about God and sin, would I go to hell?"
Priest: "No, not if you did not know."
Eskimo: "Then why did you tell me?"

Annie Dillard

"Religion is not insanity but it is born of the stuff which makes for insanity...all religions perform the function of delusion."

George A. Dorsey

"How can the Church be received as a trustworthy guide in the invisible, which falls into so many errors in the visible?"

John W. Draper

"It has no more special status than the belief of a particular West African tribe that was created from the excrement of ants."

Richard Dawkins

Futility

We must learn to live with what is, rather than our biased,
prejudiced, and idealistic beliefs of what life should be.

WE have gotten ourselves so wrapped up in the creation and promotion of religious faiths and gods that we have denied or nearly negated what life is! We are so busy trying to promote our individual faiths and gods that we have lost the truth of what a religious faith should accomplish. We do not understand what we are trying to promote or improve!

We should be trying to make human beings more humane, if not, we have no need for the religion! The futility of creating misdirected faiths, gods, religions, doctrines, and doctrinaires has erased most truth, honesty, and love from our lives. We are fighting war after war in the name of our religious faiths and beliefs. Our desperate searches for the meaning of our existence, has caused us to create all manner of fundamental faiths each claiming to be the one and only. There is little reality in any of our faiths. We shall never discover the truth of our creation as long as we deny the reality of truth and the truth of reality.

Of what good is a religious faith and its god that is based on fantasy and untruths? Do we actually believe that a god *worth his salt* would bless bigots and hypocrites who claim themselves superior to others? I know that the god which Moses created is very proud and vindictive but has proven itself ineffective! Will we ever be able to prove that our religious faith and its god is the one and only? I don't believe so!

A true religious faith and its god(s) have never existed in the world of reality. A true faith cannot be simply a matter of creating a collection of fairytales, sorcery and fantasy such as that of Christianity, Judaism or Islam. A religious faith needs to express a way of life for the betterment of all of mankind, not only the members of the particular faith.

A faith should strive to make its members the best humane animals that they can become. Humaneness comes from truthful and honest man.

A truly spiritual person does not claim to be superior and to have chosen the one and only religious faith and god. If one's religion is teaching him such concepts as superiority, it is best to cleanse oneself of that satanic faith.

Many of our most destructive wars have been fought for religious reasons. This truth should be enough of a warning to mankind. There is little love and compassion in us! Man needed to erase truth from his life when he started creating his gods and religious faiths. Not one of our religious faiths can produce the truth. Man cannot create, alter, or destroy truth.

One cannot profess to have a meaningful religious faith when he himself is filled with hate or disrespect for the religions of others. It is impossible for an honest person to look another in the eye and say, "Your religion is no good because it is not the one I have adopted." No one is born with a religious faith. We learn and adopt our faith from the teachings of others. No one religious faith has ever been proven to be better than another. No one religious faith has an exclusive hold on truth!

No religion can be proven to be anything more than faith. Faiths are simply theories, they are not truths or proven facts. Facts can be proven as truth. Religious faiths and their gods are not based on the truth of reality or the reality of truth. To claim that a faith is the truth is to prove that one knows and understands a god. No man has ever been able to do this. Faith is not proof of truth.

The creative force has created no religious faith or god. Natural law and Mother Nature cannot be controlled or owned by any religious faith. Mother Nature creates; she does not lead or judge man. The societies of mankind judge the words and actions of man.

All the faith that we place in false theories of superiority and piety would be better placed in mankind. We declare that we have adopted the correct faith and then condemn others for not believing as we. The creative force created the universe, the earth and all its flora and fauna. Man and his world are infinitesimal when compared to the total or sum of the universe.

We are not likely ever to know or understand the total truth of man's creation. The creative force does not communicate with man. Mankind would be doing itself a great service if it were to become more humane. Thousands of years of serving false gods and religious faiths have not proven to be very beneficial toward the development or improvement in the life of man. In reality religious faiths have proven themselves to be regressive and destructive.

....

"Science has never sought to ally herself with civil power. She has never subjected anyone to mental torment, physical torment, least of all death, for the purpose of promoting her ideas."

John W. Draper

"Religion is all Bunk."

Thomas Edison

"I have never seen the slightest scientific proof of the religious theories of heaven and hell, of future life for individuals, or of a personal God."

Thomas Edison

Evangelicalism

There is no greater example of the blind
leading the blind, than evangelicalism.

Many evangelists, especially those on TV, mean well! They actually believe that they are messengers of their adopted god and faith. They believe that they were meant to be the intermediaries of a savior. They may mean well but their success rates are in question! Many of these saviors of mankind haven't yet attained the first step up the ladder of spirituality as proven by the likes of Jimmy Swaggert and those numerous Catholic priests recently arrested and defrocked for their pedophilic actions. Most of these sinners against mankind believe that their man-made gods and religious faiths are truth.

The Rev. Robert Schuller is one of the very few evangelists who display faith in and an understanding of the reality of life. Robert appears to know the truth of reality, is honest, truthful, and humane. These qualities are hard to find in most of the imposters posing as evangelists. We truly need less biased and prejudiced men of faith such as the Pope of Rome, Pat Robertson, Jerry Falwell and George W. Bush. Men such the aforementioned are not honest or truthful enough to understand truth. That well thought of hypocrite, Billy Graham, proved himself as evil, when he was caught in the Nixon tapes, bashing and deriding the Jews.

Too many of these so-called evangelists are in the business of religion solely for the expressed purpose of bilking the unsuspecting faithful out of their hard earned cash so that they can build up their personal financial empires. Pat Robertson and Jerry Falwell have amassed fortunes by bilking the poor. The saving of souls is merely a cover for their devious schemes.

Many evangelists believe that if they shout loud enough and berate their flocks as the Calvinists do, the poor lost sheep will turn over all life savings to their cause. They continue preaching at, rather than to, their sheep.

Most of these shysters would not recognize a **true** god if that god were to bite them on their unholy asses. The invocation of their god's name is used only as a means of lending credibility to their underhanded schemes.

False Concepts

If only we understood all that we presume to know!

I remember and can picture in my mind the movie *Bambi*. I can still hear Thumper declare, "If you can't say something nice, don't say nothing at all!" These words sound so sweet, innocent and wise. This is the kind of unfortunate teaching that is having a devastating effect on the mental health of our children. This manner of teaching is causing our children to be untruthful and dishonest. Christianity imposes this kind of teaching.

The greatest fault in our method of teaching children is our untruthfulness and dishonesty. Children should be encouraged to tell the truth no matter the consequences. If we, the adults, cannot accept their truth, it is we who need teaching.

Of course, we should stress politeness, but at times the truth cannot be *buttered up*. We should insist on tact as well as truthfulness, not at the expense of honesty, however!

When we force a child to apologize for his words or actions, we have done nothing to improve the situation but merely transferred that anger toward ourselves. The child will now direct his anger in a different direction. The child, at times, is not ready to apologize. We need to teach children that there are more acceptable ways to solve problems than by using angry words and actions. Let the child know that you believe he could handle his emotions a little better and then give him time to do so. The world is not going to come to an end if he does not apologize but he may feel better knowing that he has done the right thing.

Most Christians believe that their faith teaches them to be moral and ethical. This trust is sadly misplaced. Most religious faiths teach mankind to be dishonest. Since religions are based on faith rather than fact or truth, most of our religious learning is based on false concepts of ideality, not reality. The world is in no way close to the concepts taught to us from the Bible or any other religious writings.

Christians falsely deceive themselves into believing that they are living not for this life, but the next. Therefore, they consider themselves above this earthly existence. This false concept of life is going to be the downfall of mankind, if our downfall ever comes to a reality.

Fallacies of Christianity

The fantasies of fairytales, make-believe, mysticism, and sorcery
which makes up the greater part of Judaism and Christianity
are not part of the reality of truth or the truth of reality.

To list all of the fallacies and fantasies of Judaism and Christianity would require a very large tome, probably as large as the bible itself! Therefore, I shall mention only the most obvious and flagrant falsehoods and distortions of truth. The greatest pretense is the one which promotes Christianity as the chosen faith of a god. The creative force of the universe has created **no** religious gods or faiths. Christ is the fairytale son of the god which Moses himself created. Christ is an entertaining fantasy for the minds of the faithful, produced from the creative minds of the mortal men who created Christianity. There might have been a boy whose mother named him Jesus. Claiming this Jesus to be the son of this mortal woman and a god, is the stuff of fantasy, not reality. Fairytales are not truths.

The creation of the universe of which the earth is a very minor part, is the work of a creative force far greater than any god that man has created to meet his personal needs. No intelligent mind could possibly, truthfully, and honestly accept the fairytale of Judaism or Christianity as having one ounce of credibility. Any religion that man has created must be accepted on faith alone as it cannot possibly be accepted on its truthfulness. No religious faith has ever been proven to be truth.

The **spiritless** Christian Coalition, the **immoral** Moral Majority, the **satanic** Southern Baptist, and the **hypocritical** Church of Christ are four of the most reckless and deceitful organizations of bigots and hypocrites spreading false doctrinaires of faith. These irresponsible and inhumane lost one would not recognize a **true** god if it were to bite them one their unholy asses!

Christians, such as Reverend Albert Mohler Jr., believe that they own the heaven of Judaism, Islam and Christianity. The hypocrites of the Baptist Church would never be allowed to soil the environment of a **true** heaven. How can these bigots be so audacious as to suggest that heaven belongs solely to the Southern Baptist? Is Mohler the true gate keeper of heaven?

The Garden of Eden is such a tragic comedy of errors. All of this creative energy of mortal man in an effort to explain his own evolution! Claiming that man is made in sin! Denouncing the realities of Mother Nature and her natural and universal laws! All sin is the creation of mortal man such as those who create false gods and religious faiths.

Mother Nature has created all mortal men equal one to the other, the heterosexual, bisexual, homosexual and such servants of the Catholic Church, the asexual! Sex is natural for all of mankind. It is only denied to the supernatural servants of the Catholic Church by the illogical Popes of Rome, not Mother Nature. There is no such thing as one accepted sex. Sex is not under the control of any religious faith or god. The only sinful sex is that controlled by unreal religious faiths.

Moses went up the mountain and came down with his tablets of stone on which the hand of god had inscribed the Ten Commandments! Come now, how much wine had Moses swilled before he made this declaration of faith? This ridiculous tale of Moses sounds more like that of Jack and Jill, in which Jack had fallen down and broken his crown!

Noah and his ark is a great work of fiction developed by Moses or other creative minds of the time. Can any truthfully intelligent person believe that the creative force of the universe would need to destroy its work to impress mortal man? How could a **compassionate** and **just** god kill thousands upon thousands of innocent people simply to impress mortal man with his power? The creative force of the universe nor Mother Nature play childish and asinine games with its creations!

....

"I do not believe that any type of religion should ever be introduced into the public schools of the United States."

Thomas A. Edison

"There is no expedient to which man will not go to avoid the real labor of thinking."

Thomas A Edison

"No idea is divinely inspired."

Albert Einstein

"I do not believe in the immortality of the individual, and I consider ethics to be an exclusively human concern with no supernatural human authority behind it."

Albert Einstein

"A man's ethical behavior should be based effectually on sympathy, education, and social ties; no religious basis is necessary. Man would indeed be in a poor way if he had to be restrained by fear of punishment and hope of reward after death."

Albert Einstein

"The religion of one age is the literary entertainment of the next."

Ralph Waldo Emerson

False Books

Religions are belief systems based on faith,
not necessarily truth.

I do not possess and do not care to have knowledge of the tenets of religious faiths since I consider them to be evils. I do have some knowledge of Christianity since I at one time was a member of the United Methodist Church. I assume that most religious texts have been written for the expressed purpose of creating and promoting a faith and a god and thus are not based upon provable facts or truth. Faith remains faith no matter how much faith is expressed!

Religious faiths are not truths no matter how many men claim that they are. The Bible starts out as fantasy and folklore with a lot of sorcery and mysticism. As it progresses, men add more books of fantasy in which is presented words that are supposedly those of the lord god of Moses. The make-believe, sorcery, and witchcraft within the five books of Moses must be swallowed along with a few grains of salt from that famous Red Sea!

The creative force nor Mother Nature has written any part of a religious text. Nature is the truth of reality, not any theory or religious faith that man has created. I would personally like to know how much wine Moses had swilled before he made his ridiculous claims about his tablets! Was Moses a real person and if so was he an honest and truthful man? We shall never know! I do not know who wrote the books of Moses. I do not believe Moses wrote them himself. I believe they are the creation of other men much later in time.

The Bible would have us accept as truth that the lord god of Moses created the universe, the Garden of Eden, Adam and Eve, placing them in this paradise filled with all manner of temptations, threatened them, and chased them from this paradise because they had partaken of his temptations.

What kind of a sick fairytale is this! Are the members of Judaism and Christianity trying to tell us that their god was involved in entrapments since the beginnings of Biblical time? The creative force and Mother Nature do not play foolish, childish, or fiendish games with their creations.

Since nature does not play ridiculous and asinine games with man, why would a **just** god need to stoop to such childish tactics as those portrayed in the fairytale of the Garden of Eden? This is a foolishly created fantasy from the mind of unenlightened mortal man.

I understand some Christians believe that lepers presented in the Bible were afflicted because they had sinned against their god. I do know that the Bible states that lepers were not allowed to take part in religious services and were driven from the cities even though god had created them to be this way! I also know for a fact that when AIDS was first detected and became known as a new disease, many Christians claimed that it was a punishment from their god for the homosexuals. The bigot, Jesse Helms, declared on the floor of the Senate that the homosexuals were being punished by his god. He was very quick to put the blame for this disease on a group of individuals whom he claimed were sinners rather than on his god who had created the disease!

As time passed, we learned the truth of this disease. For the Christian homophobes, such as Jesse, it remains a curse from their vindictive god. Fundamental Christian fanatics, like Jesse, refuse to admit that their sacred faith is dangerously flawed. No faith can successfully deny the truth of reality.

The Bible has far too many contradictory statements by various so-called experts. The mortal men who wrote the Bible perceived events as told to them by others in a manner according to their own biases and prejudices. The Christians can thank their lucky stars that we do not all hold the same biases and prejudices and therefore we do not all think like they!

Christians believe that since Christ was proclaimed the son of a god by those who created him, the entire Bible is the truth! How is this for rational Logic? There is no proof in the Bible that Jesus was the son of a god, merely an expression of faith that he was. Faith is not necessarily truth. Mortal man has in blind faith decided to accept Jesus as Christ, the son of the god of Moses.

A Christian will proclaim me to be a heretic as Christians are proclaimed infidels by the members of Islam. The words heretic and infidel were used by the members of these religions to describe those not believing in their individual faiths and gods. These terms are negative and thus are the products of mortal man, not nature.

One can be the most holy Christian on this earth and still be devoid of spirituality and humanity. One's arrogance and feelings of superiority should be the concern of a truthful society. Mother Nature created us all equal one to the other. It is only our arrogance which allows us to feel superior towards others. A truly spiritual person does not feel superior to another.

If we care to create false gods and religious faiths, that is our decision. Societies will judge our actions. **Just** societies need to be honest and truthful in their deliberations. **Humane** societies need to realize the difference between natural truth and the truth of religious faiths.

The creative force is the source of that *Big Bang* twelve to fifteen billion years ago. The creative force of the universe and its Mother Nature, have never ceased creating. The universe is constantly changing and expanding, creating, and destroying heavenly bodies and it shall forever do so. The universe shall continue for all eternity with or without the earth, man, and his religious faiths and gods.

Judging You, Me, and Them

Religious leaders, who are critics of other faiths,
are simply bigots and hypocrites.

While I am no better than you, you are not better than any other, and there has never been anyone walk the face of this earth better than you or me. Many men have been more intelligent, more handsome, more powerful, possess more wealth, have a higher status, but not one has been better.

The determining factor of a man's worth in this world is how well he treats his fellow man. Our personal accomplishments are of little consequence in the lives of others. The creator of the universe nor Mother Nature is a false god of man and neither judges or even knows of our personal lives.

Although I enjoy shaking hands with equals, I never wish to meet the Pope of Rome or any members of royalty for I could never lower myself to bow before another human being or kiss the rings on the hand of an imposter! Popes and royalty are examples of individuals who have received their positions not through their own efforts but by the use of force or cronyism. Never on this earth has any one human being deserved such idolization. We are all put on this earth by Mother Nature, one equal to another. Royalty and religious leaders **are not** the chosen of the creative force of the universe.

I could not condemn one for being less than me and then expect any **just** god to accept me. My judgment of others means absolutely nothing in the scheme of things. Nature is no god of man. Nature has created no religious faiths or gods. Faiths and gods are the creations of desperate man lost in the idea of his own importance.

Critics are bigots and hypocrites who believe that they know or have adopted the proper standards of behavior. We have these unreal ones telling you and me how to live our lives according to the standards that they or others have concocted. These standards of theirs may or may not have any validity. What makes any critic believe that he has adopted the proper standards?

I have often watched ugly as a mud fence, Joan Rivers and her homely daughter, comment on the clothes, hair and make-up of others when the two of them look like something the cat drug in from the alley! Have I made a fair and honest assessment of this mother and daughter? Are my standards fair and correct?

The reference to
God
in a few of the documents
of the United States
is no endorsement
of Christ
or Christianity.

Frederick J. Azbell

The establishment of religion clause of the First Amendment means at least this: Neither a state nor the Federal Government can set up a church. Neither can pass laws which aid one religion, aid all religions, or prefer one religion over another. Neither can force nor influence a person to go to or to remain away from church against his will or force him to profess a belief or disbelief in any religion.

Justice Hugo Black, Majority opinion, Everson v. Board of Education

Part Four Contents: Church and State

Ideality Verses High Ideals

The reality of Idealism is negativism.

Since it shall never be accomplished, idealism is, to me, a negative concept. Many idealists, however, do not accept the fact that their dreams shall never be fulfilled. Idealism is on a plane or in a state reserved for such things as fairy tales told by Anderson or those stories told in the Bible.

Embracing idealism is not the same as having high ideals. Having high ideals is a positive force since the goals are generally or for the most part, reachable. We all need to set our goals high but we have to set those goals at a level that can be accomplished.

Many people set the goals for themselves and others so high that they will never be happy or contented with the outcomes. Many parents set the goals for their children so high that the children become discouraged and quit trying to reach them when they believe they shall never succeed. They are the ones to realize that the goals are far too extreme.

The reason that the Republican Party is suffering these days (2009) is the fact that it has become like their companions, the Christian right, so idealistic that it is beginning to falter. The world never has been nor ever will be as portrayed by the goals in the Bible or the Christian right and the Republican Party.

Children growing up today are being bombarded with information true and false from all angles of society. Conservatives and religious right believers are overwhelmed by some of the "evil" things our children are acquiring from television, the internet and other modern day communication devices, although much of this information is the truth of the modern day world.

In an ideal life, teenage girls do not have sex and become pregnant because they never indulge in that "nasty and dirty" activity called intercourse. In reality, today's teenagers follow what they observe of their parents and society. They are taught that sex is great stuff.

We had a surgeon general a few years ago who told the truth and lost her job over it because the religious right demanded that Clinton fire her. Christianity does not believe that the truth shall set you free if that truth is not their truth. If we followed that surgeon general's advice and taught children the truth that mutual masturbation can be fulfilling we may have fewer out of wedlock pregnancies. For it is a fact of life that we will never stop what is natural.

Idealists say that these "children" should be taught to simply abstain. There are means to prevent these unwanted pregnancies but many of our idealistic Christian followers will not allow their use. They say that if teenagers are taught to use condoms, they will only be encouraged to have more sex. Let's get real, which is better for society and the teenagers involved, unwanted pregnancies and disease or safe sex? Which is more moral or ethical? But the religious right is more concerned with their doctrinaires than morals and ethics or safe sex.

....

"The whole religious complexion of the modern world is due to the absence from Jerusalem of a lunatic asylum."

Havelock Ellis

"God found out about the Trinity in 325 A.D."

Rocco A. Errico, Ph. D.

"I may as well level with you. There's no god, nobody makes everything right in the next world, and when you die you rot. On Easter all that really happened is that Jesus rolled back the stone, saw his shadow, and the Holy Land had six more weeks of winter."

Tom Flynn

"I do not believe in belief."

Edward M. Forster

"The absurdity of a religious practice may be clearly demonstrated without lessening the number of persons who indulge in it."

Anatole France

"It is an unusual book which begins with two contradictory stories and with a narrative whose time and place are false. [Yet] for centuries that book [the Bible] has been read as the source of truth."

Robin Lane Fox

"The Pope should be reminded that if God wanted us to pray outdoors, he wouldn't have given us multimillion cathedrals. The process of creating new scripture by constructive abuse of the old reaches its climax in the letters ascribed to Paul."

Robin Lane Fox

"The happy do not believe in miracles."

Johann Wolfgang von Goethe

Blind Faith Destroys

Blind faith is doing us in.
Blind faith is a religious sin
of the unthinking!

Blind faith is a crime.
It has no reason or rhyme
for existing!

The likes of Robertson and Falwell
have cast their evil spell.
Their religion is condescending!

Pat Robertson is insane!
His religious faith is inhumane:
blind faith unbending!

Jerry Falwell wears sheep's clothing as a disguise.
He pretends to be wise!
His hypocrisy is disgusting!

Bob Jones says, "In the antichrist Pope,
I have lost all hope!"
Christianity declining!

Albert Mohler believes he owns heaven!
Islamic and Jewish faiths are *unleaven*!
These two faiths are uninviting!

James C. Dobson created *Focus on the Family!*
His holier-than-thou families are a calamity;
exposing his bigoted right *"wingery!"*

Since the likes of Newt took control,
we have been drowning in a cesspool!
Our House is stinking!

George W. Bush has been successful in finding his god!
His head is either floating in the clouds or buried in the sod!
A righteous airhead planting!

Tim La May, the right wing creator,
is trying to destroy the U.S.A. with his words and behavior!
What a Christian leaning!

Ralph Reed is in a desperate fix!
Pat Robertson has been able to mix
his brain into an unintelligible meaning!

Rev. Sheldon wants to ban *Harry Potter!*
I believe that Sheldon *"oughtta"*
Understand the true source of sorcery and make-believing!

Rep. Tom Delay has lost all moral right!
Like Dubya, he is owned by the Christian right!
Their morals and ethics are evaporating!

Senator Frist would rule with an iron grip!
His sanctimonious attitude a rip!
His manner demeaning!

Senator Rick Santorum
is in a sorry state of decorum!
His reasoning blinding!

Fundamental Christian hypocrisy
is destroying our beautiful democracy!
The United States is waning!

I am rather dismayed, somewhat afraid
that too many of the thinking,
are not complaining!

Frederick J. Azbell

The United States and Religion

Thank our lucky stars
that Christianity does not rule supreme in the United Sates.

Religion in the United States was begun by men of various Christian faiths. Mostly these men were members of very strict Protestant churches. The first religious men and their families left Europe to escape persecution by the Church of England or the Catholic Church of Rome. The King of England, the figurehead of the Church of England, and the Pope of Rome, spiritual head of the Catholic Church, were both persecuting non believers. The fugitives from the tyrannies of the two churches, created their individual faiths along the manner of Luther and Calvin. Later peoples from other areas of the world arrived with their own forms of religious faiths. The United States then became a land of as many faiths as we have peoples.

Some of the early faiths, such as that of Calvin, believed that it was possible to drive the devils out of individuals by shouting at and berating them. This kind of idiotic religion still exists but lost much of its followers after the faithful realized that they had control of their fates and these wild men doing their senseless screaming were no more pure than they.

The humane among us realize that no amount of yelling or screaming is going to change reality. The wicked, who are the truly needy, will simply ignore this ridiculous screaming and go right on doing as they damn well please!

The founders of this country were, for the most part, Deists. They may have belonged to a church but did not follow strictly the tenets of the church. Most thought that church and state were separate entities and should remain so. When it became necessary to declare their independence from England, they were careful not to introduce the words of any particular religious faith into the documents of our government. Yet the Christians believe that since the term God was used in a few of our governmental documents, the founding fathers had implied Christianity to be the religious faith of this land. Fundamental Christians believe that Christianity and its god is the one and only. In our governmental documents we do find references to a god but there is no reference anywhere to Christ or Christianity.

To these self blinded individuals, their god and Christ are what our forefathers had placed into our government. How utterly ridiculous and presumptuous of them! Christianity has never been voted the law of the land. Christianity is not mentioned in any of our documents. No religious faith or its god shall ever own the U.S.A.

A number of religious faiths existed long before Moses created his lord god for his sinful people! Thousands of years after Moses created his lord god, Christians created their Christ to separate Christianity from Judaism. Since Christianity was going to also claim the lord god of Moses, it needed a way to distinguish itself.

Many religions shall exist long after the last Christian or member of Judaism have gone to meet their maker! We must remember that gods and religious faiths are the creations of man in his desperate believe that he needs to control his own behaviors and a feeling that he needs an explanation for his existence. We must also remember that many religious faiths and their gods have come and gone in this world of mortal man and they shall continue to do so.

The truth is; man creates all manner of gods and faiths as he wishes them to be. In my reality, no god of man has ever created anything in this universe or of the world of Mother Nature. The universe was created by the creative force. Mother Nature and her laws are the products of that creative force as well. The creative force has never created a god for man to follow.

....

"Doubt grows with knowledge."

Johann Wolfgang von Goethe

"I would like to call your attention to...an evil that, if allowed to continue, will probably lead to great trouble. It is the accumulation of vast amounts of untaxed church property."

Ulysses S. Grant

"[Pope] John the 23rd... fled and was brought back as a prisoner, the most scandalous charges were suppressed; the Vicar of Christ was only accused of piracy, murder, rape, sodomy, and incest."

Edward Gibbon (1737-1794)

"God is not all that exists. God is all that does not exist."

Remy de Gourmont

"For two thousand years Christianity has been telling us: life is death, death is life; it is high time to consult the dictionary."

Remy de Gourmont

"No theory is too false, no fable too absurd for acceptance when embedded in common belief. Men will submit to torture and death, mothers will immolate their children [for] beliefs they accept."

Henry George

To Be, Or Not To Be, Concerned

The United States is in a constant state of unrest as a result of
bigoted and hypocritical religious faiths fighting one another.

Should we in the United States be concerned that now we have a Christian fundamentalist President, George W. Bush, and a Congress amply supplied with bigots and hypocrites of the Christian right who pretended to deplore the sexual exploits of

President Clinton even though many of them were also indulging in nearly the same activities;

When we had a very influential bigot, Jesse Helms, sitting in one of our plush Senate offices, using his seniority power to deny legal rights to ten per cent of the population simply because his hypocritical religious faith teaches him that homosexuality is evil;

When we had hypocrites, such as Bob Barr, who were owned by the *irresponsible* National Rifle Association and the *spiritless* Christian Coalition, fighting against sensible gun control legislation while proclaiming that the plastering of *unconstitutional* Christian propaganda, such as the Ten Commandments, on the walls of our public schools would rid them of violence;

When we have numerous Christian leaders appearing constantly in and on the media condemning anyone not following their religious doctrinaires of hatred and intolerance;

When we have members of Congress, controlled by the *spiritless* Christian right voting for or against legislation simply because it does or does not conform to the theories of their religious faith;

When that so-called "honest and fair minded" Mr. Hyde, the leader of the conspirators that tried to overthrow President Clinton, claims that his personal fall from grace was the result of youthful indiscretions and then we later discover that these fornications took place while Henry was in his forties;

When the Republicans whose efforts to get rid of that *son-of-a-bitch* in **their** White House failed, they then refused to consider any legislation Clinton proposed even though that legislation was intended for the benefit of we the people;

When so many bigots and hypocrites in Congress were exposed during their satanic Impeachment of doing nearly the same thing as Clinton and most of them remain in office;

When the conservatives in the House passed their inflated tax cuts favoring the rich even though they had been instructed not to do so by the majority of us;

When we have unthinking people accepting the veracity of others simply because they profess to have a Christian faith;

When our great Supreme Court Justices refuse to hire non-white aides and clerks;

When Christianity is considered to be the religion of the land and the god of Moses and Christ are considered to be the only acceptable gods;

When there are so many dishonest activities continually being promoted by those hiding behind their Christian faith and our Old Glory;

When the general public accepts the bigoted and hypocritical propaganda of such Christians as Jerry Falwell, Pat Robertson, and George W. Bush even though many of us doubt that they have a spiritual bone in their bodies;

When our legislative bodies pass laws and regulations the reality of which encourage

Men and women both young and old to live together as singles rather than marry and lose benefits;

When we had religious lunatics predicting everything from the coming of Christ to the end of the world with the coming of the new millennium, as if the creative force of the universe could be confined within the limits of the Christian calendar;

When the United States joined the world and the Pope of Rome in celebrating the beginning of the third millennium on January 1, 2000 even though the second millennium did not end until the stroke of midnight on December 31, 2000;

When we have Christian fundamentalists, such as Jerry and Pat, blaming the destruction of the trade center on the A.C.L.U., secularists, liberals, gays, lesbians, feminists, and any and all groups that their satanic faith has taught them to be evil?

Should we not be, concerned?

. . . .

"The perfection preached in the Gospels never yet built an empire. Every man of action has a strong dose of egotism, pride, hardness, and cunning."

Charles de Gaulle

"So long as the universe had a beginning, we could suppose it had a creator. But if the universe is completely self-contained, having no boundary or edge, it would neither be created nor destroyed...it would simply be. What place, then for a creator?"

Cosmologist Stephen Hawking

"One does not have to appeal to God to set the initial conditions for the creation of the universe, but if one does He would have to act through the laws of physics."

Stephen Hawking

"Science uncovers questions that may never be answered. Religion is based on answers that may never be questioned."

Ken Harding

Religion and Politics

Christianity is not a political party in the United States even though
the present day Republican Party is controlled by the Christian right.

These past few years have become rather interesting although discouraging in the matter of religion and politics. Much of the American public, including me, has said that the Republican Party needs to divorce itself from the bigoted and hypocritical Christian right. We, the thinking ones of the general public, are getting extremely tired of being preached at by this sinful and spiritless faith-based administration of Bush. The Fascist style doctrinaires of Bush, Cheney and their Christian right buddies has to cease!

In this great freedom loving nation of ours, religion and politics do not mix well. As James Madison declared, "The civil government...functions with complete success...by the total separation of church from the state." We do not all have the same religious faith or beliefs. Some of us do not have any faith at all in any religion that mortal man has created. I, personally, distrust all persons who use their religion as a cover for their actions which are quite often very unethical and immoral. The founders of the United States did not form a church state. Religion controls only the minds of the self-blinded faithful. Most of mankind does not need nor want a particular religious faith sticking its nose into our personal lives and especially our bedrooms and then telling us how and with whom we can do **it**!

It's rather ironic that the Republican Party declares itself to be in favor of less government intervention into our lives yet wants to create new laws governing all aspects of our personal lives. The GOP might recruit more members if they would tell the Christian right fundamentalists to go to hell where they belong and then inform them that they must form their own party. Of course this will never happen since fanatic fundamentalist organizations, such as the *satanic* Southern Baptist, the *immoral* Christian Coalition and the *hypocritical* Church of Christ are buying access worth big bucks and we all know how money talks! A Christian right party could never survive on its own record since bigoted and hypocritically narrow-minded individuals that support such communities as Virginia Beach and Lynchburg do not have enough of a following outside of these communities.

It was utterly amazing for me to watch all of these parasites crawling out of the woodwork to run for President of the United States in the year 2000! Did any of them actually believe that the American public would be so stupid as to vote nationwide to support their ridiculous Christian right agendas?

Most of these termites had nothing good to say about the people from whom they were seeking votes. They also had very little good things to say about the country in general.

Most of the doctrinaires from these despots expressed their disgust with the country.

They were very critical of us. They seemed to think that they had mandates from hell to enslave us. People such as Bill Bennett with his hypocritical and immoral *Empower America* still refused to accept the truth. Bill could not accept the fact that three-fourths of us did not wish the President to be impeached. Bigots such as Bennett believe that they have to show us where *we* have gone wrong. Most of us live in the real world. It is not too clear in which part of hell Bennett dwells! Bennett needs to realize that we are not all blinded by the doctrinaires of our party or religious faith. Bill needs to understand that it is hypocrites such as he who are making life on this earth a living hell!

Did Gary Bauer actually believe that he had a snowball's chance in hell of winning the presidency? Wake up Gary! Most of us are not all living in the Dark Ages of Christianity!

Did Pat Buchanan truly believe that the majority of us were willing to regress to the Stone Age? Alan Keyes needs to abandon politics and create his own bigoted god, hypocritical faith, and satanic church!

We, the majority of the thinking public, have enough of bigots such as those House members who had to leave in disgrace for indulging in nearly the same acts as Clinton. That white-haired henchman who tried to overthrow the President had been active in the **nasty!** It is refreshing, however, to hear that one's forties are considered by Hyde to be youthful! By Henry's standard, I, in my late seventies, am in mid-life!

When is the last time that you heard any words from the mouth of Dan Quayle that was rational or made any sense? I still am at a loss as to how he ever was chosen a running mate! The only reason I can come up is that Bush needed a pay a debt to the Christian right. Imagine, if you can, what would have happened to this country if Quayle had become President!!!!!

These poor lost ones, of the spiritless Christian Coalition, get a few bigots like themselves to agree with their doctrinaires from hell and they believe that they can fool the entire voting population. They never truly pay attention! They continue to preach the same old clatter-trap and expect all of us to swallow this bullshit! These scatterbrained idiots can only help the economy of the country by spending money trying to make their pipe-dreams come true.

Nature had blessed our forefathers. The founders of our country had declared that religion and politics needed to be kept separate. It is about time that we make sure the bigoted and spiritless Christian right is shown the door and told where they can take their hypocritical and satanic faith.

The Christian right and their henchmen in the House should have been charged with the cost of Kenny-boys' senseless investigations and his satanic witch hunt. The so-called fair-minded Mr. Hyde and his junta should have been charged with treason for trying to overthrow our legal President.

America needs to wake-up before the time comes when we will not be able to take a piss without the approval of the Christian right. We need to exterminate these termites before they eat up the fabric of our constitution and contaminate us all with their satanic Christian right faith that is filled with hatred, bigotry, hypocrisy, and a host of other spiritless sins.

Conditions within the societies of mankind shall continue to deteriorate until we realize and accept the fact that the teachings of superiority and righteousness by religious fundamentalists within Christianity, Judaism, Islam and other satanic faiths of man are the roots of the greatest evils in this world.

No god has ever created any religious faith superior to any other. In my world of reality, no god of man has ever created anything in this universe. Religious faiths and their gods are the creations of unenlightened and hypocritical man. If there should happen to be such a thing as a *fair* and *just* god, these Christian fundamentalists who teach superiority shall find themselves in the hell that their kind had created.

The Christian right in the United States is a Fascist-style organization of would be dictators. They wrap themselves in their Bible and Old Glory and then wave their sinfully false doctrinaires in our faces. We need to take a much closer look at this hypocritical religion of theirs. The Christian right believes that we have to be led by the nose at all times. The faith of men such as Pat, Jerry, and George W. Bush is one of condescension.

The Christian right believes it needs to control our minds as well as our bodies. They believe the church should have the right to decide what we may or may not think or do. They believe that only they know what is good and that their god has given them the right to subjugate us in the name of their faith. You and I are too stupid and irresponsible to be in charge of our lives! The Christian faith teaches that we are filled with evil. The truth is that they are the evil ones who would like to be our dictators. Man is no more evil than he is good. Some of us, such as members of the Christian right, just happen to be more evil than others. If the *inhumane* Christian right displayed more faith in mankind, they would possibly be more successful in their goal of being in total charge.

It is very frightening to think that we are living in the third millennium, with the world progressing at an exceedingly fast pace scientifically, while we still have a caveman mentality within the Christian faith. Their philosophy is a greater threat to the advancement of mankind with the loss of our freedoms and liberties than that of a world full of Clintons. Clinton, at least, was a realist.

We should not allow these sly foxes, in the clothing of sheep, convince us that this country is going to their hell simply because our President lied about receiving blow-jobs from that bimbo. The President did not create any up-roar or waste our valuable time and resources. The Christian fundamentalists tried their best to convince us that we had become the laughing stock of the world. They were partly correct. We were the laughing stock because we showed excessive interest in the sexual exploits of the President. Many Presidents and leaders of various countries of the world have been known for their sexual exploits. The sexual affairs of others are frivolous matters, except to sex perverts such as Henry Hyde and his fellow conspirators, Kenneth Starr, and the Christian right fundamentalist devils.

"Disingenuity"

The Christian right would like to subjugate
all citizens of the United States of America.

Just how disingenuous can the members of the Christian right become? First they try to impress upon us the fact that it is their unbending Christian faith which gives them their family values, morals, and ethics. With the stem cell issue, they try to say it is not their religious faith but simply an issue of common morals and ethics. They have said that their morals and ethics are the result of their belief in the god of Moses and their Jesus Christ. They are now trying so hard to confuse us and keep us blind as to their real intentions. Trying to hide their evil doctrinaires and plans to subjugate us!

Dubya makes this great speech to the nation in an effort to confuse us by talking about his great soul searching. What a whopping lie! Dubya went to see the pope of Rome who told him that stem cell research was evil since it was against the doctrinaires that he and others had written on that subject. George W. was courting the Catholic vote for his run for office in 2004. He knew that he could not afford to offend not only the Catholics in the United States but all Christian fundamentalists.

The Pope of Rome referred to the United States as a country which strives to be great. The Pope of Rome was living in the Dark Ages of Christianity. The United States *is* the greatest country to have blessed this earth despite the words and actions of the Pope and George W. Bush!

Poor George has listened to the inhumane and unenlightened Christian right hypocrites again. The Christian right members of Congress put this idiot in front of them holding a set of twins. This fool asks, "Which one would you kill?" Really, now! A ball of cells in a Petri dish is a far cry from a baby one holds in his arms! Dubya's good buddies in crime, Pat, Jerry, the Pope of Rome, and other hypocrites of the Christian faith have convinced the uneducated among us that a ball of cells is a baby! The real issue, of which they are afraid, is that the fallacy of their god may be exposed.

That group of cells that we are talking about is incapable of creating a new life even if it were implanted in a woman's womb. Stem cells are not the same as sperm cells from a man. Also, the cells from which we get stem cells would probably be destroyed and thrown into the rubbish if they are not used to produce much needed medicines to fight the disease Christians say their god creates to punish man.

It is time that we start getting concerned when our government is being controlled by bigots and hypocrites of Christian fundamentalism. The god mentioned in a few of our governmental documents is that of the universal god of the founders of the United States, not the inhumane god of these Christian hypocrites. Jefferson, Adams, Madison, Washington, Franklin, Thomas Paine and most of the true founding fathers were Deists first, religious second.

··

"The advance of Western civilization has been partly a story of gradual victory over oppressive religion. The rise of humanism slowly shifted society's focus away from obedience to bishops and kings, onto individual rights and improved living conditions."

James A. Haught

"In the year 415, the woman scientist Hypatia, head of the legendary Alexandria Library, was beaten to death by Christian monks who considered her a pagan. The leader of the monks, Cyril, was canonized a saint."

James A. Haught

"Christ rode on an ass, but now asses ride on Christ."

Heinrich Heine

"The true believer is an archenemy to three things, all for the same reason. He believes totally in what he totally believes in – thus he is an enemy of himself, of truth and all that crosses his path."

Eric Hoffer

"What is preached in the churches is mainly untrue and unimportant, tiresome hostile to genuine progress, and in general not worthwhile."

Rupert Hughes

"Theology: An attempt to explain a subject by men who do not understand it. The intent is not to tell the truth but to satisfy the questioner."

Elbert Hubbard

"The great masses of the people...will more easily fall victim to a big lie than to a small one."

Adolph Hitler

"The Christian religion not only was first attended with miracles, but even at this day cannot be believed by any reasonable person without one."

David Hume

Creatively Selecting One's Intelligence

Once a hypocrite, always a hypocrite!

A few years ago, Rick Santorum, a fundamental Christian right advocate, caused a big stir when he equated homosexuality with incest and bestiality! One must realize, however, that those of Santorum's ilk have self blinded themselves from the truth of reality and the reality of truth. Santorum does not realize the fact that truth cannot be created, altered, or destroyed by man or his religious god and faith although fanatic Christians such as he are constantly trying to do so.

In Leviticus, Chapter 18, verse 22, we are advised by Moses, the creator of the Biblical lord god, "You shall not lie with a male as with a woman, it is an abomination."

Verse 23 says, "And you shall not lie with a beast and defile yourself with it, neither shall any woman give herself to a beast, to lie with it, it is perversion." It is evident that this fundamentalist gets his holier-than-thou attitude from the book of Leviticus, believing it to be the truth!

Moses, in Leviticus, also informs us in 15, 2, "Say to the people of Israel, when any man has a discharge from his body, his discharge is unclean."

15, 16, "And if a man has an emission of semen, he shall bathe his whole body in water, he shall be unclean until evening."

15, 17,"and every garment and every skin on which the semen, comes shall be washed with water, and be unclean until evening."

15, 18, "If a man lies with a woman and has an emission of semen, both of them shall be unclean until evening."

15,24, "And if a man lies with her in her impurity, her impurity is on him, he shall be unclean seven days and every bed on which he lies shall be unclean."

19,20. "If a man lies carnally with a woman who is a slave, betrothed to another man and not yet ransomed or given her freedom, an inquiry shall be held. They shall not be put to death because she was not free."

20, 10, "If a man commits adultery with the wife of a neighbor, both have committed an abomination, they shall be put to death, their blood is upon them."

20, 13, "If a man lies with a male as with a woman, both have committed an abomination, they shall be put to death, their blood is upon them."

20, 15, "If a man lies with a beast, he shall be put to death, and you shall kill the beast."

20, 16, "If a woman approaches any beast and lies with it, you shall kill the woman and the beast, they shall be put to death, their blood is upon them."

24, 14, "Bring out of the camp him who cursed, and let all who heard him lay their hands upon his head, and let all the congregation stone him."

24,16, "He who blasphemies the name of the lord shall be put to death, all the congregation shall stone him, the sojourner as well as the native, when blasphemes the name, shall be put to death."

24, 17, "He who kills a man shall be put to death."

24, 20 "...fracture for fracture, eye for eye, tooth for tooth, as he has disfigured a man shall he be disfigured."

It appears that Senator Santorum has selectively chosen his intelligence! I thus have five questions for the Senator from Pennsylvania.

1. Just how literal shall we be when interpreting the Bible?
2. Whom shall we ask to do the interpretations?
3. Whom shall we appoint as the judges?
4. Which commandments of Moses shall we follow to the letter and which ones do we deliberately overlook?
5. Are you positive sir, that using your strict interpretation of the Bible as you have so far, that you, the members of your family, your good friends and fellow fundamentalists would still be walking the face of this earth with all body parts intact?

Also sir, we need to suspend the legal laws of each state and those of the United States in order to use the laws of your Bible!

....

"Saints fly only in the eyes of their disciples."

Hindu Proverb

"Calling Atheism a religion is like calling bald a hair color."

Don Hirschberg

"Agnostics repudiate as immoral the doctrine that there are propositions which men ought to believe, without logically satisfactory evidence, and that reprobation ought to attach to disbelief."

Thomas H. Huxley

"IT may be that ministers really think that their prayers do good, and it may be that frogs imagine that their croaking brings spring."

Robert Ingersoll

Really, Now!

With some, there is no logical reasoning.

I have been reminded quite often lately just how illogical some of us can be! There are friends who try to convince me that it is possible to rationally discuss matters of consequence with people such as religious fundamentalists, terrorists, or other like fanatics.

Fanatics of various kind have previously determined all the truths of the universe for themselves and to be in their favor. The truths of others mean nothing to them. How could one expect to hold a logical conversation or discussion with one who has already decided all the truths of this world and beyond to be in his favor?

Some of my good friends believe that it was possible to negotiate with a terrorist such as Arafat! A number of our Presidents spent countless hours trying to negotiate peace accords with him. Just as one believed that he may be getting close to cutting a deal with him, Arafat comes up with another of his truths. It was impossible to negotiate with Arafat since he had determined all his own truths to be in his favor. Terrorists only understand the advantage of physical and material force.

Fanatic religious fundamentalists such as Pat Robertson, Jerry Falwell, the Pope of Rome, and George W. Bush are determined in claiming that their Bible is a book of truth. They claim their Bible to be the only truth! These fanatics refuse to face the truth that their Bible is a book of faith, not necessarily truth.

We have other religious fundamentalists such as Albert Mohler Jr. of the Southern Baptist Seminary, informing the members of Judaism and Islam that they must accept his Jesus Christ as their personal savior before they can enter heaven! How does one hold a reasonable discussion with a man who believes he owns heaven?

The terrorists that attacked the United States and took down the twin towers had decided all the truths of this world for themselves. No amount of reasoning could have changed their minds. Some of my friends try to justify Islamic fundamentalist beliefs and actions by blaming our government policies or the lack of Christ in our lives.

Bob Jones III has the audacity of calling the Pope of Rome the antichrist and then George W. Bush and other conservatives beat a path to the door of his university of bigoted and hypocritical philosophies to receive his **blessings** and **money.** Only those with their brains up their asses would believe it possible to logically converse, discuss, or negotiate with those who have previously determined all the truths of the universe to be in their favor! There is nothing to discuss.

Really, now!

"Theology is not what we know about God, but what we do not know about Nature."

Robert Ingersoll

"...why should we worship our ignorance, why should we kneel to the Unknown, why should we prostrate ourselves before a guess?"

Robert Ingersoll

"My objection to Christianity is that it is infinitely cruel, infinitely selfish, and, I might add, infinitely absurd."

Robert Ingersoll

"Any man who follows faithfully all...[the New Testament's]...teachings is an enemy of society and will probably end his days in prison or an asylum."

Robert Ingersoll

"The crime called blasphemy was invented by priests for the purpose of defending doctrines not able to take care of themselves."

Robert Green Ingersoll

"I tell Christians, 'If you had two children and one had to be bribed (heaven) and threatened (hell) to do what he was supposed to do, and the other one just did it because that's what he knew was the right thing to do, which would you consider the better person?' "

Greg Irwin, humanist

"The day that this country ceases to be free for irreligion, it will cease to be free for religion."

Robert S. Jackson

"I believe in treating others as I want to be treated – but I certainly don't believe in turning the other cheek and the truth is that I never knew any Christian who did either."

James Hervey Johnson

"God said: 'Let us make a man in our own image'; and man said: 'Let us make God in our own image.' "

Douglas Jerrold

It's Downright Scary

The truth of the bigotry and hypocrisy of
George W. Bush

Certain things that I have seen, heard, or read about lately are puzzling and nearly scaring the life out of me! Take for example, my two favorite bigots and hypocrites of the Christian right, Jerry Falwell and Pat Robertson. They and their fellow good buddies in crime, such as George W. Bush, actually believe that their words and actions are the truth and nothing but the truth since their Bible is the only truth! What a sense of reasoning! Very scary, indeed!

These three Christian fundamentalists also believe that they will be spending eternity in heaven. I have good friends who are praying and believing that they will go to that same heaven. It's scary that these friends are planning to spend eternity with bigots and hypocrites who believe themselves better than they.

George W. Bush believes that reading with children while terrorists are trying to destroy the financial center of the country in New York, our top military and civilian brass in the Pentagon, and an attempt to hit the capitol building, is real teaching. Bush does not understand that reading with children is only the beginning of a motivational process which we hope will convince children the importance of reading and education. Being able to reason and understand that Bush knows little to nothing about teaching or education is an example of real learning. With his poorly developed *No Child Left Behind,* all children will be left blind. Now this is a scary future for our children and the nation.

Education is a discipline. Without discipline, there is no education! There is no discipline, when we have children raising children, drunks and drug addicts raising children, pedophilic priests abusing our children, holier-than-thou religious fundamentalists raising bigoted children, while telling the rest of us how to raise our children! These Christian fundamentalists are teaching intolerance of other faiths. This last statement of fact is the scariest of all.

Pat, Jerry, and Dubya believe that if a man and a woman profess to be heterosexual and are considered to be Christian, they are necessarily good parents! How scary is this reasoning?

Around half of the heterosexual marriages in this country end in divorce. If the Christian faith, in this Christian nation, was as it is advertised, this figure would be far less. There are millions of single moms and dads raising kids. The households of single parents, gays, and lesbians are considered bad and are not even thought of as families by the hypocritical James Dobson and his *Focus on the Family.* Not very realistic thinking! How scary!

Bush is pushing for a Constitutional Amendment which declares that a marriage can be only that between a man and a woman. Bush is informing us that the most important aspect of marriage is heterosexual sex with the production of children. Even if the couple is not fit to reproduce their kind! How very, very, sad and scary!

You can be a child abusing pedophile, wife beater, drunk, or drug addict but if you are in a heterosexual marriage, you are OK with the world of Bush. How scary, Mr. President!

The Catholic Church has proven to us that going against Mother Nature does not work. Man is a sexual animal who cannot and will not be denied his natural desire and need for sex. All of those pedophilic priests prove this point. Only the supernatural religious try to suppress this desire, sadly with very little success. This proven fact may be scary to some but it is the real truth.

The scientific fields of psychology and psychiatry have proven that homosexuality is not the cause of pedophilia. Pedophiles are more likely to be those that are considered to be heterosexual such as Fathers, mothers, brothers, sisters, uncles, aunts, priests, nuns, reverends, counselors, teachers, or other trusted friends of the family. The fact that these are the animals that Christians choose as good family members and friends is very scary indeed!

• •

"The great enemy of truth is very often not the lie – deliberate, contrived, and dishonest – but the myth – persistent, persuasive, and unrealistic."

John F. Kennedy

"Organized religion: The world's largest pyramid scheme."

Bernard Katz

"Theology is a parasite eating at a table set by others."

Joachim Kahl

"I'd rather navigate the seas of uncertainty than be mired in the concrete of dogma
Patricia Livingston."

"The theory that you should always treat the religious convictions of other people with respect finds no support in the Gospels."

Arnold Lunn

Our Greatest Threat

Religious fundamentalism has no equal in its destructive power.

The greatest threat to our personal freedoms and security is religious fundamentalism. Fundamentalists of various religions have been fighting for the control of the mind of the individual man since man first created his gods and religious faiths. In the United States it is the fundamentalists of the Christian right that is threatening to destroy all competing faiths and subjugate the citizens of this country. They keep preaching that this country was founded by Judeo Christians although the true founders were mostly Deists that belonged to various churches. The fundamentalists of Judaism are threatening the Middle East. They might possibly cause a third world war and get us involved since the United States is tied to their apron strings. Islamic fundamentalists are a threat to the Middle East and the world.

The Crusades, the Inquisitions, and exorcisms of the Catholic Church and the witch hunts of the Protestants were examples of religious fundamentalists who had decided that their truths were the only truths of this world. Together these actions of the Catholics and Protestant Churches killed many innocent people simply because these *heretics* were determined to be free of the church.

Religious fundamentalists are those fanatics who have self-deluded themselves into believing that they have created the only god and religious faith.

In the United States, we have religious fundamentalists such as Pat Robertson, Jerry Falwell, Bob Jones III, Albert Mohler Jr., and George W. Bush who are worshipping a bigoted and hypocritical god and practicing a satanic faith.

A short time ago, after the destruction of the twin towers, Jerry Falwell appeared on pat Robertson's 700 Club and informed the people of the United States and the world that this attack was the result of his vindictive god becoming angry with our secular views, the ACLU, gays, lesbian, liberals, and any and all groups that his satanic faith has taught him to be evil. Pat agreed that their revengeful god had done this evil deed to punish the wicked.

Bob Jones III calls the Pope of Rome the antichrist and then many of our conservative Christian right leaders, such as George W. Bush, beat a path to the front door of his university of hypocritical philosophies to receive his blessings and money.

Albert Mohler Jr., the president of the Baptist Seminary, tells us that he holds the sole key to the gates of heaven! He declares that only those who accept his Jesus Christ as their personal savior shall be admitted to heaven! Judaism was the creator of heaven thousands of years before the Christians created their Christ. Of which heaven is Mohler speaking?

The conflict in Ireland is the result of Christian Protestants fighting Christian Catholics over their conflicting fundamentalist views. The war in the Middle East is Islamic fundamentalist fighting fundamentalists of Judaism. The conflict over Kashmir is Hinduism fighting Islam.

The attack on the United States on September 11, 2001, was committed by those who follow the fanatic fundamental beliefs of Islam. It was not simply evil terrorists as George first tried to make us believe. These Islamic fundamentalists did not like to be dictated to and controlled by the evil forces of the Christian fundamentalists that were trying to subjugate them.

The United States attack upon Iraq is partly the result of George W. Bush believing that he had the Christian God on his side. He was confident that he could defeat the secular government of that country. When the Islamic terrorists decided to join the fight and drive the Christian Bush and his fellow *infidels* out of their country, Bush had no idea of what to do and never did learn.

I see no greater threat to the security, civil rights and liberties of the people of the United States than the fundamentalism of the Christian right.

Conditions within the societies of mankind shall continue to deteriorate until we realize and accept the fact that the teachings within the fundamentalism of Christianity, Islam, Judaism and other faiths are the root of the majority of the evils committed against one another.

....

"When your heart is full of Jesus, there's little room for anything else."

Bill Lueders

"The Church says that the earth is flat, but I know it is round, for I have seen the shadow on the moon, and I have more faith in a shadow than the Church."

"If the triangles made a god, they would give him three sides."

Charles de Montesquieu

"If you eat sausage, you are better off not knowing the inner workings of sauage factories, and if you are a Christian, that of the Christian church."

Rev. Donald Morgan

The Satanic Faithful

If the people of the United States are going to hell, it is most likely the result of satanic beliefs and actions of Christian fundamentalism! If there be such a thing as a *just* and *honest* god, the following men shall surely spend eternity in the hell which they and their faith have created.

Pat Robertson tops my list of the worst offenders against humanity. The only reason this sorry excuse of a man has for professing to be Christian is that his religion provides him the cover he needs for hoodwinking the stupidly unsuspecting out of their millions of dollars for his personal benefit. This evil man has used those millions of dollars sent to him in the name of his god for building his personal financial empire. This hypocrite of the highest order condemns those in America approving of selective abortion while he is doing millions of dollars of business with China where the government forces women to have abortions.

My second choice is that satanic Christian wearing the clothing of a sheep, Jerry Falwell. He is so hypocritical that he has convinced himself of the truth of his satanic god and faith. This poor homophobic man actually believes that homosexuality is a *chosen* lifestyle and not the sexuality that Mother Nature provided. Jerry would not recognize a *true* god if it were to bite him on his unholy ass!

Bob Jones III has tried to convince the peoples of the world that the Pope of Rome is the antichrist. I personally believe the Pope to be an imposter, but no more so than this *escapee* from the happy farm!

Albert Mohler Jr. really should not flaunt his stupid satanic views for the people of the world to witness. This moron is trying to threaten the population of the world with the nonsense that if they do not accept his Jesus Christ as their personal savior, he will not allow them to enter his heaven! Judaism was speaking of heaven thousands of years before the Christians created Albert's Christ. Of which heaven is Albert speaking? Who in their sane mind would be praying to spend eternity in the heaven that Albert claims to own?

Rev. Walter C. Dobson created what he calls, *Focus on the Family.* He is pushing for church action on partisan political activities. How can this man focus on the family when the only family he is willing to acknowledge is the one with a father, mother and their children? Christian ideology does not reign supreme in the United States. Half of the Marriages, Christian or of any other faith, end in divorce, thus half the households in the United States lack one or more of the members necessary for a family according to Dobson.

Gary Bauer never ceases to amaze me with his hypocritical stupidity. This poor lost one honestly believed that the members of the general public of the United States were stupid enough to adopt him and his satanic outlook on life. Just as with that Vice President of the first burning Bush, I have yet to hear a sensible word come from this devil worshipper.

P. James Kennedy is another of those TV evangelists hoodwinking the stupidly faithful out of their livelihoods. This evil man honestly believes that what he reads in his hypocritical religious textbook is gospel. He might be believable if he were to become an honest man.

U.S. Representative Ernest Istook (R. Okla.) wants the government to sponsor religion in our public schools. Of course, the only religion allowed to be taught would be Christianity. This hypocrite knows but does not understand that Christianity is only one of the many religions being practiced in this country.

Tim La Maye, the so-called key architect of the Christian right, which consists of the most bigoted and hypocritical groups of satanic organizations to have ever existed, is trying to destroy our democracy and replace it with his Fascist brand of religion. Heaven help us!

Ralph Reed is the former director of Pat Robertson's satanic Christian Coalition. This man had blinded himself from reality ages ago. Poor Ralph would not know truth if it surrounded him!

Rev. Luis P. Sheldon wants to ban all Harry Potter books. Since his Bible is replete with the fantasies of make-believe, sorcery, and witchcraft, the fanatic condemnation by this Christian fundamentalist of the Harry Potter books only proves that he does not understand all that he presumes to know of the five books of Moses which are the foundations of Judaism and Christianity.

U. S. Senator Rick Santorum (R. PA) has dove to the deep end. He truly wants to destroy the government of the United States and set up a new church state. I would like to know which of his satanic buddies he would pick to be the dictator of his Fascist country?

Rep. J. C. Watts (R. Okla.) has missed his calling. I am sure that there must be a far out church there in Oklahoma that is in desperate need of a bigoted Christian leader! J. C., please find that church and practice your hypocrisy far away from Washington D. C.!

··

"The Belief that man is outfitted with an immortal soul, differing from the engines which operate the lower animals, is ridiculously unjust to them. The difference between the smartest dog and the stupidest man – say a Tennessee Holy Roller – is really very small, and the difference between the decentest dog and the worst man is still all in favor of the dog."

H. L. Mencken

The Christian Right and Their Impeachment

If this country is going to hell, it most likely is the result of the satanic practices of our fundamentalist Christian right government.

I could not understand the great circle shoot that the Republican members of the House insisted upon promoting! Why had the party of honest Abe sold itself to bigots and hypocrites of the Christian right such as Pat Robertson, Jerry Falwell and James Dobson? The members of the Christian right were shooting down each other so badly that the antichrist, Pat Robertson, pulled himself out of the fray for fear that his hypocrisy would be exposed.

Many reasonable people of the United States had told the religious right to get over Bill and get on with the business of the country. The sensible population of this nation understood that our government is not supposed to be controlled by any religious junta. Christianity has no mandate for dictating doctrinaires to us. The nation is not solely Christian, thank our lucky stars.

The Christian right members in the House believed that their Bible of superstitious, propaganda and evil doctrinaires gave them the right to subjugate us as well as the government. Sorry to disappoint those hypocrites, the framers of our government were a far more intelligent group than the current members of Congress. The creators of our Constitution made sure that the law of the land is governed by the people, not any certain religious faith. The creative force and its natural law are not Christian. The laws of the universe and Mother Nature are not slaves to the whims of man.

When the Impeachment hearings for President Clinton began in the House, most of the media declared that Representative Henry Hyde was this great, honest, and revered person. Hyde himself declared that if the Impeachment was to be successful, the House had to remain unbiased. What a Farce!

Because Hyde had the numbers with him in the House, he was assured success at whatever he decided to do. So, this hypocrite, who had also dabbled in extra-marital sex, proceeded with the Impeachment of Clinton. The *spiritless* Christian coalition and their good buddies decided the outcome for Henry. Hyde, understanding on which side his bread was buttered, readily complied with their doctrinaires from hell and proceeded to impeach the President. Henry, along with his fellow henchmen, the House Managers, was successful in their satanic ritual.

Thank our lucky stars, the Senate in its slow and deliberate wisdom, listened to the American public and finally recognized that this was not what the vast majority of we the people wanted. Henry Hyde, along with his fellow conspirators, had decided to hell with the public, we have a mandate from the satanic Christian right and we are going to impeach this *son-of-a-bitch* and no rational public is going to stop us!

The American public knew well and understood the difference between immoral sex and this sneaky attack upon our government. The Hypocritical Christian right had nearly succeeded in its satanic attempt to subjugate the people of the United States.

Most peoples of the world could not understand our all consuming interest in the sex life of our President! These peoples were able to make their logical determinations based upon reason, sensibility, and reality. They were not being led by the nose by the spiritless, bigoted, and hypocritical Christian right.

The Republican Party needs to decide if it wishes to be the party of honest Abe or the party of bigoted and hypocritical Christian right devils from hell. It cannot serve the masters of opposing ideologies.

It is both amusing and amazing that these spiritless fanatics try to convince us that the troubles in this country are the results of moral decay emanating from the lack of Christ in our lives. The truth is that our problems are the result of untruths promoted by the likes of Pat, Jerry, Dubya and their ilk. The lack of truthfulness and honesty is the reason this country may be going to their hell. "We have seen the enemy and he is us!" Pogo spoke the truth.

No one can listen to the likes of Pat Robertson and Jerry Falwell and then honestly declare these are rationally sane persons. Being fundamental Christians does not make them sane. It is morons such as these Christian right devils of which we should be afraid. These men do not know the reality of truth or the truth of reality. Members of the Christian right are not living in this world of humane mankind.

For me, there are no such places as the heaven and hell of the Christians. Heaven and hell exist solely in the heads of the blinded faithful. If there should happen to be such a place as hell, I am positive that reservations are awaiting all fanatic fundamentalists of the Christian right such as Pat, Jerry and Dubya.

We can thank our lucky stars that the members of the *spiritless* Christian right are the majority of the devils in this country. Until we wake up and rid ourselves of these devils in the clothing of sheep, our societies shall continue down that slippery slope to their hell.

Those infamous House Managers, their esteemed head henchman, and other Christian hypocrites tell us that they voted their consciences in that satanic Impeachment. If they were to be honest and truthful, they would admit to the fact that a traitor or a conspirator does not have a conscience.

....

"Why does the Christian right believe that it should have the right to fuck whomever it pleases but I shouldn't have that same right?"

Frederick J. Azbell

Clinton and The Bar

Bigots and hypocrites galore!

What laws had Clinton broken? What laws had he broken which many of his accusers had not also broken? Who were those accusers? Who was it that wanted Clinton disbarred and why?

Clinton had committed the sin of extra marital sex and then tried to hide the fact. According to the material that I have read or know about this subject, I suspect that he is not alone! The number of the men of the Congress that have been exposed lately confirms my suspicions. Many members of the House and the Senate have been enjoying the **nasty** as of late. But it is not new. Remember JFK, his brother and Marilyn! This thing called extra-marital sex has been going on since the beginning of man on this earth, however. With modern communication and prying noses, it is made public more often these days. It is getting harder to hide our transgressions!

But when he was caught with his pants down, Clinton lied about it! How outrageous of him! He could have been more creative by declaring temporary insanity or that the devil made him do it like any good Christian would do, such as Jimmy Swaggert! He could have blamed it on a youthful indiscretion as did his chief judge and accuser, Henry Hyde. Why did he have to lie about receiving head from some bimbo other than his wife? Why?

Did you happen to notice how many termites came crawling out of the woodwork during the Impeachment? It is no wonder that poor Newt had remained as quiet as one of his fellow church mice! He knew that his own cover was about to be blown by his wife who had found out about his fornications with his young mistress.

That great white-haired savior of the nation, Mr. Hyde, declared that his own fall from grace was the result of a youthful indiscretion. A short time after he made this statement, we found that he had committed these **indiscretions** while in his forties. It is so heartwarming for me to learn that one's forties are considered youthful! By Henry's standards, I in my late seventies am in mid-life!

Mr. Livingston, the blessed of the Christian right and the conservative House members, was to replace Newt. When Larry Flint exposed his extra-marital exploits he lost the job before he ever assumed the office.

Now, I am not denouncing nor defending any of these *fallen* men for their immoral activities. I am simply stating the fact that many married men and women, plus their judges, indulge in the **nasty.** The lord god of Moses declares that they should all be stoned to death! Rather a harsh sentence for such a common practice, don't you think? Most of these men and women pray to their god that their sins are never disclosed in the hopes that they are protecting themselves and their loved ones. Many of us choose to suffer the sin of omission, such as Hyde, Gingrich, and Livingston and then pray that our sins are never discovered.

However, it is true that Clinton lied to his judges no matter how evil the judges may be. He also did not know that the rat, Linda, had pumped poor **loose lips** Monica for all the *juicy* details so that she could make a good deal of money from that publisher and instigator, Luci. When that publishing deal fell through, Linda sold herself, Monica, and the President to that sex deviate, Kenneth Starr.

Does anyone reading this article actually believe that Bill Clinton intended to practice law once he left the White House? Why should he have been disbarred? Billy is making a good living by being paid extremely well for giving speeches. He is being asked to give more speeches than his busy schedule will allow.

••

"Jesus' last words on the cross, 'My God, my God, why hast thou forsaken me?' hardly seem to be the words of a man who planned it that way. It doesn't take a Sherlock Holmes to figure there is something wrong here."

Rev. Donald Morgan

" 'God' – who is said to have created everything from nothing, and to have done so with no help from anyone is now completely helpless to do anything at all without the assistance of an army of clergymen and the charity of a flock of faithful followers."

Rev. Donald Morgan

"Resurrection: The means by which his friends became convinced that Jesus was the Messiah. Though they never got together on the details of the story, faith teaches us that it is nonetheless a historical fact."

Rev. Donald Morgan

"The biblical concepts of sin and salvation are an intrinsic part of Christian doctrine. Christianity first creates a problem (sin) and then offers a 'solution' (salvation). This is not unlike the protection racket – you either buy 'protection' – or else!"

Rev. Donald Morgan

"Moral: A peerless maxim enumerated by God in his Holy Bible, such as that of Deut. 23:1, if you testicles are crushed or your male member missing, you must never enter a sanctuary of the Lord."

Rev. Donald Morgan

The Importance of One

An over estimation of one's importance
is a sin of bigoted, hypocritical man.

It never ceases to both amuse and amaze me how important some people believe themselves to be. People, such as George W. Bush, are so full of themselves. Dubya actually believes that he is a favorite of a god and that he is making a difference. The true fact is, things might be moving at a better pace without him and his interferences in the progress of the nation.

Congress makes the laws. The only time a President makes a difference is when he has a willing or a rubber-stamp Congress. So far, Dubya has not vetoed a single law, but does have the rubber-stamp of a Christian right Congress.

Since George W. believes that his god is on his side and guiding his every move, he has gotten us into a terrible war based on his and the lies of his cronies. He has managed to cause the death of nearly three thousand American service personnel. The wounded is in the tens of thousands. The country of Iraq has lost many times these figures.

With the absence of a government in Iraq, which Bush caused, he has managed to multiply by many times over the number of terrorists and has caused a civil war in Iraq.

George managed to take the huge surplus of funds left by Clinton and turn it into a record deficit proving that he can make a difference.

Because of his fundamental Christian faith, the influence of the Pope of Rome and his fundamentalist buddies, George has hindered the advancement of the medical field by taking a strong stance against fetal and stem cell research, again proving that he could make a difference.

He has been successful in sending our manufacturing companies to communist China and our internet and communication jobs to India, putting thousands of Americans out of work. What a difference, George!

Dubya stood silently by while many U. S. businesses set up their headquarters in the Bahamas and the Caribbean so that they could avoid paying their fair share of taxes to the U. S.

The compassionate conservatism of Dubya has caused the citizens of the United States to become extremely partisan. Democrats and Republicans fight each other over the simplest of issues. We should not be too surprised with the direction George has taken, however. He told us that his god was his champion. He stated that the most influential person in his life was Jesus Christ.

Since this admission by this Christian fundamentalist President, the philosophy of Pat

Robertson, Jerry Falwell, James Dobson and other Christian right members have been leading George by his Christian nose ring.

Dubya's most admired Supreme Court judges are the very extreme conservative ones. One of these conservative Supreme Court judges is a known sexual pervert who preys on and takes advantage of innocent women.

George refuses to confer with other than his hand-picked cronies whom he knows will agree with anything he suggests. He believes it is his right and duty to direct Congress and the courts. Congress, for George, is his personal legislative body to do with as he wishes. George believes the courts also should answer to him.

The voters were led to believe that they were voting for a compassionate conservative when in fact, they voted for a Christian right wing fundamentalist.

· ·

"The resurrection is something that should have been demonstrated to all of Jerusalem, not just a handful of faithful followers. This was an irresponsible oversight on the part of God Incarnate."

Rev. Donald Morgan

"Church: A place where, once a week or so, hired prayer-makers lead the least worthy of us in granting to the infinite Presence the praise without which He would feel slighted."

Rev. Donald Morgan

"Theology: A prolonged and passionate study of nearly everything that could possibly be said about nothing."

Rev. Donald Morgan

"How many things we held yesterday as articles of faith, today we tell as fables?"

Michael E. de Montaigne

"America's favorite religion is scientifically unsupported, philosophically suspect at best, disreputable at worst, and historically fraudulent."

Delos B. McKown

"The invisible and the non-existent look very much alike."

Delos B. McKown

"There has never been a kingdom given to so many civil wars as the Kingdom of God."

Charles de Montesquieu

Hirohito and Bush

Similarities!

For some time, I have wracked my brain to see
of whom bush reminds me.
Amid all the confusion,
I have reached my conclusion.

Hirohito was a living god;
a descendent of the sun!
George W. Bush believes
himself to be the Christian one!

Hirohito had Tojo and
other would-be war lords.
Dubya has Rove, Rumsfeld, Rice
and the Christian hordes.

Hirohito bombed the hell out of Pearl Harbor.
to prove his godliness.
Bush bombed Bagdad into submission
to prove his righteousness.

Hirohito nearly destroyed Japan
before losing the strife.
Dubya is destroying the U.S.A.
with his senseless plight.

The U.S.A. was successful in
restoring Japan to a peaceful state.
I hope the U.S.A. can be saved
before it is too late!

Frederick J. Azbell

False Concepts

A fundamentalist will believe what he wishes
regardless of stronger counter evidence!

For some time now, the people of the United States has been living under the false premise put forth by the Bush Administration, using Christian fundamentalism as a guide, that there is such a thing as a black and/or white philosophy.

The black and/or white philosophy is one of extremes. As Bush says, "You are either with me or against me!" This philosophy of arrogant man suggests that one is one hundred percent correct in his philosophy and if we do not agree, then we are one hundred percent incorrect!

AS for me, I maintain that, "The philosophies of man are forever muddled in countless shades of gray." There is no black or white when it comes to philosophy. My pragmatic realism suggests that there are no absolute truths in any philosophy that man has developed.

The only fields one can find absolute truths are those of mathematics and pure science. These fields do not depend on the interpretation of man. Man simply needs to know and understand these truths as facts.

Shortly after Bush took office, I discovered that Bush would consider me undemocratic since I did not believe in many or most of his policies which he considered sacred. He told us that he believed he was favored by his god. He said that Jesus Christ was the most influential being in his life. Soon after nine eleven, I also discovered that I would be considered unpatriotic since I did not believe in his cowboy philosophy of go it alone, my way or the highway, or his belief that the only way to deal with dictators or tyrants was to join them in their philosophy of using material and physical force. He put no faith in negotiations. These thoughtless philosophies, void of any sense of reasoning, caused George W. Bush to go to war in Iraq without any good evidence.

Bush and his administration believe that the only way the United States can influence the world of thugs is to join them and use physical and/or military force to beat the devil out of them. The Bible teaches them an eye for an eye, tooth for tooth... This flawed Texas cowboy philosophy has earned him and the United States the disrespect of most of the nations of this world.

The Muslim world does not care for our presence in their land of fundamental Islam! I'm sure that this modern day crusade of Bush is not going to be any more successful than the current one being waged by Israel against the Palestinians, or the past crusades of the Christians against the *heretics*. After two thousand years of Christianity and a host of religious faiths, the world still has many disillusioned religious followers, disbelievers, tyrants and thugs, including Bush!

Most of the failed policies of Bush come from his belief in Christian fundamentalism. The Christian fundamental belief is that which is displayed by the likes of Pat Robertson, the late Jerry Falwell, James Dobson and a profusion of others.

Albert Mohler Jr., the President of the Southern Baptist Seminary, declares that, "If you do not accept Jesus Christ as your personal savior, you cannot enter heaven!" This fundamentalist, with his brains up his ass, is trying to force the members of Judaism and Islam to become Christian or he will not allow them to enter the heaven he owns! Judaism and Islam also claim heaven as their final resting places. In fact, the Jews were the creators of heaven and were speaking of it thousands of years before the creation of Christ and Christianity!

I maintain that there is no black and/or white in the world of philosophy. This means that there is no absolute right or wrong in philosophical thought. Religions are philosophies based in faith. No religious faith has ever been proven to be fact or truth. One must use faith, not reason, in order to accept a religious philosophical belief system.

One is not born with a philosophy of religious belief. All of man's philosophies, he has adopted. For every philosophy of one, there is a philosophy of another.

Bush's policies, based on his Christian right religious philosophy, have failed him and us. If we continue following all of those lost souls who believe in these false premises of the black and/or white philosophies, we will continue down the path to the Christian hell and lose all respect of the world community.

The world of man has adopted many philosophies dealing with all aspects of life. One can adopt any philosophy by simply denying the existence of others. However, the simple denial of a thing does not make that thing any less real. Faith and faith alone is not the answer to the problems of man. There is nothing as important in the life of man as the use of the brain power he has been provided with whether you believe that that brain was given to you by a god or Mother Nature.

There is no such thing as a black and/or white philosophy. One's intelligence and awareness should tell him that there are many conflicting philosophies of life. Not one can be proven to be the absolute or only one. The individual must choose which of the conflicting philosophies to adopt. You have no assurance that you will pick the best one.

The Evil Ones

Bush needs to understand who his real enemies are.

Dubya says that he is fighting forces of evil! He declares that the terrorists he is fighting hate our liberty and freedom. He says that the terrorists have hi-jacked Islam!

The terrorists that Bush is fighting hate him and all that he stands for. Dubya represents the *infidels* who have been trying to destroy the world of Islamic fundamentalism. In philosophical belief, these fundamentalists of the Islamic faith are no different than members of Christian fundamentalism. Christian fundamentalists killed thousands of innocent men, women and children during their Crusades. Each fundamentalist believes that his god is the one and only. Some fundamentalist just happen to be more extreme in their actions.

We have fundamentalists of Judaism and Islam fighting each other in the Middle East. We have fundamental Christian Protestants fighting fundamental Christian Catholics in Ireland. We have fundamentalists of Islam and Hinduism fighting each other in Kashmir. We have a variety of religious and ethnic wars going on in Africa.

The Islamic fundamentalists have decided to drive out the Christian *infidels* that have been trying to dominate their lands and steal their oil. They began hating the United States years ago when it backed that dictator in Persia, who called himself the Shah of Iran. Bush is just the latest of hypocritical Americans. He won't be the last and they realize this. Their disrespect for liberty and freedom is not what is driving them. They could care less about our liberties and freedoms. They do not want Christian fundamentalism in their land of Islam. Christianity is not their *cup of tea!*

George W. Bush and his Christian right good buddies are not going to win this Christian Crusade until they become more honest and discover who their real enemies are. I am afraid that Dubya's religious crusade is going to be about as successful as the Christian Crusades of a few hundred years ago or even the present day crusade of Israel. Man cannot solve irrational disputes with irrational philosophies of religious beliefs.

In the United States, not long ago, our Attorney General, John Ashcroft, and the President's Solicitor General, Ted Olson, were two of the Christian fundamentalists whose goal appeared to be to remove our personal freedoms and liberties and subjugate us with their brand of Christian doctrinaires. Our Christian fundamentalist President is employing Fascist techniques to install his military industrial complex.

Immediately after Bush landed on that aircraft carrier and declared the end of hostilities in Iraq, we had a Southern Baptist minister appear on CNN and declare that his goal was to go to Iraq and convert those evil followers of Allah to Christianity. Just how Christian can one become!

Tell me who the evil ones are!

....

"It is a truism that almost any sect, cult, or religion will legislate its creed into law if it acquires the political power to do so."

Robert A. Heinlein

"If you believe in the existence of fairies at the bottom of the garden you are deemed fit for the bin. If you believe in parthenogenesis, ascension, transubstantiation and all the rest of it, you are deemed fit to govern the country."

Jonathan Meades

"One should not go into churches if one wants to breathe pure air."

Frederick Nietzche

"The Christian church has left nothing untouched by its depravity; it has turned every value into worthlessness, and every truth into a lie and every integrity into baseness of soul."

Frederick Nietzche

"The Christian faith from the beginning, is sacrifice of all freedom, all pride, all self-confidence of spirit; it is at the same time subjection, self-derision, and self-mutilation..."

Frederick Nietzche

"In the beginning was nonsense, and the nonsense was with God, and the nonsense was God."

Frederick Nietzche

"God is a thought who makes crooked all that is straight."

Frederick Nietzche

"It is curious that God learned Greek when he wished to turn author – and that he did not learn it better."

Frederick Nietzche

"A casual stroll through a lunatic asylum shows that faith does not prove anything."

Frederick Nietzche

Devious Religiosities

Man can be s devious animal.

Devious shields of belief are not reserved for the religious. Man, since his evolution, has been adopting untested and sometimes shady philosophies. Religions just happen to be systems of belief which cannot be proven since they are based on faith alone and thus lack reason, fact, or reality. There is no way to prove the truth or factuality of a god or faith which all religions rely on for their existence. The deviously religious among us use their faith in order to hide their immoral and ethically bankrupt schemes.

But many of our beliefs and philosophies can be proven true or false through the passage of time and the use of scientific tests to determine their factuality. The lack of evidence to support many of our beliefs is proof of their fallacy.

The Christian right maintains that gay marriages will destroy what they claim composes a true family. They have no proof of this statement but constantly claim it as truth. The only **truth** they have is the fact that the Bible claims homosexuality to be an abomination. The Bible cannot be proven. It is a fact that the Bible exists but it is also a fact that the Bible cannot be proven as truth or being truthful. The reason the Bible, as well as all religious texts, cannot be proven truth is the fact that they are not reality or factually based.

We have had a number of circumstances which have led to the financial crises of today, (2008). The Democrats are blaming the Republicans and vice versa. Main Street is blaming Wall Street. There is no one black or white answer here. The factors are plentiful, not anything as simple as a single fault.

I maintain the main reason for the crisis is the fact of wrong philosophies of those in charge. Congress has neglected to be the over seer or protector of *We the People*. We have far too many of us using our devious Christian right religiosity as a shield to hide our shady dealings.

I believe that much of the problem began with Ronald Reagan. This foolish President has incorrectly been revered as a wise man. This man was about as good a President as he was an actor. His *Trickledown Economics* have proven to have been disastrous for this country.

This country had been built from the bottom up not from the top down. Main Street built Wall Street. It was not the other way around. Reaganomics tried unsuccessfully to deny reality. We can see where this untested philosophy of Reagan has gotten us! The big businesses of the conservative Christian right and the shysters on Wall Street have only become money grabbers without any morals. The middle class has lost out.

Reagan fired the air traffic controllers when they went on strike for more money and a need to relieve overtime working conditions. This job is very stressful for those having to work prolonged overtime hours.

From the time that Reagan took action against the air traffic control officers, there has been a systematic drive to break up the unions and let big business pay the lowest possible wages in all labor fields. The greed of big business was accelerated and set into full force by the untested philosophy of Reagan's Economics.

Big Business did not make this country great. It was the sweat and determination of the blue collar laborers that made this country what it is. Wealthy men may have supplied the money to start the factories but it was the ingenuity of the laboring class who made this country what it is today.

But with the conservatives and big business now in the driver's seat, and with nothing or no one to stop them, they began hiring cheaper, non-union, and unskilled laborers.

Big agricultural conglomerates forced out the small independent farmers and then began the hiring of illegal cheap laborers. Mainly from Mexico, to work in their fields since these poorly educated peons would work for very low wages. These poor migrants could and would work for very low wages since they were barely making enough to exist in Mexico.

This action of these agricultural giants had a snowballing effect. The more workers that the big business of agriculture could hire for less, the more they hired in order to make greater profits. This practice spread to all areas of the economy.

We, the average Americans, went along with this as it required us to pay less for our food and other necessary items. We did not realize what these big business men had up their sleeves. Greed really began in earnest. CEOs were now making hundreds of times more than a blue collar or peon field worker. Growers, like those in the Central Valley of California, were reaping millions off of the sweat from workers willing to work for next to nothing.

Meanwhile, the conservatives, always the devious friends to big business, began pushing for less and less government regulations into the affairs of these businesses that were becoming bigger by the day. They, like their champion President Reagan, believed that big business could do a better job of taking care of us by regulating itself! If big business did well, the country would prosper. This was Reagan's dream which turned into a nightmare for the United States and the world economy.

The religious right saw its opportunity of taking control of the Republican Party. Pat Robinson's dream was about to come true. The conservatives of the Republican Party along with Christian right saw a great opportunity of claiming themselves the moral and ethical leaders of the country. The Christian right and the Republican Party embraced each other and the hoodwinking of the American population began in earnest. The American public was made to feel insecure and fearful if they did not comply with the beliefs of the Christian right. Pat Robertson, Jerry Falwell and their good buddies, such as George W. Bush, began claiming that this country was founded on Judeo-Christian principles. They led the public to believe that only the Christian right possessed the necessary morals and ethics to guide this country. The hoodwinking of the United States was now in full force.

But the Christian right and the conservatives could not cover up the true the facts. This country has changed drastically since its beginning. We no longer have slavery and women have the right to vote. We are not as we were when this country was founded. In reality, the founders of this country were mostly Deists in philosophy although they may have belonged to various mostly Protestant churches. They were Anglican, Episcopalian, Unitarian,

Presbyterian, Roman Catholic, Congregationalist, Lutheran, Dutch Reform, Methodist, and Freemasonry. Some, such as Jefferson, were hostile toward Christianity, since they distrusted the clergy.

The problem with the Christian right philosophy is the fact that it is idealistic. Idealism is a negative philosophy since its goals can never be accomplished. Idealism is void of reality. Reality is all we have. We cannot continue to prosper or survive by striving for that which is impossible to achieve. Morals and ethics do not come from any religion. Morals and ethics are determined by reasonable men who understand mankind.

The many disgraceful, devious schemes, such as the pedophilic actions of religious men, like Catholic priests and members of Congress, prove to us that the religious right is a failure. Too many of our elected officials have been found guilty of child molestation. Most of these criminals are using their religious garb as shields.

Religion should not be used as a shield to hide our human failures. We cannot blame a devil for our personal immoral acts.

Corruption began to be the way to go with big business, the Christian right and members of Wall Street. The CEOs were now rolling in money. The reverends and the priests of the holy religious were raking in the hard earned money of the unsuspecting sheep. Men, such as Pat Robertson and Jerry Falwell, collected millions to invest for their personal fortunes. Trading in shady deals was the way to make it rich. After all, Congress had neglected their job and had given big business and the Christian right the green light to do as they damn well wished.

Then many CEOs of big business discovered that if they moved their assets to banks in the Caribbean, they could avoid paying their fair share of taxes and thus grow greater profits for themselves. Then they started moving their factories to cheap labor countries such as China. Pat and Jerry learned how to invest in China and other lucrative tax shelters for their personal gain. They, and others of their ilk, became extremely wealthy.

One of the greatest downfalls to our economy was the Free Trade Agreements that Clinton pushed. I never could understand these and I at this time was a Democrat. How can a country with a high economy and high wages like the United States trade equally or on the same basis with a country which uses slave labor and has a low economy? Then Clinton failed to put limits on this *free* trade. Trade imbalances became the standard for the United States. It has gotten so bad that before too long now China and India are going to own the United States. These were two of the poorest countries in the world and now they own us. This is what free trade has accomplished!

The Devil Made Me Do It

Who is the real devil?

How did man survive for all those thousands of years before the birth of the Christian devil? Civilizations from the Sumerians, the Greeks, the Egyptians, the Romans, the Mongols, and Ancient Chinese all existed before Christianity.

Religions such as Hinduism, Buddhism, Chinese Folk, Tribal, Judaism, Shamanists, Confucianism, Jainism and a few others were in existence before Christianity.

But the Christians decided that they needed someone to blame for all the evil in them! So they created the devil to be a fall guy. In blaming the devil for all of the evil in themselves, they felt guilt free for their words and actions.

Can one imagine not being able to say, "The devil made me do it!" Some of we comedians and satirists would be devoid of material! I wonder if Flip Wilson ever really understood that he owed his success to the devil? Did he pay the devil the respect he deserved for being his fall guy? Flip took the devil's name in vain quite often.

Are we aware that the devil is responsible for any and all of our sinful thoughts and actions? He is also responsible for all the other sinful religions outside of Christianity!

The devil is responsible for our taking the lord god's name in vain.

The devil also made me eat all those double whoppers with cheese, thus is responsible for my obesity.

The devil is the one who made me drink that bottle of Black Label and then drive my car into that electric pole, knocking out the electricity for blocks around.

The devil is responsible for me calling Jerry Falwell, Pat Robertson, the Pope of Rome, and George W. Bush four of the greatest hypocrites that have ever graced this earth.

The devil was responsible for the Impeachment of Clinton. The devil made Clinton receive those blow-jobs from that dim-wit.

The devil is the force that caused Dubya to drink and take drugs and then become a born again Christian.

It is obvious to all who are not blind that the devil is actually a force for good. His actions cause us to realize the errors of our ways as did Clinton and Bush.

But if one cannot mend his wicked ways, he can always claim, "They devil made me do it!"

Bigotry in Red Neck Country

Bigotry in the Midwest Thrives

This year (2008) I was amazed at the hypocrisy of many of the reporters and analysts in the media. The members of the media talked all around the issue but refused or were afraid to link the bigotry and hypocrisy to the Christian right. Religion is not the only factor causing this bigotry and hypocrisy but it a major one. They knew what the problem in the Midwest was but were too chicken shit to state the facts as presented to them.

After Clinton had won several of these redneck counties or states, the media could not "understand" how she could beat out Obama in Indiana, Ohio, Pennsylvania, Kentucky, West Virginia and the like. They evidently believed that this bigotry and hypocrisy existed solely in the southern part of the United States.

I was born and raised in south central Ohio, Lancaster, to be exact. I know and understand that there are thousands of bigoted and hypocritical red neck Christians living there.

In the southern part of these Midwest states, there are many poorly educated and religious right non thinkers. Most of these backward folks never think for themselves. They are told how to believe by their church. Also many are still fighting the Civil War. These people believe that the blacks should never be considered on the level with them. Equal rights, for all is a threat to their superiority as a race. The blacks were their slaves and the "niggers" should have remained that way.

You say, "These people live in the north, how could they believe this way?" Well, they are taught this by their Bible and their preachers. Many of these people are also what you might call "conservative" in their views. In their eyes, nothing should ever or will ever change. In their world, time stands still. What was good for their ancestors is good enough for them.

Today the world may be moving at an extremely fast pace but many of the red necks in these states, especially those in the "rolling hills" are content to remain in the time of their ancestors.

Many of these Christian right hypocrites believe that the modern world is just too evil for them. A black President of the United States is beyond belief! It will never happen!

Sense of Humor

You're not that important!

One of the greatest needs of you so-called men of a god, such as **"my good friend"** Jerry, is a good sense of humor. You natural buffoons need to realize that you are about the biggest jokesters around these days.

I'm talking to you, Jerry, Pat, Bob, James, Albert, and Dubya. You need to take your bows. No one else could possibly receive as many belly laughs at Comic Central than you six good buddies. You quacks need to acquire a better sense of humor and stop taking yourselves so seriously. You are supposed to be part of the human race. Too many of us are laughing at your buffoonery and we do not believe that you actually possess a religious bone in your bodies. You hypocrites of the first order need to take your well deserved bows and show some faith in your ridiculous speech and antics.

If you natural clowns do not wish us laughing at you, you need to get real. Your views toward life and your laughable doctrinaires from hell are so ridiculous because they are too far off the nuthouse wall to be taken seriously. Jerry, you, Pat and Dubya impress no one but yourselves and your fellow hypocrites. Come on *youse* guys get some spirit, get real and you could be laughing all the way to the bank as those mocking your stupidity.

The Congress which took control with that hypocrites Newt, also needs to acquire a sense of humor. Some members of this comical Congress actually believe that the plastering of Christian propaganda on the walls of our public schools can solve the violence in them. This is the most laughable group of misfits to have ever graced the halls of Congress. The butt of their jokes, however, is we the people!

These Christian right dickheads want to arm the lunatics of the country, subjugate the populace with their ridiculous doctrinaires from hell and turn us into hypocrites such as they. They haven't a clue as to what it is that they should be doing. They are about as amusing as watching a group of monkeys masturbate themselves.

Come on youse guys, get real! Get a sense of humor before you destroy the United States of America with your hypocritical doctrinaires from hell!

The Founding Fathers

Debunk

The Untruths and Lies

Christianity Employs

in Exalting and Promoting

Church and State

Fredrick J. Azbell

Part Five Contents: **The Founding Fathers**

168

The Founding Fathers

The most important founders had philosophies
that leaned more toward that of Deism.

There are many men who had a hand in the founding of the United States but the most important were George Washington, Thomas Jefferson, John Adams, Alexander Hamilton, John Hancock and Benjamin Franklin.

Wikipedia, the free encyclopedia, states that the founding fathers of the United States are the political leaders who signed the Declaration of Independence or otherwise participated in the American Revolution as leaders of the Patriots, or who participated in the drafting the United States Constitution eleven years later.

Some authors or historians make the distinction between the founders, who signed the Declaration of Independence, and the Framers, who drafted the United States Constitution that replaced the Articles of Confederation.

Lambert, who examined the religious affiliations and beliefs of the Founders states that some of the delegates had no affiliation. The others were Protestants except for three Catholics. There were Episcopalians, Presbyterians, Congregationalists, Lutherans, Dutch Reform, and Methodists. Some of the more prominent Founding Fathers were anticlerical or vocal about their opposition to organized religion, such as Jefferson.

George Washington, John Adams, and Benjamin Franklin often related their anti-organized church leanings in their speeches and correspondence. Thomas Jefferson even created his own Jefferson Bible. He could not accept the trinity!

Founders, such as Patrick Henry, were strong proponents of traditional religion. Several of the Founding Fathers considered themselves to be Deists, such as Franklin, Jefferson, and Ethan Allen.

There were many founders who were Freemasons, such as Samuel Adams, John Blair, Benjamin Franklin, James Mchenry, George Washington, Abraham Baldwin, Gunning Bedford, William Blount, David Brearly, Daniel Carroll, Jonathan Dayton, Rufus King, John Langdon, George Read, Roger Sherman, James Madison, Robert Morris, William Paterson and Charles Pinckney.

The claim by the present day religious right that the United States was founded on Judeo-Christian values and principles is only partly correct. The Founders were mostly from Europe. But only a few of the true founders believed in organized religion.

George Washington

**"Every man conducting himself as a good citizen
and being accountable to God alone for his religious opinions,
ought to be protected in worshipping the Deity according to
the dictates of his own Conscience."**

George Washington was an Episcopalian. He was a member of the Episcopal Church, the American province of Anglican Communion. His family was originally Anglicans. The Episcopal Church was founded as a separate church from Anglicanism in 1789. The Episcopal Church was part of the Church of England.

George Washington has been frequently described as a Deist. Washington never described himself in this way but others labeled him such after reading his writings concerning religion.

George Washington has been reported to never take communion and was not considered to be an official "communicant" or full-fledged adult church member. He was not dedicated to the Episcopalian Church nor did he have a strong Anglican or Episcopalian self-identity. Washington's theological belief placed him within the mainstream Christianity of the time. His religious beliefs were relatively broad and non-specific.

Some commentators labeled Washington non- Christian because of his disinterest or disbelief in some mainstream Protestant Christian beliefs.

Jon Butler, Dean of the Graduate School of Arts & Sciences at Yale University, stated "Washington had no deep, personal involvement with religion. He did, however, believe that religion was important for the culture and was important for soldiers to instill good discipline. He was often bitterly disappointed by the discipline that it did or did not instill."

MR. Butler further states that Washington was not a pious man. He wasn't someone who was given to daily Bible reading. He was not evangelical. He was simply a believer.

Jon Butler further states: "the principal Founding Fathers – Washington, Jefferson, Adams, Franklin – were in fact deeply suspicious of a European pattern of governmental involvement in religion."

Some interesting insights from About.com, Agnosticism / Atheism:

In 1793 Washington thus summarized the religious philosophy he was evolving during his Mount Vernon years. How happenings would "terminate is known only to the great ruler of events; and confiding in his wisdom and goodness, we may safely trust the issue to him, without perplexing ourselves to seek for that which is beyond human ken, only taking care to perform the parts assigned to us in a way that reason and our conscience approve of." George Washington was, like Benjamin Franklin and Thomas Jefferson, a deist. [*The Forge of Experience* Volume One of James Thomas Flexner's four volume biography of Washington, Little Brown & Company; pps. 244-245]

George Washington's conduct convinced most Americans that he was a good Christian, but those possessing first-hand knowledge of his religious convictions had reasons for doubt. [Barry Schwartz, George Washington: *The Making of an American Symbol,* New York, 1987, p. 170]

Washington subscribed to the religious faith of the Enlightenment: Like Franklin and Jefferson, he was a deist. [Flexner, James Thomas Flexner, *Washington, The Indispensible Man,* New York, 1974: New American Library, 1974, p. 216]

...That he was not just striking a popular attitude as a politician is revealed by the absence of the usual Christian terms: he did not mention Christ or even use the word "God." Following the phraseology of philosophical Deism he professed, he referred to "the invisible hand which conducts the affairs of men," to "the benign parent of the human race." [James Thomas Flexner, on Washington's first inaugural speech in April 1789, in *George Washington and the New Nation* {1783-1793}, Boston: Little, Brown and Company, 1970, p. 184]

George Washington thought he belonged to the Episcopal Church, never mentioned Christ in any of his writings and he was a deist. [Richard Shenkman, *I love Paul Revere whether He Rode or Not.* New York: Harper, Collins, 1991.]

Some interesting Quotations of Washington from About.com:

Of all the animosities which have existed among mankind, those which are caused by difference of sentiments in religion appear to be the most inveterate and distressing, and ought to be deprecated. I was in hopes that the enlightened and liberal policy, which has marked the present age, would at least have reconciled Christians of every denomination so far that we should never again see the religious disputes carried to such a pitch as to endanger the peace of society, [George Washington, letter to Sir Edward Newenham, October 20, 1792; from Geoge Seides, ed., *The Great Quotations,* Secaucus, New Jersey: Citadel Press, 1983, p. 726]

There is nothing which can better deserve our patronage than the promotion of science and literature. Knowledge is in every country the surest basis of public happiness. [George Washington, address to Congress, January 8, 1790]

Religious controversies are always productive of more acrimony and irreconcilable hatreds than those which spring from any other cause. [George Washington, letter to Sir Edward Newenham, June 22, 1792]

...the path of true piety is so plain as to require but little political direction. [George Washington,1789, responding to clergy complaints that the Constitution lacked mention of Jesus Christ, from *The Godless Constitution: The Case Against Religious Correctness,* Isacc Kramnick and R. Laurence Moore, W. W. Norton and Company, pps. 101-102

If they are good workmen, they may be from Asia, Africa or Europe; they may be Mahometans, Jews, Christians of any sect, or they may be Atheists...[George Washington, to Tench Tighman, March 24, 1784, when asked what type of Workman to get for Mount Vernon, from *The Washington papers* edited by Saul Padover]

To give opinions unsupported by reasons might appear dogmatical. [George Washington, to Alexander Spotswood, November 22, 1798, from *The Washington papers,* edited by Saul Padover]

...I beg you be persuaded that no one would be more zealous than myself to establish effectual barriers against the horrors of spiritual tyranny, and every species of religious persecution. [George Washington, to United Baptists Churches of Virginia, May 1789 from *The Washington papers* edited by Saul Padover]

As the contempt of the religion of a country by ridiculing any of its ceremonies, or affronting its ministers or votaries, has ever been deeply resented, you are to be particularly careful to restrain every officer from such imprudence and folly and to punish every instance of it. On the other hand, as far as lies in your power, you are to protect and support the free exercise of religion of the country, and the undisputed enjoyment of the rights of conscience in religious matters, with your utmost influence and authority, [George Washington, to Benedict Arnold, September 14, 1775 from *The Washington papers* edited by Saul Padover]

The blessed Religion revealed in the word of God will remain an eternal and Monument to prove that the best institutions may be abused by human depravity; and that they may even, in some instances, be made subservient to the vilest of purposes.

Thomas Jefferson

"Ignorance is preferable to error,
and he is less remote from the truth who believes nothing
than he who believes what is wrong."

Jim Walker, in *Thomas Jefferson on Christianity & Religion,* writes, "In spite of right-wing Christian attempts to rewrite history to make Jefferson into a Christian, little about his philosophy resembles that of Christianity. Although Jefferson in the Declaration of Independence wrote the Laws of nature and of Nature's God, there exists nothing in the Declaration about Christianity.

Jefferson believed in a creator, but his concept resembled that of the god of deism. The Deists referred to god as "Nature's God." Jefferson possessed a scientific bent and thus sought to organize his thoughts on religion in a scientific bent. He rejected the superstitions and mysticisms of Jesus in his *Jefferson Bible.* He left only the correct moral philosophy of Jesus as he deemed it to be.

Many Christians distort history whenever they see the word "God" embossed in statue or memorial concrete. Jefferson wrote, "I have sworn upon the altar of God eternal hostility against every form of tyranny over the mind of man."

Many Christians believe the word "God" is "poof" of Jefferson's Christianity. God can have many definitions ranging from nature to supernatural. Jefferson was attacking the tyranny of the Christian clergy.

Jefferson believed in individual freedom. He felt that any form of government control, not only of religion, consisted of tyranny. He thought that our civil rights have no dependence on our religious opinions, any more than our opinions in physics or geometry.

Jefferson had a complex view of religion. These quotes of Jefferson give us a glimpse of how Thomas Jefferson viewed the corruptions of Christianity and religion.

Millions of innocent men, women, and children, since the introduction of Christianity, have been burnt, tortured, fined, imprisoned; yet we have not advanced one inch towards uniformity. [Notes on Virginia, 1782]

But it does me no injury for my neighbor to say there are twenty gods or no God. It Neither picks my pocket nor breaks my leg. [Notes on Virginia, 1782]

What is it men cannot be made to believe! [Thomas Jefferson to Richard Henry Lee, April 22, 1786 on the British regarding America, but quoted for its universal appeal.]

Question with boldness even the existence of a god; because if there be one he must approve of the homage of reason more than that of blindfolded fear. [Thomas Jefferson, letter to Peter Carr, August 10, 1787]

Where the preamble declares, that coercion is a departure from the plan of the Holy author of our religion, an amendment was proposed by inserting "Jesus Christ," so that it would read "A departure from the plan of Jesus Christ, the holy author of our religion;" the insertion was rejected by the great majority, in proof that they meant to comprehend, within the mantle of its protection, the Jew and the Gentile, the Christian and Mohammedan, the Hindoo and the Infidel of every denomination. [Thomas Jefferson, Autobiography, in reference to the Virginia Act for Religious Freedom]

I concur with you strictly in your opinion of the comparative merits of atheism and demonism, and really see nothing but the latter in the being worshipped by many who think themselves Christians. [Thomas Jefferson, letter to Richard Price, January 8, 1789]

I never submitted the whole system of my opinions to the creed of any party of Men whatever in religion, in philosophy, in politics, or in anything else where I was capable of thinking for myself. Such an addiction is the last degradation of a free and moral agent. [Thomas Jefferson, letter to Francis Hopkinson, March 8, 1789]

They [the clergy] believe that any portion of power confided to me, will be Exerted in opposition to their schemes. And they believe rightly; for I have sworn upon the altar of god, eternal hostility against every form of tyranny over the mind of man. But this is all they have to fear from me: and enough too, in their opinion. [Thomas Jefferson to Dr. Benjamin Ruch, September 23, 1800]

Believing with you that religion is a matter which lies solely between man and his God, That he owes account to none other than his faith or his worship, that the Legislative powers of government reach actions only, and not opinions, I contemplate with sovereign reverence that act of the whole American people which declared that their legislature should 'make no law respecting an establishment of religion, or prohibiting the free exercise thereof,' thus building a wall of separation between church and State. [Thomas Jefferson, letter to Danbury Baptist Association CT., January 1, 1802]

History, I believe, furnishes no example of a priest-ridden people maintaining a free civil government. This marks the lowest grade ignorance of which their civil as well as religious leaders will always avail themselves for their own purposes. [Thomas Jefferson to Alexander von Humboldt, December 6, 1813.]

The whole history of these books [the Gospels] is so defective and doubtful that it seems vain to attempt minute enquiry into it: and such tricks have been played with their text, and with the texts of other books relating to them, that we have a right, from that cause, to entertain much doubt what parts of them are genuine. In the New Testament there is internal evidence that parts of it have proceeded from an extraordinary man; and that other parts are the fabric of very inferior minds. It is as easy to separate those parts, as to pick out diamonds from dunghills. [Thomas Jefferson, letter to John Adams, January 24, 1814]

Christianity neither is, nor ever was a part of the common law. [Thomas Jefferson, Letter to Dr. Thomas Cooper, February 10, 1814]

In every country and every age, the priest has been hostile to liberty. He is always in in alliance with the despot, abetting his abuses in return for protection to his own. [Thomas Jefferson, letter to Horatio G. Spafford, March 17, 1814]

If we did a good act merely from love of God and a belief that it is pleasing to Him, whence arises the morality of the Atheist?...Their virtue, then must have had some other foundation than the love of God. [Thomas Jefferson, letter to Thomas Law, June 13, 1814]

Ridicule is the only weapon which can be used against unintelligible propositions. Ideas must be distinct before reason can act upon them, and no man ever had a distinct idea of trinity. It is the mere Abracadabra of the mountebanks calling themselves the priests of Jesus. [Thomas Jefferson, letter to Francis Adrian Van der Kemp, July 30, 1816]

My opinion is that there would never have been an infidel, if there had never been a priest. The artificial structures they have built on the purest of all moral systems, for the purpose of deriving from it pence and power, revolts those who think for themselves, and read in that system only what is really there. [Thomas Jefferson, letter to Mrs. Samuel H. Smith, August 6, 1816]

You say you are a Calvinist. I am not. I am of a sect by myself, as far as I know. [Thomas Jefferson, letter to Ezra Stiles Ely, June 25, 1819]

As you say of yourself, I too am an Epicurian. I consider the genuine (not the imputed) doctrines of Epicurus as containing everything rational in moral philosophy which Greece and Rome have left us. [Thomas Jefferson, letter to William Short, October 31, 1819]

Priests...dread the advance of science as witches do the approach of daylight and scowl on the fatal harbinger announcing the subversions of the duperies on which they live. [Thomas Jefferson, letter to Correa de Serra, April 11, 1820]

Among the sayings and discourses imputed to him [Jesus] by his biographers, I find many passages of fine imagination, correct morality, and of the most lovely benevolence; and others again of so much absurdity, so much untruth, charlatanism, and imposture, as to pronounce it impossible that such contradictions should have proceeded from the same being. [Thomas Jefferson, letter to William Short, April 13, 1820]

To talk of *immaterial* existences is to talk of *nothings.* To say that the human soul, angels, gods, are immaterial, is to say they are *nothings,* or that there is no god, no angels, no soul. I cannot reason otherwise: but I believe I am supported in my creed of materialism by Locke, Tracy, and Stewart. At what age of the Christian this hersey of *immaterialism,* this masked atheism, crept in, I do not know. But heresy it certainly is. [Thomas Jefferson, letter to John Adams, August 15, 1820]

Man once surrendering his reason, has no remaining guard against absurdities the most monstrous, like a ship without a rudder, is the sport of every wind. [Thomas Jefferson to James Smith, 1822]

I can never join Calvin in addressing *his god.* He was indeed an Atheist, which I can never be; or rather his religion was Daemonism. If ever man worshipped a false god, he did. [Thomas Jefferson, letter to John Adams, April 11, 1823]

And the day will come when the mystical generation of Jesus, by the supreme being as his father in the womb of a virgin will be classed with the fable of the generation of Minerva in the brain of Jupiter. But may we hope that the dawn of reason and freedom of thought in these United States will do away with this artificial scaffolding, and restore to us the primitive and genuine doctrines of this most venerated reformer of human errors. [Thomas Jefferson, letter to John Adams, April 11, 1823]

It is between fifty and sixty years since I read it [the Apocalypse], and I then considered it merely the ravings of a maniac, not more worthy nor capable of explanation than the incoherence of our own nightly dreams. [Thomas Jefferson, letter to General Alexander Smyth, January 17, 1825]

May it be to the world, what I believe it will be, (to some parts sooner, to others later, but finally to all), the signal of arousing men to burst the chains under which monkish ignorance and superstition had persuaded them to bind themselves, and to assume the blessings and security of self-government. All eyes are opened, or opening, to the rights of man. The general spread of the light of science has already laid open to every view the palpable truth, that the mass of mankind has not been born with saddles on their backs, nor a favored few booted and spurred, ready to ride them legitimately, by the grace of God. [Thomas Jefferson, letter to Roger C. Weightman, June 24, 1826 (in the last letter he penned)]

John Adams

"The question before the human race is,
whether the God of nature shall govern the world by his laws,
or whether priests and kings shall rule it by fictitious miracles?"

John Adams is regarded as one of the most important Founding Fathers of the United States of America. Before becoming the second President of the United States, John Adams served as the first Vice President under President George Washington. He had been a signer of the Declaration of Independence as a delegate from Massachusetts.

John Adams was a devout Unitarian, which was a non-trinitarian Protestant Christian denomination. He was identified as a Congregationalist by the Congregationalist Library. They stated that he later became a Unitarian.

Adams was raised a Congregationalist, but ultimately rejected many fundamental doctrines of conventional Christianity. He did not accept the Trinity and the divinity of Jesus. He became a Unitarian in his later life. Adams' father wanted him to become a minister. Adams refused, considering the practice of law to be a more noble calling. Adams view of religion was rather ambivalent. He recognized the abuses, large and small, that religious beliefs lends itself to, but he also believed religion could be a force for good in individual lives and in society at large. He read extensively. His reading of the classics, led him to believe that his view applied no only to Christianity, but to all religions.

Adams was aware of the risks, such as persecution of minorities and the temptations to wage wars, an established religion poses.

The Jeffersonians drove the Federalist out of office in 1880 and Adams retired to Quincy. John Adams died at the age of 90 just a few hours after Thomas Jefferson on July 4, 1826. This was the 50th anniversary of the adoption of the Declaration of Independence. Charles Carroll was the only signer of the Declaration to outlive John Adams and Thomas Jefferson.

The principal Founding Fathers, Washington, Jefferson, Adams, and Franklin, were deeply suspicious of a European pattern of governments involvement in religion. They believed that government was corrupting religion.

In the Treaty of Peace and Friendship with Tripoli, which the Senate ratified during the presidency of John Adams, Article XI states that:

> As the government of the United States of America is not founded on the Christian Religion – as in itself no character of enmity against the laws, religion of tranquility of Musselmen, - and as the said States never have entered into war or act of hostility against any Mehomitan nation, it is declared by the parties that no pretext arising from religious opinions shall ever produce an interruption of the harmony existing between the two countries.

Some famous quotes of John Adams as compiled by Positive Atheism:

The United States of America have exhibited, perhaps, the first example of governments erected to the simple principles of nature; and if men now sufficiently enlightened to disabuse themselves of artifice, imposture, hypocrisy, and superstition, they will consider this event as an era in their history. Although the detail of the formation of the American governments is at present little known or regarded in Europe or in America, it may hereafter become an object of curiosity. It will never be pretended that any persons employed in that service had more than those at work upon ships or houses, or laboring in merchandise or agriculture; it will forever be acknowledged that these governments were contrived merely by the use of reason and the senses. [John Adams, "A defense of the Constitutions of Government of the United States of America" (1787-88), from Adrienne Koch, ed., *The American Enlightenment: The Shaping of the American Experiment and a Free Society* (1965) p. 258, quoted from Ed and Michael Buckner, "Quotations that Support the Separation of State and Church."

Thirteen governments [of the original states] thus founded on the natural authority of the people alone, without a pretense of miracle or mystery, and which are a great point gained in favor of the rights of mankind. [John Adams, "A Defense of the Constitutions of Government of the United States of America." (1787-88), from Adrienne Koch, ed., *The American Enlightenment: The Shaping of the American Experiment and a Free Society* (1965) p. 258, quoted from Ed and Michael Buckner, Quotations that Support the Separation of State and Church."

We should begin by setting conscience free. When all men of all religions...shall enjoy equal liberty, property, and equal chance for honors and power...we may expect that improvements will be made in the human character and the state of society. [John Adams, letter to Dr. Price, April 8, 1785, quoted from Albert Menendez and Edd Doerr, *The Great Quotations on Religious Freedom (1991)]*

As I understand the Christian religion, it was, and is, a revelation. But how has it happened that millions of fables, tales, legends, have been blended with both Jewish and Christian revelation that have made them the most bloody religion that ever existed? [John Adams, letter to FA Van der Kamp, December 27, 1816]

The frightful engines of ecclesiastical councils, of diabolical malice, and Calvinistical good-nature never failed to terrify me exceedingly whenever I thought of preaching. [John Adams, letter to his brother-in-law, Richard Cranch, October 18, 1756, explaining why he rejected the ministry.]

I shall have liberty to think for myself without molesting others or being molested myself. [John Adams, letter to his brother-in-law, Richard Cranch, August 29, 1756, explaining how his independent opinions would create much difficulty in the ministry,, in Edwin S. Gaustad, *Faith of Our Fathers: Religion and the New Nation* (1987) p. 88, quoted from Ed and Michael Buckner, "Quotations that Support the Separation of State and Church."

When philosophic reason is clear and certain by intuition or necessary induction, no subsequent revelation supported by prophecies or miracles can supersede it. John Adams, from Rufus K. Noyes, *Views of Religion,* quoted from James A. Haught, ed., 2000 Year of Disbelief.

Indeed, Mr. Jefferson, what could be invented to debate the ancient Christianism which Greeks, Romans, Hebrews, and Christian factions, above all the Catholics, have not fraudulently imposed upon the public? Miracles after miracles have rolled down in torrents. John Adams, letter to Thomas Jefferson, December 3, 1813, quoted from James A. Haught, ed 2000 *Years of Disbelief.*

Cabalistic Christianity, which is Catholic Christianity, and which has prevailed for 1,500 years, has received a mortal wound, of which the monster must finally die. Yet so strong is his constitution , that he may endure for centuries before he expires. John Adams, letter to Thomas Jefferson, July 16, 1814, from James A. Haught, ed., 2000 *Years of Disbelief.*

Let the human mind loose. It must be loose. Superstition and dogmatism cannot confine it. John Adams, letter to his son, John Quincy Adams, November 13, 1816, from James A Haught, ed., 2000 *Years of Disbelief.*

The Church of Rome has made it an article of faith that no man can be saved out of the church, and all other religious sects approach this dreadful opinion in proportion to their ignorance, and the influence of ignorant or wicked priests. John Adams, *Diary and Autobiography.*

God is an essence that we know nothing of. Until this awful blasphemy is got rid of, there never will be any liberal science in the world. John Adams, "this awful blasphemy" that he refers to is the myth of the Incarnation of Christ, from Ira D. Cardiff, *What Great Men Think of Religion,* quoted from James A. Haught, ed., 2000 *Years of Disbelief.*

James Madison

"Freedom arises from the multiplicity of sects which pervades America
and which is the best and only security for religious liberty in any society.
for there is such a variety of sects, there cannot be a majority of any one sect
to oppress and persecute the rest."

James Madison was the fourth President of the United States. He was one of only two Presidents (along with Washington) who signed the U. S. Constitution. Madison also served as a Representative in the First Federal Congress.

James Madison was a n Episcopalian but believed firmly that Church and State needed to be kept separate. Some sources classify Madison as a Deist.

James Madison was thought of as a brilliant political philosopher and pragmatic politician who dominated the Constitutional Convention. He won the epithet "Father of the Constitution."

James was taught by his mother, from tutors, and at a private school. He graduated in 1771 from the College of New Jersey which later became Princeton. Madison demonstrated a special interest in government and law. He stayed on for a year of postgraduate study in theology.

He returned to Montpelier and was still undecided on a Profession. He soon embraced the patriot cause. State and local politics began absorbing much of his time.

Although Madison remained a slave owner all his life, he was active during his later years in the American Colonization Society whose mission was the resettlement of slaves to Africa.

Some telling quotations of James Madison:

An alliance or coalition between Government and religion cannot be too carefully guarded against...every new and successful example therefore of a Perfect Separation between ecclesiastical and civil matters is of importance...religion and government will exist in greater purity, without (rather) than with the aid of government. [James Madison in a letter to Livingston, 1822, from Leonard W. Levy – *The Establishment Clause, Religion and the First Amendment*, p. 124]

That diabolical, hell-conceived principle of persecution rages among some; and to their eternal infamy, the clergy can furnish their quota of impas for such business...[James Madison, letter to William Bradford Jr., January 1774]

Ecclesiastical establishments tend to great ignorance and corruption, all of which facilitate the execution of mischievous projects. [James Madison, letter to William Bradford Jr., January 1774]

What influence, in fact, have ecclesiastical establishments had on society? In some instances they have been seen to erect a spiritual tyranny on the ruins of the civil authority; on many instances they have been seen upholding the thrones of political tyranny; in no instance have they been the guardians of the liberties of the people. Rulers who wish to subvert the public liberty may have found an established clergy convenient auxiliaries. A just government, instituted to secure and perpetuate it, needs them not. [President James Madison, *A Memorial and Remonstrance*, addressed to the General Assembly of the Commonwealth of Virginia, 1785]

Experience witnesseth, that ecclesiastical establishments, instead of maintaining the purity and efficacy of religion, have had a contrary operation. During almost fifteen centuries has the legal establishment of Christianity been on trial. What has been its fruits? More or less, in all places, pride and indolence in the clergy; ignorance and servility in the laity; in both, superstition, bigotry and persecution. [James Madison, *A Memorial and Remonstrance*, addressed to the general Assembly of the Commonwealth of Virginia, 1785]

The number, the industry, and the morality of the priesthood, and the devotion of the people have been manifestly increased by the total separation of the church from the state. [James Madison, 1819, in Boston, *Why the Religious Right is Wrong about the Separation of Church and State.*]

Strongly guarded as is the separation between religion and government in the Constitution of the United States, the danger of encroachment by ecclesiastical bodies, may be illustrated by precedents already furnished in their short history. [James Madison, *Detached Memoranda*, 1820]

Religious bondage shackles and debilitates the mind and unfits it for every noble enterprise [sic], every expanded prospect. [James Madison, in a letter to William Bradford, April 1, 1774, as quoted by Edwin S. Gaustad, *Faith of Our Fathers: Religion and the New Nation*, San Francisco: Harper & Row, 1987, p. 37]

The purpose of separation of church and state is to keep forever from these shores the ceaseless strife that has soaked the soil of Europe in blood for centuries. [James Madison, 1803? Origin Questionable]

The experience of the United States is a happy disproof of the error so long rooted in the unenlightened minds of well-meaning Christians, as well as in the corrupt hearts of persecuting usurpers, that without a legal incorporation of religious and civil polity, neither could be supported. A mutual independence is found most friendly to practical Religion, to social harmony, and to political prosperity. [James Madison, letter to F. L. Schaffer, December 3, 1821]

To the Baptist Churches on Neal's Greek on Black Creek, North Carolina I have received, fellow-citizens, your address, approving my objection to the Bill containing a grant of public land to the Baptist Church at Salem Meeting House, Mississippi Territory. Having always regarded the practical distinction between Religion and civil Government as essential to the purity of both, and as guaranteed by the Constitution of the United States, I could not have otherwise discharged my duty on the occasion which presented itself. [James Madison, letter to Baptist Churches in North Carolina, June 3, 1811]

It was the belief of all sects at one time that the establishment of Religion by law, was right & necessary; that the true religion ought to be established in exclusion of every other; and that the only question to be decided was which was the true religion. The example of Holland proved that a toleration of sects, dissenting from the established sect, was safe & even useful. The example of the colonies, now states, which rejected religious establishments altogether, proved that all Sects might be safely & advantageously put on a footing of equal & entire freedom...We are teaching the world the great truth that governments. Do better without Kings & Nobles than with them. The merit will be doubted by the other lesson that Religion flourishes in greater purity, without than with the aid of Gov. [James Madison, letter to Edward Livingston, July 10, 1822, *The Writings of James Madison, Gaillard Hunt]*

Alexander Hamilton

"I have a tender reliance on the mercy of the almighty,
the merits of the Lord Jesus Christ. I am a sinner.
I look to Him for mercy; pray for me."

Hamilton made this remark before his death on July 12, 1804 after being shot by Aaron in a duel. Hamilton was considered to be more religiously inclined than most of the founding fathers. Some aspects of his personal life, however, suggested he may not have been so fundamental in his belief. I believe Hamilton used his religiosity to hide or disguise his moral shortcomings!

Alexander Hamilton was one of the most influential of the United States' founding fathers. He was the first Secretary of the treasury and placed the country on a firm financial footing. His advocacy of a strong national government brought him into bitter conflict with Thomas Jefferson and others but his political philosophy ultimately prevailed in governmental development.

Hamilton was born on the West Indian island of Nevis. He was the illegitimate son of Rachel Fawcett Lavien and James Hamilton, both of West Indian trading families. His exact birth date as well the circumstances of his early life are difficult to determine. It is believed that he was born in 1755 and not in 1757 as his children had supposed.

Hamilton was a precocious child. His guardian sought to enroll him in the College of New Jersey at Princeton. He was refused permission to accelerate his program of studies there so he enrolled instead at King's College which later became Columbia University in New York City. When he was not yet twenty, he entered the growing dispute between the American colonies and the British government. He wrote many fervent tracts filled with doctrines of rebellion and natural rights derived from the philosopher, John Locke.

Hamilton enlisted in the militia and fought in battles around New York City in 1775 and 76. George Washington recognized his organizing ability and he received a commission in March 1777, as lieutenant colonel in the Continental Army. He led a regiment of New York troops at the Battle of Yorktown in October 1781.

He gained a high social position when he married Elizabeth Schuyler in December of 1780. Elizabeth was the daughter of General Philip Schuyler, a wealthy and influential of New York society. He was admitted to legal practice in New York shortly after leaving the army. Before his 30th birthday, Hamilton had had a distinguished military career, knew most of the leaders of the American Revolution, had achieved high social standing, and was recognized as one of the leading lawyers in the country.

Hamilton was elected as a member to the Continental Congress in 1782. He was a prominent proponent of a stronger national government than what had been provided in the Articles of Confederation.

Along with John Jay and James Madison, Hamilton wrote many of the Federalist Papers in which he urged the people of New York to ratify the new constitution.

Hamilton distinguished himself as the first Secretary of the Treasury. He set guidelines for the staff and all departments of the government. Hamilton believed that if the nation was to prosper, its credit would have to be sound to encourage both foreign and domestic investment.

On leaving the government Hamilton resumed a busy and lucrative law practice. Hamilton opposed Adam's reelection for what he thought had been erratic leadership. But when it appeared that Aaron Burr might win the Presidency over Jefferson, he threw his support to Jefferson.

This action so angered Burr that he challenged Hamilton to a duel. Hamilton was mortally wounded and died the next day.

There are not many quotes of Hamilton but these two help us to understand his philosophy of life:

> For my own part, I sincerely esteem it a system which without the finger of God, never could have been suggested and agreed upon by such a diversity of interests. [Alexander Hamilton shortly after the Constitutional Convention of 1787]

> "I now offer you the outline of the plan they have suggested. Let an association be formed to be denominated 'The Christian Constitutional Society,' its object to be first: The support of the Christian religion, Second: The support of the United States."

Douglas Adair and Marvin Harvey identify four religious phases in Hamilton's life: He had a conventionally religious youth. From 1777 to 1792, he seemed totally indifferent to religion. From the period of the French Revolution onward, he had an "opportunistic religiosity," seeking to use Christianity for political ends, and then after the death of his son Philip in 1801, truly became a repentant orthodox Christian. They state that the first three phases of his life were consistent with theistic rationalism.

They also state that from 1777 to 1792 there are only two letters where Hamilton mentions God or religion at all. One of them, a letter to Anthony Wayne, July 6, 1780, he discusses a military chaplain:

> "He is just what I should like for a military parson except that he does not whore or drink. He will fight and he will not insist upon your going to heaven whether you will or not."

John Adams called Alexander Hamilton a "bastard brat of a Scotch pedlar," who had a "superabundance of secretions which he could not find whores enough to draw off." Adams decried, "the profligacy of his life; his fornications, adulteries and his incests."

John Adams' wife, Abigail wasn't much nicer, stating, "Oh, I have read his heart in his wicked eyes. The very devil is in them. They are lasciviousness itself!"

When Hamilton was caught having an affair with Maria Reynolds, a grafter, he made a self-serving, less than forthcoming apology about the matter.

It is clear to me, that although Alexander Hamilton was a great and good influence in the production of the nation, he was less than honest about his personal conduct and morals.

....

I wish that President Bush had read and understood what Theodore Roosevelt had written. He would then have understood the brains up his ass Fascist style attitude he himself displayed!

"Patriotism means to stand by the country. It does NOT mean to stand by the President or any other public official save exactly to the degree in which he himself stands by the country. It is patriotic to support him insofar as he efficiently serves the country. It is unpatriotic not to oppose him to the exact extent that by inefficiently or otherwise he fails in his duty to stand by the country."

Theodore Roosevelt

John Hancock

"There I guess King George will be able
to read that without his spectacles!"

The statement above is accredited to John Hancock by some and disputed by others. On my search for quotes of John Hancock, I found very few.

His flamboyant signature on the Declaration of Independence made him and American legend. John Hancock was a Harvard graduate and a prosperous businessman who favored American independence from Great Britain.

He became a Massachusetts representative to the Continental Congress. He was elected to the president of the Continental Congress in 1775. He was the first to sign the Declaration of Independence in July of 1776. He wrote his name in the center of the page in extra-large script. He had referred to the bounty the British had put on the heads of revolutionaries and stated, "The British ministry can read that name without spectacles; let them double their reward," (Hence, "John Hancock" became a slang term for any signature.)

Later Hancock was elected the first governor of the commonwealth of Massachusetts, serving in that position from 1780-85 and from 1787 until his death in 1793.

John Hancock was born at Braintree, Mass., on January 23, 1737. He was reared in the piety and penury of a Congregational minister's household. He was 7 when his father died and he became a ward of his uncle, a prominent Boston merchant. After graduating from Harvard in 1754, he served for a time in his uncle's office as a clerk, and was sent to London in 1760 as the firm's representative. He returned to Boston in 1763 and became a partner in his uncle's prosperous importing and provisioning business.

When his uncle died in 1764, he inherited property that made him very wealthy. As a merchant prince he resisted Britain's attempt to restrict colonial trading via the Stamp Act. Later this Stamp Act was repealed but Hancock was involved in mercantile ventures which led to evasive tactics that were, in fact, smuggling.

Hancock's public career began with the election to his election to the office of Boston selectman in 1765. He then aligned himself with Samuel Adams and the Patriot opposition to the Stamp Act. When his sloop, Liberty, was seized for smuggling during the opposition to the Townshend Acts in 1768, Hancock stood up as champion of resistance to British measures.

The following year Boston elected Hancock as one of its representatives to the Massachusetts legislature. Hancock was reputed to be the chief financial backer of the Patriot group. In 1774, he gave a rousing oration commemorating the Boston Massacre of 1770. When the British troops marched to Lexington and Concord on April 19, 1775, one of their missions was to capture Hancock and Samuel Adams.

Hancock's steadfast service to Massachusetts led to his being sent in 1775 to the Second

Continental Congress, where he served as its president but he was dismayed not to be chosen commander of the Continental army which went to George Washington. However, he spent two years in Baltimore and Philadelphia supplying the American forces and creating a navy.

Hancock played a crucial role in the ratification of the U. S. Constitution. He urged the ratification with the addition of a bill of rights. Hancock died in office at the age of fifty-six, being the foremost popular politician in Massachusetts.

....

"He therefore is the truest friend to the liberty of this country who tries most to promote its virtue, and who, so far as his power and influence extend, will not suffer a man to be chosen into any office or power and trust who is not a wise and virtuous man...The sum of all is, if we would most truly enjoy this gift of Heaven, let us become a virtuous people."

Samuel Adams

Benjamin Franklin

"Resolve to perform what you ought;
perform without fail what you resolve."

Benjamin Franklin was known for his writings on moral issues. He organized the virtues he felt necessary or desirable into thirteen categories. The list of virtues were temperance, silence, order, resolution, frugality, industry, sincerity, justice, moderation, cleanliness, tranquility, chastity, and humility. He had a description for each of these virtues.

When Benjamin was 15, his brother, James, started The New England Courant, the first newspaper in Boston. The two other newspapers at this time only reprinted news from abroad.

Benjamin wanted to write articles but was not permitted to do so by his brother. So, Benjamin wrote articles under the name of "Silence Dogood," a fictional widow. He wrote 16 of these letters before he admitted he was the author.

His brother was not pleased and became jealous of the writing ability of Ben.

James found himself out of favor with the Puritan Mathers family and ended up going to jail for his writings. Although Ben had kept the newspaper going while James was in jail, he lost favor with his brother. Ben decided to run away in 1723.

He ended up in Philadelphia penniless. He met his future wife there. He became an apprentice printer. The governor of Pennsylvania liked Ben's work, promising to set him up in business if he would got to London to but fonts and printing equipment. Ben went to London but the governor reneged on his promise and Ben had to spend several months in London doing print work.

When he returned to Philadelphia Ben borrowed some money and set himself up in the printing business. He seemed to work all the time and was soon receiving contracts to do government work.

Ben fathered a child in 1728, named William. The mother was unknown. In 1730 Ben married his childhood sweetheart, Deborah Read. Besides his printing work, between them, the couple ran a store in which Deborah sold a variety of goods. They also ran a book store.

Ben bought the newspaper, the *Pennsylvania Gazette,* in 1729. This newspaper became the most successful in the colonies.

In 1733 he began publishing: *Poor Richard's Almanac.* Almanacs were printed yearly and had things like weather reports, recipes, predictions, and homilies. What distinguished Franklin's almanac were his witty aphorisms and lively writing. Franklin used his almanac to launch his most famous phrases such as, "A penny saved is a penny earned."

During the 1730's and 1740's, Franklin helped launch projects to clean and light the streets of Philadelphia. Books were expensive in these days so Franklin started the Library Company in 1731. The members could pool their resources and thus be able to buy books from England. In 1743 he was instrumental in forming the American Philosophical Society. Franklin brought together a group of people who started Pennsylvania Hospital in 1751. These are all in existence today.

In 1736 he organized the Philadelphia Union Fire Company. Ben's expression, "An ounce of prevention is worth a pound of cure," was actually fire-fighting advice.

In 1752, Franklin retired from the printing business and started concentrating on science, experiments, and inventions. Franklin had already invented in 1743, a heat-efficient stove, called of course, the Franklin stove. He refused to take out a patent as it was developed to improve society.

Franklin also invented swim fins and bifocals. He invented a glass musical instrument called the armonica.

In the early 1750's, he turned to the study of electricity. His kite experiment, which verified the nature of electricity, brought Franklin international fame.

In 1757, Franklin who had become interested in politics, went to England to represent Pennsylvania in its fight with the Penn family over who should represent the colony.

On his return to Pennsylvania, Franklin started working actively for independence. Franklin and his son who had become the Royal governor of New Jersey, became estranged since William remained a Loyal Englishman.

Franklin was elected to the Second Continental Congress and worked on a committee of five that helped draft the Declaration of Independence. He sailed to France as an ambassador to the court of Louis XVI.

The French loved this humble backwoodsman that was a match for any wit in the world. Franklin spoke French, although stutteringly. His wife had died and Franklin became known as a notorious flirt.

In his seventies, Franklin returned to America. He became a delegate to the Constitutional Convention and signed the Constitution. One of his last public acts was writing an anti-slavery treatise in 1789.

Franklin was known for his wit as well as his deep-thinking philosophy. He was a very modest man who never took himself too seriously. He wrote much. His virtues, with their precepts, were:

Temperance: Eat not to dullness; drink not to elevation.

Silence: Speak not but what may benefit others or yourself; avoid trifling conversation.

Order: Let all your things have their places; let each part of your Business have its time.

Resolution: Resolve to perform what you ought; perform without fail what you resolve.

Frugality: Make no expense but to do good to others or yourself; i.e., waste nothing.

Industry: Lose no time; be always employed in something useful; cut off all unnecessary actions.

Sincerity: Use no hurtful deceit; think innocently and justly, and, if you speak, speak accordingly.

Justice: Wrong none by ding injuries, or omitting the benefits that are your duty.

Moderation; . Avoid extremes; forbear resenting injuries so much as you think they deserve.

Cleanliness: Tolerate no uncleanliness in body, clothes or habitation.

Tranquility: Be not disturbed at trifles, or at accidents common or unavoidable.

Chastity: Rarely use venery but for health or offspring, never to dullness, weakness, or the injury of your own or another's peace or reputation.

Humility: Imitate Jesus and Socrates...

Addendum

Azbell's Reality Quotes

Azbell's Reality Quotes

Since I believe that all we ever had and all we ever shall have is reality,
there is no supernatural thinking in my quotes!

These quotes are all mine, and although I have been influenced by others,
no one else should be *blamed* for them!

I am the pessimistically optimistic realist with a bent of humanistic pragmatism, a Deist.

The last thing that Jesus would have prayed to become, a Christian!

Why does the Christian right believe that it should have the right to fuck whomever it pleases but I should not have that same right?

A bigot is one who believes that his philosophy is the one and only. A hypocrite is one who believes that his philosophy makes him better than others. The best examples of bigots and hypocrites are Pat Robertson, Jerry Falwell, Bob Jones, Albert Mohler Jr., George W. Bush, the Pope of Rome, and two billion of their good buddies.

Since I do not believe in any god or religious faith, I automatically distrust anyone that suggests a god or his religious faith is responsible for his words or actions.

It appears to me, that if the gods of man were as omnipotent as are proclaimed, we would be living in a paradise by now!

Man's refusal to accept the truth of the universe and Mother Nature has caused him to create all manner of gods and religious faiths.

Deities exist in the minds of those who have conveniently blinded themselves as to the truth of reality and the reality of truth.

Organized religions are the most regressive and destructive forces that man has ever created,
While one's religious faith may be the most important aspect in life to him, civilized humanity is more concerned with the humaneness of that one.

All of those who have received communion and the blessings from men such as Cardinal Law, have received the blessings of a Satan."

The pope of Rome can claim no moral authority as long as he allows one pedophile priest, and those who protect him from the arms of justice, to remain in the church.

The evilness in the U. S. A. is no more the result of the lack of Christ in our lives than is the presence of superiority concepts being taught to us daily in our hypocritical Christian churches.

I wish to live only as long as I can rationally think and do for myself, move my body on my own, and have the strength to make both emotional and physical love.

If the Christian fundamentalists believe that the time spent in prayer within their churches and homes is insufficient, thus requiring prayer in our public schools and work sites, the fanatic faithful are displaying a definite lack of faith in the sustaining power of their faith.

In reality, reality TV is nothing more than the depiction of disillusioned man in attempts to escape his true reality.

Reality TV is one man trying to out-macho his fellow man and women trying to out-macho the men. The stupidity of much of mankind never ceases.

Man's most valuable attribute is the ability to understand that which he presumes to know.

The reality is, truth is reality: not all of reality is the truth.

The creative force of the universe has been and forever shall be; having no beginning or end.

Truth stands alone: truth cannot be created, altered, or destroyed by man.

What is so frightening about George W. Bush is the fact that he knows but does not understand the rhetoric he espouses.

The futility of creating countless gods and religious faiths has erased most truth, honesty and love from the world of man.

The cost for the adoption of a religious faith is the forfeiture of one's natural humanity. Faith is no synonym of truth.

The banning of a thing only raises the value of that thing to a higher level.

The reason for the banning of a thought is usually that that thought is too real for some hypocrites.

Since the Bible is replete with the fantasies of make-believe, sorcery, and witchcraft, the fanatic condemnations of the Harry Potter books, proves that the Christian hypocrites do not understand the contents of the Bible, especially the five books of Moses, and those of Matthew, Mark, Luke, and John.

Most religious faiths have two major flaws, one is truth, and the other is reality.

If man were truthful, he would feel less need for the creation of blind religious faiths.

In man's world of philosophical thoughts, there is no black or white: man's world of philosophies and faiths are a reality of countless shades of gray.

Blind faith is blind: I could not agree more!

By my nature, I automatically distrust anyone who believes that a certain philosophy is a matter of pure black or white.

The greatest threat to personal freedom or world security is religious fundamentalism.

Nothing could cure quicker our sick Christian family values than a few massive doses of reality based truth and honesty.

If we could only understand that which we proclaim to know of this world and beyond, we would be living at the level for which the religious are constantly praying.

Religious faiths have proven themselves to be the greatest obstacles to the intellectual and scientific development of mankind.

As with all books, the Bible is only as truthful as were the mortal men who wrote it.

The adoption of a blind faith necessitates the negation of reason and realistic sensibilities.

Religious faiths are not based on fact, known truths, or reality, thus have no legitimacy.

We must learn to live with the reality of what is, not that which we may wish it to be.

I often contemplate the fact that without man there would be no gods.

At times, I get to thinking that this world would be a much better place without man.

Religious faiths and their deities are created by mortal man in his desperate attempts to alter truth; an impossibility at best.

Man is not the creation of a god: gods are the creations of man!

Man is tangible but that which he calls his god is intangible. Man and god do not appear on the same plane, thus the two are unable to communicate one with the other.

There is only one soul for all of mankind. The individual temporary self becomes part of the one soul of mankind when it no longer exists in life.

Since faith is belief, belief is theory, theory is unproven as to fact, it is impossible to prove as fact, a religious faith.

Organized religious faiths are in a state of stagnation, while the universe of man is in a constant state of flux.

Why does a natural and otherwise intelligent man blind himself as to the truth of reality in order to adopt a supernatural religious faith and its god?

A religious person is one who is able to irrationally synchronize his adopted faith with his natural self.

The true fact is; that in fact, I am the truth.

I am no better than you and you are no better than me, and in the same breath I can say, that there has never been one to walk the face of this earth better than you or me.

Truth comes solely from natural laws of Mother Nature and the universe.

All things in opposition to natural and universal law are invalid.

Since it is not all animals but only man who worships gods, all gods are simply the visions of man.

Though man shall never know how the matter which comprises the universe ever came to be, the creator of the universe and all that is, was the force which created the Big Bang billions of years ago.

Only matters of belief which can be scientifically proven become matters of fact. Religious beliefs remain theories of faith since they cannot be proven to be fact.

Man, and what man calls his soul, do not exist on the same plane, thus man and soul are incongruous.

Man has not yet been able to find himself despite his creation of countless gods and religious faiths.

Since man has refused to accept that which Mother Nature and fate has presented to him, man is simply searching for that which he is willing to accept.

How can we trust the words of the *Family Research Council* when their description of a family has little to do with reality?

In reality, when one claims to know all the answers, he most assuredly has very little understanding of the problem.

Have evil gods created hypocritical religious faiths or has evil man created them?

What does one call Bob Jones III when he calls the Pope of Rome the antichrist?

What should we call Albert Mohler Jr. who claims that he is replacing Saint Peter as the gatekeeper to heaven?

Regular doses of reality tend to cure the evil ills man assimilates through false religious faiths.

How can a twenty-first century Christian man, Pat Robertson, justify the use of slave labor in his gold and diamond minds in Africa and his clothing factories in China?

Realities of the Crusades, Inquisitions, and witch hunts of the past, along with the present day exorcisms confirm the inhumanity of Christianity.

Man is no more evil than he is good.

It is a challenge to decide whether more bad or good has come from the 2000 years of Christianity. It seems, to me, that history leans toward bad as the winner!

With so many gods to choose from it would be a challenge to know which one to adopt.

Christians proclaim that there is only one god which happens to be a combination of the one that the Jew Moses created and his Christian son, the one they created.

Fundamental religious faiths appear to be counter-productive since they spend much of their time in futile attempts to denounce one another.

Those who adopt fundamental faiths create their own unrealistic, supernatural truths.

A troubling truth of Bush; he honestly believes that humanitarian charities must be based on religious faith rather than natural humanity.

The more that man strives to escape universal law and Mother Nature, the more he strays from the truth of the universe in which he lives.

The truth is, man chooses his truths.

When Bush displays faith in we the people, we the people may display more faith in him.

A critic is nothing more than a frustrated would-be dictator.

What we need in the media today is better reporting of fact with fewer prejudiced assessments. Give me the unembellished truth and let me decide its importance and its consequences.

A politician is at his best when he is less of one.

Never do today that which can be put-off until tomorrow for that which can be put-off may not be worth the doing.

Who in their sane mind would pray to spend eternity with Christian fundamentalist hypocrites such as Jerry Falwell, Pat Robertson, the Pope of Rome, and George W. Bush?

Politician would be better with less 'I'.

The greatest argument for the regressive and destructive nature of Christianity is the continual *spiritless* doctrinaires flowing from the mouths of Christians such as Falwell, Robertson, Bush, the Pope of Rome, and the total of the Christian right.

Mortal man writes his philosophies as he wishes, declaring them to be the truth after he has determined that truth.

My truths cannot be determined by others as I am the truth.

The truth dwells within me, however, that which I declare as truth and what in reality is truth, may be quite different.

What truth is there in the truth formed by biased and prejudiced man?

When we sin, it is against our fellow man and nature. What is sinful to one, however, may not be so to another, since sin is a matter of individual perception.

Man's greatest sin is the feeling that his adopted faith and god make him better than non-believers or those of other faiths.

Communications from gods are the result of self-delusions, self-illusions and hypnotic misconceptions of the one receiving such messages.

The goal of any worthwhile religious faith should be the increase in the humanity of the faithful.

Faiths are not truths no matter how much faith is expressed.

Spirituality is achieved naturally through being one with self, Mother Nature, and the universe; it cannot be taught by religious faiths since faiths are not natural.

To become spiritual one must know oneself through meditation, not prayer.

One must be at peace with self, nature and the universe in order to find one's self.

My belief system has but one tenet which happens to be the Golden Rule, "Do unto others as you would have others do unto you." That's it, there ain't no more!

The Bible presents the creation of the universe, earth and man as a fairytale with little reality.

Science and the knowledge that it has provided to mankind, have seen to the fact that we are no longer the stupid and ignorant ones we were in the days of Moses and Jesus.

Man existed thousands of years before he was forcefully thrust into Christianity.

Since I do not believe in Christianity, it has no right to be in my life.

The creative force of the universe, through Mother Nature, is the creator of all life on this earth.

One may choose to be whomever one wishes, just do not expect me to choose the same.

A true sadist is one that adopts a god he fears.

Only the unthinking religious faithful among us blame others for the intolerance and hatred that the religious faith they adopted teaches them.

Religious fanatics are nothing more than bigots and hypocrites who believe that they have adopted a true god and its fundamental faith.

The importance of one is determined by the manner in which he treats any and all of mankind and other creations of Mother Nature.

Like most critics, Joan Rivers comments on the clothes, hair, and make-up of others when she herself looks like something the cat drug in from the alley.

Man, with the help of others, makes his own heaven and hell here on earth.

If heaven be the home of the good, many of us do not have much remaining time to prepare for our eternity.

Organized religious faiths and their gods are the creations of idealistically driven spiritless men who have little to no faith in their natural selves or mankind.

The religious faiths of man need to become more real, truthful, and honest so that their adopted morals and ethics reach a purposeful level of importance.

The Bible is void of truth, fact or reality; therefore, it never shall succeed in its goal to subjugate real man.

Mother Nature creates man and gives him brains, consequently man creates his own world of good and evil.

It is the false religious faiths of man, rather than man; that are in need of salvation.

In the philosophical world of man, there is no black or white: all philosophies of man are composed of countless shades of gray.

Dysfunctional individuals such as Jerry Falwell, Pat Robertson, and George W. Bush are prime examples of men who have never developed a meaningful respect for mankind.

Violence within our schools is the result of the intolerance, hatred, and superiority concepts being taught daily by our religious faiths.

Rather than our ill-conceived idealistic beliefs of what life should be, we must learn to live with what is natural.

The futility of creating countless false gods and religious faiths has erased most of the truth, honesty, and love which Mother Nature had presented to man.

The faith we place in our false gods and religious faiths would be better spent on faith in natural man.

Millions of us are planning our lives based on falsehoods of faith and then wondering why our lives are not progressing in a manner for which we have been praying.

While life is a reality, religious faiths deal only with the fantasy of ideality.

An idiot can be just as devout as a genius.

The creative force of the universe and its Mother Nature, have never operated with the confines of any religious calendar of man.

If only we understood all that we presume to know.

Heretics and infidels are the champions of the intelligent.

We need to exterminate the termites of the Christian right before they eat up the fabric of our Constitution.

What I think of myself is of little consequence: what others think of me determines my worth to society.

I calculate that George W. Bush, along with his Fascist based Christian right-winged morally and ethically bankrupt administration, has set the United States back some fifty years.

Since I believe that religious gods and faiths are the most sinister of all philosophies, it is my belief that the pure, honest and free peoples are those without a religious faith or god.

Pray to your god that I become religious and you shall see, over a period of time, just how useless your prayers are.

The fundamental fanatics of the god of Islam have decided to war against the fundamental fanaticism of Bush and his Christian god.

When it comes to choosing, I choose the reality of reality over the unreality of the ideality.

For his ideological and religiously based doctrinaires against the use of condoms, the Pope of Rome needs to be held responsible for the deaths of millions of his innocent sheep.

Gods and religious faiths are no more or no less than what is intended by the will of the one who creates them.

Faith and truth are not synonymous facts.

The reality is, truth is reality: not all of reality is truth.

Deities exist in the minds of those who have conveniently blinded themselves as to the truth of reality and the reality of truth.

Possibly the most valuable attribute of man is his ability to understand that which he presumes to know.

Truth reigns supreme: truth cannot be created, altered, or destroyed.

The fact that a religious faith exists is no proof of its truth or truthfulness.

Without peanut butter, my life would not be worth living!

....

Since they believe there is more truth in their unproven faiths than proven science, the religious are choosing their own path to destruction and obliteration!

Frederick J. Azbell

May the creative power of the universe be with you!
azbellfj@yahoo.com